Modern Cryptography – Current Challenges and Solutions

Edited by Menachem Domb

Published in London, United Kingdom

IntechOpen

Supporting open minds since 2005

Modern Cryptography - Current Challenges and Solutions
http://dx.doi.org/10.5772/intechopen.78088
Edited by Menachem Domb

Contributors
Ayan Mahalanobis, Anupam Singh, Sushil Bhunia, Pralhad Shinde, Anthony Overmars, Shlomi Dolev, Youssou Faye, Herve Guyennet, Ibrahima Niang, Samed Bajric, Riccardo Bernardini

First published in London, United Kingdom, 2019 by IntechOpen
IntechOpen is the global imprint of INTECHOPEN LIMITED, registered in England and Wales, registration number: 11086078, 7th floor, 10 Lower Thames Street, London, EC3R 6AF, United Kingdom
Printed in Croatia

British Library Cataloguing-in-Publication Data
A catalogue record for this book is available from the British Library

Additional hard and PDF copies can be obtained from orders@intechopen.com

Modern Cryptography - Current Challenges and Solutions
Edited by Menachem Domb
p. cm.
Print ISBN 978-1-78984-470-2
Online ISBN 978-1-78984-471-9
eBook (PDF) ISBN 978-1-78984-365-1

For EU product safety concerns:
IN TECH d.o.o., Prolaz Marije Krucifikse Kozulić 3, 51000 Rijeka, Croatia, info@intechopen.com or visit our website at intechopen.com.

Meet the editor

Prof. Menachem is an Associate Professor and the Head of the Computer Science Department at the Ashkelon Academy College [AAC], Israel. He obtained his BSc degree in Mathematics and Computer Science from Bar-Ilan University, Israel. He obtained an MSc degree in Applied Mathematics from the Currant institute of Mathematical Sciences, New York University, USA, an MSc degree in Computer Science from Queens College, USA, and an MBA from Tel-Aviv University, Israel. He obtained his PhD in Operational Research from the Technion, Israel and his Post Doctorate at Washington University, USA. His research interests are: cyber security, IoT, and telecommunications. In recent years, he has published many articles and conference papers covering topics related to these fields. In parallel, he has 35 years of professional experience in executive positions in international companies in the security, health and telecommunication fields.

Contents

Preface

The challenges in and solutions for cryptography are the core subject of this book. Core security concepts and solutions were proposed decades ago. However, mainly due to technology advancements, the increase of data transmission volume and the evolving of Internet infrastructure, challenges to cryptography systems have been found, calling for adjustments and solutions. In this book, we start with improvements proposed to symmetric cryptography by construction of Boolean functions for generating orthogonal variable spreading factor codes used in cryptographic applications. We proceed with asymmetric cryptography by outlining RSA voluntaries followed by ECC performance improvements of its Fast Scalar Multiplication and improved performance of the encryption used in numerical problem applications. We conclude the book with two proposals to cope with the quantum computing challenge to Internet security. One approach uses a combination of overlay security, Blockchain, and Merkle trees to provide a quantum safe Internet. The second employs the MOR cryptosystem in a asymmetric cryptography, by generalizing the discrete logarithm problem from a cyclic group to an arbitrary group.

I would like to acknowledge AAC for its help and Mrs. Nina Kalinic Babic for her assistance as the Author Service Manager of this project.

Menachem Domb
Ashkelon Academy College,
Ashkelon, Israel

Chapter 1

Implementing Symmetric Cryptography Using Sequence of Semi-Bent Functions

Samed Bajrić

Abstract

Symmetric cryptography is a cornerstone of everyday digital security, where two parties must share a common key to communicate. The most common primitives in symmetric cryptography are stream ciphers and block ciphers that guarantee confidentiality of communications and hash functions for integrity. Thus, for securing our everyday life communication, it is necessary to be convinced by the security level provided by all the symmetric-key cryptographic primitives. The most important part of a stream cipher is the key stream generator, which provides the overall security for stream ciphers. Nonlinear Boolean functions were preferred for a long time to construct the key stream generator. In order to resist several known attacks, many requirements have been proposed on the Boolean functions. Attacks against the cryptosystems have forced deep research on Boolean function to allow us a more secure encryption. In this work we describe all main requirements for constructing of cryptographically significant Boolean functions. Moreover, we provide a construction of Boolean functions (semi-bent Boolean functions) which can be used in the construction of orthogonal variable spreading factor codes used in code division multiple access (CDMA) systems as well as in certain cryptographic applications.

Keywords: symmetric cryptography, Boolean functions, Walsh spectrum, nonlinearity, resiliency, (fast) algebraic attack

1. Introduction

Cryptography has become a branch of information theory and is used within a mathematical approach to study the transmission of information from place to place. In a modern society, exchange and storage of information in an efficient, reliable, and secure manner are of fundamental importance. Applications of cryptography are present in many aspects of our society, and they include authentication and encryption (bank cards, wireless telephone, e-commerce), access control (car lock systems, ski lifts), and payment (prepaid telephone cards, e-cash). Behind all the previously mentioned applications, an underlying cryptographic system has to satisfy a number of security goals. Some important aspects in information security are data confidentiality, data integrity, authentication, and non-repudiation, and some of these goals will be elaborated later in the framework of Boolean functions. Therefore, cryptography is evermore important for business and industry as well as for society at large.

A classic example of a cryptosystem is depicted in **Figure 1**. Such a cryptosystem primitive is also called symmetric-key encryption algorithm, since the transmitted message (plaintext) is encrypted (into ciphertext) and decrypted with the same secret key which is shared between both sender and recipient. Symmetric cryptography is best introduced with an easy-to-understand problem: There are two users, Alice and Bob, who want to communicate over an insecure channel. The actual problem starts with the bad guy, Oscar, who has access to the channel, for instance, by hacking into an Internet router or by listening to the radio signals of a Wi-Fi communication. This type of unauthorized listening is called eavesdropping. Obviously, there are many situations in which Alice and Bob would prefer to communicate without Oscar listening. For instance, if Alice and Bob represent two offices of a car manufacturer, and they are transmitting documents containing the business strategy for the introduction of new car models in the next few years, these documents should not get into the hands of their competitors or of foreign intelligence agencies for that matter. In this situation, symmetric cryptography offers a powerful solution: Alice encrypts her message m using a symmetric algorithm, yielding the ciphertext c. Bob receives the ciphertext and decrypts the message. Decryption is, thus, the inverse process of encryption. What is the advantage? If we have a strong encryption algorithm, the ciphertext will look like random bits to Oscar and will contain no information whatsoever that is useful to him.

Symmetric-key cryptography comprises two large families of cryptographic primitives, namely, block and stream ciphers (see **Figure 2**). Since both block and stream ciphers provide significant performance improvement compared to public-key encryption techniques, they are commonly used as encryption schemes in practice. However, the design rules for these two primitives are quite different.

In general, symmetric-key cryptography is much more computationally efficient than public-key cryptography (approximately 1000 faster), and it requires shorter key length to ensure the same level of security. On the other hand, every pair of users that wants to communicate using symmetric encryption must share a common secret key. If n users want to ensure a pairwise secure communication, a total of $\frac{n(n-1)}{2}$ secret keys need to be exchanged, and every user must store and keep safe $n-1$ different secret keys, which is in many cases highly impractical. In comparison, public-key cryptography offers a functionality of only keeping a single private key secret.

The security of symmetric cryptosystems is strongly influenced by Boolean functions. They are often used as nonlinear combining functions in stream ciphers based on linear feedback shift register. Those functions allow making the relationship between the plaintext and the ciphertext as complex as possible. More precisely, a bit of the ciphertext is obtained from a bit of the plaintext by adding

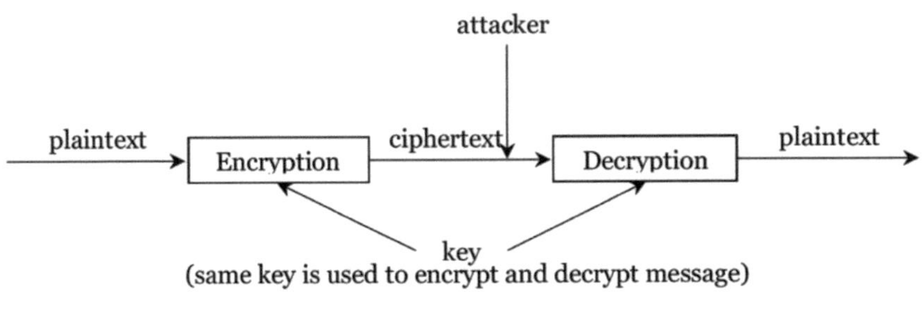

Figure 1.
Model of classic cryptosystem.

DOI: http://dx.doi.org/10.5772/intechopen.85023

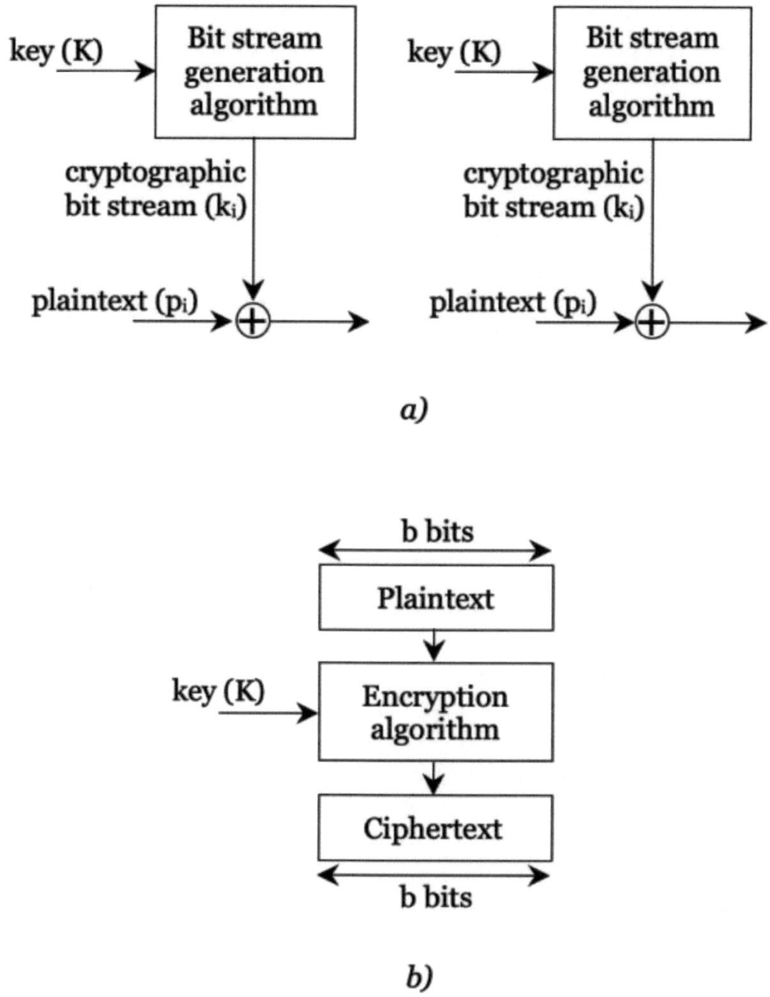

Figure 2.
Symmetric-key encryption schemes. (a) Stream cipher using algorithmic bit stream generator. (b) Block cipher.

bitwise a key digit (the output of the Boolean function) whose dependence upon the LFSR entries (the secret information) is nonlinear. Thus, the security of such cryptosystems deeply relies on the choice of the Boolean function because the complexity of the relationship between the plaintext and the ciphertext depends entirely on the Boolean function. Indeed, some properties of the Boolean function can be exploited to gain access to the contents of encrypted messages, even if the key is unknown. Therefore, Boolean functions need to have some important characteristics that are called security criteria to resist several types of attacks (see Section 3). Furthermore, the research fields of Boolean functions regarding the cryptography include the design and implementation, the properties of Boolean functions, the construction and counting of Boolean functions with certain properties, the trade-off between different properties, and the properties according to new attacks.

A special class of Boolean functions defined as semi-bent function has been introduced in 1994, by scientists Chee, Lee, and Kim [1]. The motivation for their study is firstly related to their use in cryptography (in the design of cryptographic functions). Indeed, semi-bent functions can be balanced and resilient. They also possess various desirable characteristics such as low autocorrelation, a maximal nonlinearity among balanced plateaued functions, but they cannot have high algebraic degree. In terms of linear feedback shift-register synthesis, they are usually generated by certain power polynomials over a finite field and in addition are characterized by a low cross-correlation and high nonlinearity. Besides their practical use in cryptography, they are also widely used in code division multiple access (CDMA) communication systems for sequence design [2, 3]. In this context, families of maximum length linear feedback shift-register sequences having three-valued cross-correlation are used. Such sequences have received a lot of attention since the late 1960s and can be generated by a semi-bent function. Even though a lot of work has been done on semi-bent functions, there are a few generic methods of constructing semi-bent functions that can be found in the literature. The classification of these functions is still elusive, especially their construction are challenging problems. Some open problems and an overview of the known construction related on semi-bent functions can be found in the book of Mesnager [4]. The rest of this chapter is organized as follows. In Section 2 the essential background on Boolean functions is given. Some main requirements for constructing significant Boolean function are given in Section 3. An infinity class of semi-bent function specified by employing some sufficient conditions is given in Section 4. Some concluding remarks are given in Section 5.

2. Useful definitions and terms

Let $\mathbb{F}_2^n$ denote the n-dimensional vector space over the prime field $\mathbb{F}_2$. Let $x = (x_1, \ldots, x_n)$ be a vector over $\mathbb{F}_2$ of length n.

A *Boolean function* $f(x_1, \ldots, x_n)$ *in n-variables* is an arbitrary function from $\mathbb{F}_2^n$ to $\mathbb{F}_2$. It can also be interpreted as the output column of its *truth table*, i.e., a binary string of length 2^n,

$$f = [f(0, 0, \ldots, 0), f(1, 0, \ldots, 0), \ldots, f(1, 1, \ldots, 1)]. \tag{1}$$

An n-variable function f is said to be *balanced* if its output column in the truth table contains equal number of 1's and 0's.

Any Boolean function has a unique representation as a multivariate polynomial over Galois field of two elements, called *algebraic normal form* (ANF),

$$f(x_1, \ldots, x_n) = a_0 + \sum_{1 \le i \le n} a_i x_i + \sum_{1 \le i < j \le n} a_{ij} x_i x_j + \ldots + a_{12\ldots n} x_1 x_2 \ldots x_n \tag{2}$$

where the coefficients $a_0, a_{ij}, \ldots, a_{12\ldots n}$ belong to $\{0, 1\}$.

The *algebraic degree*, denoted by $\deg(f)$, is the number of variables in the highest order monomial with nonzero coefficient. A Boolean function with $\deg(f) \le 1$ is said to be *affine*, and the set of all n-variable affine functions is denoted by $\mathcal{A}_n$. An affine function with the constant term equal to zero is called a *linear* function.

The *nonlinearity* of an n-variable function f is $N_f = \min_{g \in \mathcal{A}_n} d(f, g)$, which measures the minimum distance between f and all n-variable affine functions.

Many properties of Boolean function can be deduced from its Walsh spectra. The *Walsh transform* of $f(x)$ in point $\omega \in \mathbb{F}_2^n$ is an integer-valued function over $\mathbb{F}_2^n$ defined by

$$W_f(\omega) = \sum_{x \in \mathbb{F}_2^n} (-1)^{f(x) + x \cdot \omega}, \tag{3}$$

where $x \cdot \omega = x_1\omega_1 + \ldots + x_n\omega_n$ is the inner product of two vectors over $\mathbb{F}_2^n$. The set $\{W_f(\omega) : \omega \in \mathbb{F}_2^n\}$ is called the Walsh spectrum of f.

A Boolean function $f(x)$ is called *plateaued* if its Walsh spectrum only takes three values, 0 and $\pm 2^{\lambda}$, where λ is some positive integer.

Two Boolean functions $f(x), g(x)$ are said to be a pair of *disjoint spectra* functions if

$$W_f(\omega) \cdot W_g(\omega) = 0. \tag{4}$$

for all $\omega \in \mathbb{F}_2^n$.

In terms of Walsh spectra, the nonlinearity of f is given by

$$N_f = 2^{n-1} - \frac{1}{2} \max_{\omega \in \mathbb{F}_2^n} |W_f(\omega)|. \tag{5}$$

A function is balanced if and only if $W_f(0) = 0$, i.e., $\#\{x|f(x) = 0\} = \#\{x|f(x) = 1\}$.

An n-variable Boolean function f is said to be *bent* if its Walsh transform takes only two values $\pm 2^{\frac{n}{2}}$. Moreover, f is said to be *semi-bent* function if for all $\omega \in \mathbb{F}_2^n$

$$W_f(\omega) \in \begin{cases} \left\{0, \pm 2^{\frac{n+1}{2}}\right\}, \textit{if n is odd} \\ \left\{0, \pm 2^{\frac{n+2}{2}}\right\}, \textit{if n is even} \end{cases}. \tag{6}$$

The *derivative* of $f(x)$ at $a \in \mathbb{F}_2^n$, denoted by $D_a f(x)$, is a Boolean function defined by $D_a f(x) = f(x + a) + f(x)$, for all $x \in \mathbb{F}_2^n$. The notion of the derivative of a Boolean function is extended to higher orders as follows.

Suppose $\{a_1, \ldots, a_k\}$ is a basis of a k dimensional subspace V of $\mathbb{F}_2^n$. The k-th derivative of f with respect to V, denoted by $D_V f(x)$, is a Boolean function defined by

$$D_V f(x) = D_{a_k} D_{a_{k-1}} \ldots D_{a_1} f(x), \tag{7}$$

for all $x \in \mathbb{F}_2^n$.

3. Cryptographic requirements for constructing Boolean functions

One of the fundamental research topics in cryptography is the construction of cryptographically significant Boolean functions, that is, a function which possesses some of the following properties:

1. High ***algebraic degree*** aims to increase the linear complexity in ciphers. Using Boolean functions of high degree in block ciphers leads to more complicated systems of equations describing the cipher and hence makes cryptanalysis of the cipher more difficult. All cryptosystems using Boolean functions for confusion can be attacked if the functions have relatively low algebraic degree, i.e., the Berlekamp-Massey attack [5] or the Ronjom-Helleseth attack [6] can be applied. Note that the algebraic degree of a Boolean function in n-variables is at most n.

2. In order to prevent the system from leaking statistical dependence between the input and output, the concept of ***balancedness*** implies that a given Boolean function outputs equally many zeros and ones over all possible input values. To avoid distinguishing attacks [7], cryptographic function must be balanced.

Note that the algebraic degree of a Boolean balanced function in n-variables is at most $n - 1$.

3. High ***nonlinearity*** is one of the most important properties in the design of symmetric-key cryptosystems, since it directly affects the resistance of the cipher to majority of cryptanalytic techniques. The nonlinearity simply measures the Hamming distance to the set of all affine functions. Therefore, a high nonlinearity implies a better resistance to affine approximation attacks [8]. According to the definition of nonlinearity, all affine functions have zero nonlinearity. On the other hand, a Boolean function having nonzero nonlinearity implies the function is not affine. Thus, the nonlinearity of a nonlinear Boolean function cannot exceed 2^{n-1}. On an even size Boolean space, there is a class of Boolean functions, called *bent* functions, that have maximum nonlinearity $(2^{n-1} - 2^{\frac{n}{2}-1})$. In general, it is not an easy problem to identify all Boolean functions with high nonlinearity. However, this problem has been completely solved for quadratic Boolean functions (Boolean functions with the algebraic degree 2).

4. In order to avoid correlation attack [9], the concept of ***correlation immune*** of order m implies that any sub-function deduced from a given Boolean function by fixing at most m inputs has the same output distribution as a given Boolean function. Correlation immune has long been recognized as one of the critical indicators of nonlinear combining functions of shift registers in stream generators. Moreover, if a balanced Boolean function f is correlation immune of order m, then f is said to be *m-resilient*. When used in stream cipher systems, a Boolean function is required to have high nonlinearity and resiliency for protection against correlation attacks. It is actually very difficult to find a balanced Boolean function which has a high correlation immunity order and at the same time has a high nonlinearity.

5. Optimal ***algebraic immunity*** aims to provide resistance against algebraic attack. The algebraic immunity is the minimum value of d such that a given Boolean function f or its complement $1 + f$ admits an annihilator (a nonzero Boolean function g such that $fg = 0$) of algebraic degree d. In ciphers, Boolean functions with high algebraic immunity should be used in order to avoid the application of algebraic cryptanalysis [10]. Recall that algebraic attacks recover the secret key, or at least the initialization of the system, by solving a system of multivariate algebraic equations that describes a cipher. Although a high algebraic immunity is the necessary cryptographic requirement, it is not sufficient, because of a more general kind of attack introduced by Courtois [11] in 2003 called fast algebraic attack. It is well-known that maximum algebraic immunity of n-variable Boolean function is $\lceil \frac{n}{2} \rceil$. The problem of efficiently constructing balanced Boolean functions with optimal algebraic immunity is thus of great significance. Moreover, several examples of functions having optimal algebraic immunity could be found but no example of correlation immune Boolean function with optimal algebraic immunity.

However, the major problem in construction of cryptographically strong functions is that the multiple criteria mentioned above have to be satisfied at the same time, while there exist intrinsic trade-offs between them. Such properties allow the system designer to quantify the level of resistance of the system to attacks. Since the number of Boolean functions in n-variables is 2^{2^n}, an exhaustive search of functions which satisfy some of the properties above is practically impossible (unless the input variable space n is quite small). Indeed, the difficulty precisely lies in finding the best trade-offs between all criteria and proposing concrete constructions of functions achieving them. Thus, bringing new construction methods of these functions is still a vivid research activity.

By (n, m, d, N_f) function we specify an n-variable, m-resilient Boolean function f, algebraic degree d, and nonlinearity N_f. Siegenthaler [9] proved that $m + d \leq n + 1$ if $m \leq n - 2$. The exact nature of trade-offs among order of correlation immunity, nonlinearity, and algebraic degree has also been investigated, for instance, ([12, 13]. Using the above bounds, one may naturally try to provide the construction of an (n, m, d, N_f) function for any given n and m while at the same time attempting to optimize d and N_f . This optimization can be efficiently done for a small number of variables $n \leq 5$, but even some interesting open problems for $n>5$, related to the existence of $(8, 1, 6, 116)$ and $(7, 2, 4, 56)$ functions, were settled using some sophisticated computer search and theoretical results [14]. The importance of finding these optimized functions in small number of variables lies in the fact that one can use these functions recursively to obtain new instances of optimal functions in larger number of variables. For instance, Tarannikov [15] has provided a construction technique of optimized resilient Boolean functions with maximum possible nonlinearity. Basically Tarannikov's construction is a recursive one, and using this technique and taking an (n, m, d, N_f) optimized function, such as the $(7, 2, 4, 56)$ function, one can generate a sequence of optimal plateaued $(7 + 3i, 2 + 2i, 4 + i, 2^{7+3i-1} - 2^{2+2i+1})$ functions, $(10, 4, 5, 480)$, $(13, 6, 6, 3968)$, $(16, 8, 7, 32256)$, *etc*. A modified version of Tarannikov's construction was presented in [16]. A construction of Boolean functions with maximum nonlinearity and small order of resiliency has also been considered in [17]. Later, Carlet [18] proposed a general framework for these iterative concatenation methods, unifying most of these techniques into a single method called "indirect sum." This construction leads to a multiple branching infinite tree of functions, but in order to employ this construction in the design of optimal plateaued functions in an iterative manner, there are certain conditions imposed on the initial pairs of disjoint spectra functions.

A recursive construction method of optimal plateaued functions (the functions of the form $(n, m, n - m - 1, 2^{n-1} - 2^{m+1})$ and for $m > \frac{n}{2} - 2$) is given in [19]. The iteration once again employs a $(7, 2, 4, 56)$ function, whose 6-variable sub-functions have disjoint spectra, to construct a sequence of $(7 + 4i, 2 + 3i, 4 + i, 2^{7+4i-1} - 2^{2+3i+1})$ optimal plateaued functions (whose $(7 + 4i - 1)$-variable sub-functions are again disjoint spectra functions). Nevertheless, this iterative method generates the functions with relatively large order of resiliency ($(11, 5, 5, 964)$, $(15, 8, 6, 15872)$, $(19, 11, 7, 258048)$, *etc*.), and in addition it only gives one infinite sequence of optimal plateaued functions. For instance, in the first step of iteration, an optimal plateaued $(11, 5, 5, 964)$ function is generated whose 10-variable sub-functions are again disjoint spectra functions (two $(10, 5, 4, 452)$ disjoint spectra functions), thus leaving some open slots concerning the construction of optimal plateaued functions when $n = 8, 9, 10$. On the other hand, a modified Tarannikov construction has a slightly different effect, since the resiliency is increased by two at each step of iteration (but the degree is also increased by one) and the iteration step is three instead of four. Still, optimal plateaued functions cannot be generated for $n = 8$ or $n = 9$ using the particular $(7, 2, 4, 56)$ function.

The idea of employing a set of disjoint spectra functions in construction of highly nonlinear resilient functions was firstly elaborated in [16]. Later, the sets of disjoint spectra functions were successfully used in constructions of almost optimal resilient functions. The generalized Maiorana-McFarland (GMM) construction method for obtaining the almost optimal resilient functions has been proposed in [20]. Namely, this construction generates the functions with relatively large number of variables and small order of resiliency. The resulting functions cannot be viewed as a pair of disjoint spectra almost optimal resilient functions. Recently, Zhang and Pasalic used GMM technique to obtain the strictly optimal resilient functions with high nonlinearity and good algebraic properties [21]. The design of some balanced functions that also achieve currently best known nonlinearity can be found in [22]. Although these construction methods achieve currently the best nonlinearity for a given function, these methods are only efficient for relatively large input space of variables.

4. A construction of semi-bent Boolean functions

As it is described in the previous section, in the design of cryptographic functions, there is a need to consider various nonlinear characteristics simultaneously. But some characteristics restrict each other. Bent functions, for example, have maximum nonlinearity and satisfy the propagation criteria with respect to every nonzero vector over the Boolean spaces on which they are defined. However, bent functions are not balanced and exist only on even size Boolean spaces. Furthermore, bent functions are not correlation immune, and they are not suitable for use in cryptosystems. Partially bent functions are highly nonlinear and can be balanced. However, except for bent functions, partially bent functions have nonzero linear structures that are cryptographically undesirable. For these reasons, people study other classes of Boolean functions to try to overcome the disadvantage of bent functions or partially bent functions. The class of plateaued Boolean functions is one candidate that is defined by a series of inequalities and examines the critical case of each inequality. Compared with other functions, plateaued functions may reach the upper bound on nonlinearity given by the inequalities.

In what follows we specify a simple generic method for deriving semi-bent functions. This method is deduced from two bent functions whose derivatives differ by a constant one. It should be noticed that there are strong connections behind the concepts of bentness and semi-bentness though many questions remain unanswered. In particular, it is not settled how the cardinality of the whole class of bent functions relates to the class of semi-bent functions. Most notably, it appears that certain classes of semi-bent functions derived in [23] defined for even n are not extendable to bent functions in $n + 2$ variables. In [24] and recently in [25], a sufficient condition on two bent functions g and h used in the construction of semi-bent functions was given as the following theorem.

Theorem 1. *Let n be even, and suppose that f and g are two bent Boolean functions in n-variables. If there exists an* $a \in \mathbb{F}_2^n$ *such that* $D_af(x) = D_ag(x) + 1$, *then the function*

$$h(x) = f(x) + g(x) + D_af(x) + D_a[f(x)g(x)] \tag{8}$$

is a semi-bent function in even number of variables.

This condition immediately implies the possibility of constructing infinite classes of semi-bent functions using known classes of quadratic bent functions. Notice that all quadratic Boolean functions (including bent and semi-bent functions) are classified up to equivalence and any quadratic bent function is affine equivalent to the canonical form given by $\sum_{i=1}^{n/2} x_{2i-1}x_{2i}$.

One may define a Boolean function f with n even to be a quadratic bent function of the form $f(x) = \sum_{i=1}^{n} b_i x_i + \sum_{1 \le i < j \le n} c_{i,j} x_i x_j$ for suitably chosen $b_i, c_{i,j} \in \mathbb{F}_2$. Furthermore, let g be a Boolean function defined as $g(x) = f(x) + \sum_{i=1}^{n} \alpha_i x_i$, where $\alpha_i \in \mathbb{F}_2$. Then, if $a \in \mathbb{F}_2^n$ is such that $a \cdot \alpha = 1$, it can be shown that the function

$$h(x) = f(x) + g(x) + D_a f(x) + D_a[f(x)g(x)]$$

is a quadratic semi-bent Boolean function.

Another related approach, though without restriction on the degree of a single bent function used, is given by the following result.

Theorem 2. *Let f be bent Boolean function in even number of variables. For* $a, \alpha \in \mathbb{F}_2^n$ *such that* $a \cdot \alpha = 1$ *define the function g as either*

$$g(x) = \begin{cases} f(x) + \alpha \cdot x + d \\ f(x+a) + \alpha \cdot x + d \end{cases}, \tag{9}$$

where $d \in \mathbb{F}_2$*. Then, the function*

$$h(x) = f(x) + g(x) + D_a f(x) + D_a[f(x)g(x)]$$

is a semi-bent function.

Proof. Obviously, in both cases g is also a bent function, and if $g(x) = f(x) + \alpha x + d$, we have

$$\begin{aligned} D_a f(x) + D_a g(x) &= [f(x) + f(x+a)] + [g(x) + g(x+a)] \\ &= [f(x) + f(x+a)] + [f(x) + \alpha x + d + f(x+a) + \alpha x + a\alpha + d] \\ &= a \cdot \alpha = 1. \end{aligned}$$

A similar calculation gives that

$$D_a f(x) + D_a g(x) = 1 \text{ if } g(x) = f(x+a) + \alpha x + d.$$

By Theorem 1 we deduce that $h(x) = f(x) + g(x) + D_a f(x) + D_a[f(x)g(x)]$ is a semi-bent function. q.e.d.

This result enables us to construct, for even n, an infinite sequence of semi-bent functions from bent functions. It would be of interest to find other examples or classes of bent functions g_1, g_2, apart from using affine equivalent functions g_1 and g_2, satisfying $D_a g_1(x) = D_a g_2(x) + 1$. This appears to be a nontrivial task since apart from establishing the fact that the used bent functions are indeed affine inequivalent, at the same time, their derivatives need to satisfy the condition in Theorem 1.

Example 1. Let $f(x_1, x_2, x_3, x_4, x_5, x_6) = x_1x_3x_4 + x_2x_3x_4 + x_1x_5x_6 + x_2x_5x_6 + x_1x_2 + x_3x_5 + x_4x_6 + x_5x_6$ be a bent function of degree 3 over $\mathbb{F}_2^6$. Take $a = (0,0,1,0,0,0)$ and $\alpha = (1,0,1,0,0,0)$ such that $a \cdot \alpha = 1$. Define the function g as either

$$g(x) = \begin{cases} f(x) + x_1 + x_3 \\ f(x+a) + x_1 + x_3 \end{cases} = \begin{cases} f(x) + x_1 + x_3 \\ f(x) + x_1x_4 + x_2x_4 + x_1 + x_3 + x_5 \end{cases},$$

where $d = 0 \in \mathbb{F}_2$.

Let us take $g(x) = f(x) + x_1 + x_3$. We have

$$D_af(x) = f(x) + f(x+a) = f(x) + f(x) + x_1x_4 + x_2x_4 + x_5 = x_1x_4 + x_2x_4 + x_5,$$

so that

$$f(x) + g(x) + D_af(x) = x_1x_4 + x_2x_4 + x_1 + x_3 + x_5.$$

Then, using the idempotent property of Boolean ring,

$$\begin{aligned} f(x)g(x) &= f(x)(f(x) + x_1 + x_3) = f(x)(1 + x_1 + x_3) \\ &= (x_1x_3x_4 + x_2x_3x_4 + x_1x_5x_6 + x_2x_5x_6 + x_1x_2 + x_3x_5 + x_4x_6 + x_5x_6)(1 + x_1 + x_5) \\ &= x_1x_2x_3x_4 + x_1x_2x_5x_6 + x_2x_3x_4x_5 + x_1x_2x_5 + x_1x_3x_4 + x_1x_3x_5 + x_1x_4x_6 \\ &\quad + x_2x_3x_4 + x_4x_5x_6 + x_4x_6. \end{aligned}$$

$$\begin{aligned} f(x+a)g(x+a) &= f(x+a)(f(x+a) + x_1 + x_3 + 1) = f(x+a)(x_1 + x_3) \\ &= (f(x) + x_1x_4 + x_2x_4 + x_5)(x_1 + x_3) \\ &= f(x)(x_1 + x_3) + (x_1x_4 + x_2x_4 + x_5)(x_1 + x_3). \end{aligned}$$

After some simplification, we get

$$\begin{aligned} D_a[f(x)g(x)] &= f(x)g(x) + f(x+a)g(x+a) \\ &= f(x) + (x_1x_4 + x_2x_4 + x_5)(x_1 + x_3) \\ &= x_1x_5x_6 + x_2x_5x_6 + x_1x_2 + x_1x_4 + x_1x_5 + x_2x_4 + x_4x_6 + x_5x_6. \end{aligned}$$

Finally,

$$\begin{aligned} h(x) &= f(x) + g(x) + D_af(x) + D_a[f(x)g(x)] \\ &= x_1x_5x_6 + x_2x_5x_6 + x_1x_2 + x_1x_5 + x_4x_6 + x_5x_6 + x_1 + x_3 + x_5. \end{aligned}$$

It is easy to compute the Walsh spectrum of function $h(x)$, i.e., $W_h(\omega) = \{0, \pm 16\}$, which means that $h(x)$ is a semi-bent function.

Notice that the standard derivation rule for multiplication does not apply for our definition of derivatives. Indeed, the derivative $D_a[f(x)g(x)] = f(x)g(x) + f(x+a)g(x+a)$ is different from $g(x)D_af(x) + f(x)D_ag(x) = f(x+a)g(x) + f(x)g(x+a)$. Furthermore, using the fact that $D_aD_af(x) = 0$ for any Boolean function f, we have

$$\begin{aligned} D_ah(x) &= h(x) + h(x+a) \\ &= f(x) + g(x) + D_af(x) + D_a[f(x)g(x)] + f(x+a) + g(x+a) \\ &\quad + D_af(x+a) + D_a[f(x+a)g(x+a)] \\ &= D_af(x) + D_ag(x) + D_aD_af(x) + D_aD_a[f(x)g(x)] \\ &= D_af(x) + D_ag(x) = 1. \end{aligned}$$

Thus, the element a is always a linear structure of $h(x)$. Nevertheless, we show that under certain sufficient conditions, a is the only linear structure of $h(x)$. We have the following theorem.

Theorem 3. *Let h be defined as in Theorem 2, and assume that a bent function $f(x)$ is such that $\deg(D_bf(x))>1$, for any $b \in \mathbb{F}_2^n \setminus \{0\}$. Then h has a single linear structure, that is, $D_bh(x) = h(x) + h(x+b)$ is a constant function only for $b = a$.*

Proof. Assume that $g(x) = f(x+a) + \alpha x + d$. Without loss of generality, we can take $d = 0$. Then,

$$\begin{aligned} D_b f(x) + D_b g(x) &= [f(x) + f(x+b)] + [g(x) + g(x+b)] \\ &= [f(x) + f(x+b)] + [f(x+a) + \alpha(x+a) + d + f(x+a+b) + \alpha(x+a+b) + d] \\ &= D_b D_a f(x) + \alpha b, \end{aligned}$$

where $D_b D_a f(x) = f(x) + f(x+a) + f(x+b) + f(x+a+b)$, and therefore

$$D_b h(x) = D_b D_a f(x) + \alpha b + D_b D_a f(x) + D_b D_a [f(x) g(x)] = D_b D_a [f(x) g(x)] + \alpha b.$$

Hence, $D_b h(x)$ is constant if and only if $D_b D_a [f(x) g(x)]$ is constant. But,

$$\begin{aligned} D_b D_a [f(x) g(x)] &= D_b [f(x) g(x) + f(x+a) g(x+a)] \\ &= D_b [f(x)(f(x+a) + \alpha x) + f(x+a)(f(x) + \alpha(x+a))] \\ &= D_b [\alpha x (f(x) + f(x+a)) + \alpha a f(x+a)] \\ &= D_b [\alpha x (f(x) + f(x+a)) + f(x+a)] \\ &= \alpha x D_b D_a f(x) + \alpha b [f(x+b) + f(x+a+b)] + f(x+a) + f(x+a+b). \end{aligned}$$

Thus, if $\alpha b = 0$, then $D_b h(x)$ is constant if and only if

$$\begin{gathered} \alpha x D_b D_a f(x) = f(x+a) + f(x+a+b) \\ \alpha x [f(x) + f(x+a) + f(x+b) + f(x+a+b)] = f(x+a) + f(x+a+b) \\ (\alpha x + 1)[f(x+a) + f(x+a+b)] + \alpha x [f(x) + f(x+b)] = 0 \\ (\alpha x + 1) D_b f(x+a) + \alpha x D_b f(x) = 0 \\ \alpha x D_b f(x+a) + \alpha x D_b f(x) + D_b f(x+a) = 0. \end{gathered}$$

There are four possible cases:

1. $\alpha x D_b f(x+a) = \alpha x D_b f(x) = D_b f(x+a) = 0$, i.e.,
   $D_b f(x+a) = 0 \Leftrightarrow f(x+a) = f(x+a+b) \Rightarrow b = 0$. A contradiction.

2. $\alpha x D_b f(x+a) = \alpha x D_b f(x) = 1 \wedge D_b f(x+a) = 0$, i.e.,
   $D_b f(x+a) = 0 \Rightarrow b = 0$. A contradiction.

3. $\alpha x D_b f(x+a) = 0 \wedge \alpha x D_b f(x) = D_b f(x+a) = 1$, i.e.,
   $D_b f(x+a) = 0 \Rightarrow b = 0$. A contradiction.

4. $\alpha x D_b f(x+a) = D_b f(x+a) = 1 \wedge \alpha x D_b f(x) = 0$, i.e.,
   $D_b f(x+a) = 0 \Rightarrow b = 0$. A contradiction.

On the other hand, if $\alpha b = 1$, then $D_b h(x)$ is constant if and only if

$$\begin{gathered} \alpha x D_b D_a f(x) = f(x+a) + f(x+b) \\ \alpha x [f(x) + f(x+a) + f(x+b) + f(x+a+b)] = f(x+a) + f(x+b) \\ (\alpha x + 1)[f(x+a) + f(x+b)] + \alpha x [f(x) + f(x+a+b)] = 0. \end{gathered}$$

It is obvious that $f(x+a) = f(x+b)$ is equivalent to $f(x) = f(x+a+b)$. Thus, the above equation is constant if and only if $f(x+a) = f(x+b)$, which implies that $a = b$. The sufficiency of this condition is obvious. For the necessity, we first observe that for $a \neq b$ the functions $f(x+a) + f(x+b)$ and $f(x) + f(x+a+b)$ being derivatives of a bent function f are both nonconstant. Then, assuming that

$$D_b D_a f(x) = f(x) + f(x+a) + f(x+b) + f(x+a+b) = 0,$$

it would imply that $f(x+a) + f(x+b)$ is constant, a contradiction. On the other hand, the function $\alpha x D_b D_a f(x)$ cannot be balanced, unless $D_b D_a f(x) = \alpha x$. Because of the assumption, deg($f(x+a) + f(x+b)$)>1 and therefore cannot be equal to αx.

The proof for the case $g(x) = f(x) + \alpha x + d$ is similar as above, and it is omitted here. q.e.d.

Notice the condition in Theorem 3 that deg($D_b f(x)$)>1 is sufficient but may not be necessary. An analysis of other cryptographic criteria appears to be difficult due to the dependency of h on the choice of a bent function f and the use of the derivative $D_a[f(x)g(x)]$ in its definition, which is illustrated in the following example.

Example 2. Let n be even and $f(x,y) = x \cdot y$, where $x, y \in \mathbb{F}_2^k$ is a bent function and belongs to the Maiorana-McFarland class. Then, defining $g(x,y) = f(x+a, y+b) + (\alpha, \beta) \cdot (x,y)$ for a nonzero $(a,b) \in \mathbb{F}_2^k \times \mathbb{F}_2^k$ such that $(\alpha, \beta) \cdot (a,b) = 1$, we have

$$g(x,y) = x \cdot y + (\alpha + b) \cdot x + (a + \beta) \cdot y + a \cdot b,$$

which is clearly a bent function obtained by adding an affine function to f. Similarly,

$D_{(a,b)} f(x,y) = x \cdot b + a \cdot y + a \cdot b$, so that

$$f(x,y) + g(x,y) + D_{(a,b)} f(x,y) = \alpha \cdot x + \beta \cdot y.$$

Then, using the idempotent property of Boolean ring,

$$\begin{aligned} f(x,y) \cdot g(x,y) &= (x \cdot y)(x \cdot y + (\alpha + b) \cdot x + (a + \beta) \cdot y + a \cdot b) \\ &= (1 + a \cdot b)(x,y) + ((\alpha + b) \cdot x + (a + \beta) \cdot y)(x \cdot y). \end{aligned}$$

Note that the first term is a quadratic function and the second term is cubic. After some simplifications we have

$$\begin{aligned} D_{(a,b)}[f(x,y)g(x,y)] &= x \cdot y + (b \cdot x + a \cdot y + a \cdot b)(1 + a \cdot b + \alpha \cdot x + \alpha \cdot a + b \cdot x \\ &\quad + a \cdot b + a \cdot y + \beta \cdot y + \beta \cdot b) \\ &= x \cdot y + (b \cdot x + a \cdot y + a \cdot b)(\alpha \cdot x + b \cdot x + a \cdot y + \beta \cdot y + a \cdot b + \beta \cdot b) \\ &= x \cdot y + (b \cdot x + a \cdot y + a \cdot b)((\alpha + b) \cdot x + (\beta + a) \cdot y + a \cdot b + \beta \cdot b). \end{aligned}$$

Finally,

$$\begin{aligned} h(x,y) &= f(x,y) + g(x,y) + D_{(a,b)} f(x,y) + D_{(a,b)}[f(x,y)g(x,y)] \\ &= x \cdot y + (\alpha \cdot x + \beta \cdot y)(b \cdot x + a \cdot y + a \cdot b + 1) + (b \cdot x + a \cdot y + a \cdot b)(1 + \beta \cdot b). \end{aligned}$$

More precisely, it can be illustrated using Example 1.

Example 3. Let
$f(x_1, x_2, x_3, x_4, x_5, x_6) = x_1x_3x_4 + x_2x_3x_4 + x_1x_5x_6 + x_2x_5x_6 + x_1x_2 + x_3x_5 +$ $x_4x_6 + x_5x_6$ be a bent function of degree 3 over $\mathbb{F}_2^6$. Take $a = (0, 0, 1, 0, 0, 0)$ and $\alpha = (1, 0, 1, 0, 0, 0)$ such that $a \cdot \alpha = 1$. Define the function g as $g(x) = f(x) + x_1 + x_3$. By Example 1 we have

$$h(x) = x_1x_5x_6 + x_2x_5x_6 + x_1x_2 + x_1x_5 + x_4x_6 + x_5x_6 + x_1 + x_3 + x_5.$$

Moreover, by Theorem 2 h has a single linear structure only for $b = a$. Indeed,

$$\begin{aligned} D_a h(x) &= h(x) + h(x + a) \\ &= x_1x_5x_6 + x_2x_5x_6 + x_1x_2 + x_1x_5 + x_4x_6 + x_5x_6 + x_1 + x_3 + x_5 + \\ &\quad + x_1x_5x_6 + x_2x_5x_6 + x_1x_2 + x_1x_5 + x_4x_6 + x_5x_6 + x_1 + x_3 + 1 + x_5 \\ &= 1. \end{aligned}$$

5. Conclusions

The need for the most possible secure cryptographic primitives in cipher systems is of great importance. In the case of stream ciphers, most of the reliability and security lies in the Boolean functions. For the cryptographic point of view to be good, a Boolean function should possess several cryptographic properties mentioned in this work. Very often such properties contradict each other. Therefore, the problem of constructing Boolean functions with stronger cryptographic properties is still a vivid research activity. We may also require new properties because attacks never stop. On the other hand, semi-bent functions are interesting for defending against the so-called soft output joint attack on pseudorandom generators, which are used in the IS-95 standard of code division multiple access technology. In this work we present an infinite sequence of semi-bent functions using known classes of quadratic bent functions. The construction of other classes of infinite sequences of semi-bent functions is an interesting research challenge.

Acknowledgements

This research was supported by the Slovenian Research Agency (research program P2-0037).

Author details

Samed Bajrić
Laboratory for Open Systems and Networks, Jožef Stefan Institute, Ljubljana, Slovenia

*Address all correspondence to: samed@e5.ijs.si

References

[1] Chee S, Lee S, Kim K. Semi-bent functions. In: Advances in Cryptology-ASIACRYPT94. 1994

[2] Ding C, Mesnager S, Tang C, Xiong M. Cyclic Bent Functions and their Applications in Codes, Codebooks, Designs, MUBs and Sequences. 2018. Available from: https://arxiv.org/pdf/1811.07725.pdf

[3] Hunt FH, Smith DH. The construction of orthogonal variable spreading factor codes from semi-bent functions. IEEE Transactions on Wireless Communications. 2012;**11**(8): 2970-2975

[4] Mesnager S. Bent Functions—Fundamentals and Results. Switzerland: Springer International Publishing; 2016

[5] Massey JL. Shift-register synthesis and BCH decoding. IEEE Transactions on Information Theory. 1969;**15**(1): 1222-1127

[6] Ronjom S, Helleseth T. A new attack on the filter generator. IEEE Transactions on Information Theory. 2007;**53**(5):1752-1758

[7] Andreeva E, Bogdanov A, Mennink B. Towards understanding the known-key security of block ciphers. In: International Workshop on Fast Software Encryption. Springer; 2013

[8] Liu J, Mesnager S, Chen L. On the nonlinearity of S-boxes and linear codes. Cryptography and Communications. 2016:345-361

[9] Siegenthaler T. Correlation-immunity of nonlinear combining functions for cryptographic applications. IEEE Transactions on Information Theory. 1984;**30**:776-780

[10] Tang D, Carlet C, Tang X. Highly nonlinear Boolean functions with optimal algebraic immunity and good behavior against fast algebraic attacks. In: Transactions on Information Theory; Institute of Electrical and Electronics Engineers. 2013. pp. 653-664

[11] Courtois N, Meier W. Algebraic attacks on stream ciphers with linear feedback. In: EUROCRYPT 2003. LNCS 2656. Springer; 2003. pp. 345-359

[12] Han G, Li X, Zhou Q, Zheng D, Li H. 1-resilient Boolean functions on even variables with almost perfect algebraic immunity. Security and Communication Networks. 2017;**2017**:9

[13] Li LY, Zhang WG. Construction of resilient Boolean functions with high nonlinearity and good algebraic degree. Security and Communication Networks. 2015:2909-2916

[14] Maitra S, Pasalic E. Further constructions of resilient Boolean functions with very high nonlinearity. IEEE Transactions on Information Theory. 2002;**48**(7):1825-1834

[15] Tarannikov Y. On resilient Boolean functions with maximal possible nonlinearity. In: Indocrypt 2000. LNCS 1977. Springer-Verlag; 2000. pp. 19-30

[16] Pasalic E, Johansson T, Maitra S, Sarkar P. New constructions of resilient and correlation immune Boolean functions achieving upper bounds on nonlinearity. In: Workshop on Coding and Cryptography. Elsevier Science; 2001. pp. 425-435

[17] Sarkar P, Maitra S. Construction of nonlinear Boolean functions with important cryptographic properties. In: Advances in Cryptology EUROCRYPT 2000. LNCS 1807. Springer-Verlag; 2000. pp. 485-506

[18] Carlet C. On the secondary constructions of resilient and bent

functions. In: Coding, Cryptography and Combinatorics. Basel: Birkahauser Verlag; 2004. pp. 3-28

[19] Gao SM, Zhao Y, Zhao Z. Walsh spectrum of cryptographically concatenating functions and its applications in constructing resilient Boolean functions. The Journal of Computer Information Systems. 2011; 7(4):1074-1081

[20] Zhang W, Xiao G. Constructions of almost optimal resilient Boolean functions on large even number of variables. IEEE Transactions on Information Theory. 2009;**55**(12): 5822-5831

[21] Zhang W, Pasalic E. Improving the lower bound on the maximum nonlinearity of 1-resilient Boolean functions and designing functions satisfying all cryptographic criteria. Information Sciences. 2017;**376**:21-30

[22] Zhang F, Wei Y, Pasalic E, Xia S. Large sets of disjoint spectra plateaued functions inequivalent to partially linear functions. IEEE Transactions on Information Theory. 2018:2987-2999

[23] Carlet C, Mesnager S. On semibent Boolean functions. IEEE Transactions on Information Theory. 2012;**58**(5): 3287-3292

[24] Sun G, Wu C. Construction of semi-bent Boolean functions in even number of variables. Chinese Journal of Electronics. 2009;**18**(2):231-237

[25] Pasalic E, Gangopadhyay S, Zhang W, Bajric S. Design methods for semi-bent functions. Information Processing Letters. 2019:61-70

Chapter 2

Survey of RSA Vulnerabilities

Anthony Overmars

Abstract

Rivest et al. patented (US) RSA. RSA forms the basis of most public encryption systems. It describes a public key encryption algorithm and certification process, which protects user data over networks. The patent expired in September 2000 and now is available for general use. According to Marketsandmarkets.com, the global network encryption market size is expected to grow from USD 2.9 billion in 2018 to USD 4.6 billion by 2023, at a compound annual growth rate (CAGR) of 9.8%. Major growth drivers for the market include increasing adoption of optical transmission, an increasing demand to meet various regulatory compliances and a growing focus on shielding organizations from network security breaches. In short, RSA forms the basis of almost all public encryption systems. This, however, is not without risk. This chapter explores some of these vulnerabilities in a mathematical context and provides the reader with an appreciation of the strength of RSA.

Keywords: survey, public keys, vulnerability

1. Introduction

Rivest et al. patented (US) RSA, which forms the basis for most public encryption systems. RSA describes a public key encryption algorithm and certification process, which protects user data over networks. The patent expired in September 2000 and now is available for general use. According to Marketsandmarkets.com [1], the global network encryption market size is expected to grow from USD 2.9 billion in 2018 to USD 4.6 billion by 2023, at a compound annual growth rate (CAGR) of 9.8%. Major growth drivers for the market include increasing adoption of optical transmission, an increasing demand to meet various regulatory compliances and a growing focus on shielding organizations from network security breaches. In short, RSA forms the basis of almost all public encryption systems. This, however, is not without risk. This chapter explores some of these vulnerabilities in a mathematical context and provides the reader with an appreciation of the strength of RSA.

RSA is secure and difficult to factorize in polynomial time. Conventional sequential computing machines, running in polynomial time, take an unfeasible amount of CPU cycles to find factorization solutions to RSA keys. Quantum computing holds great promise; this, however, is realistically still some way off. Opportunities exist using conventional computing (sequential and parallel) using better mathematical techniques. A discussion on exploiting implementation flaws is also considered.

Of keen interest is our lack of understanding of prime numbers and their structure. The current perception is that there appears to be some underlying structure, but essentially, primes are randomly distributed. This is explored in Sections 8 and 12.

Vulnerabilities in the selection of primes are exploited in Section 5 using Euler's factorization.

Poor RSA key design and their exploits are considered in Section 6 using Wiener's method and in Sections 15–17 using a combination of LLL, Coppersmith and Pohlig-Hellman. All of these attacks can be mitigated by designing the RSA keys with these exploits in mind. RSA key design (Section 2) consists of two parts, a private key $(\boldsymbol{N}, \boldsymbol{d})$ and a public key $(\boldsymbol{N}, \boldsymbol{e})$. A composite number N, is derived from two prime numbers. The $(\boldsymbol{d}, \boldsymbol{e})$ numbers are selected in an ad hoc manner using Euler's totient.

Development of quantum computing is continuing at breakneck speed; however useful machines are yet to appear. Parallel computing however is here and now, and whilst factorizing RSA keys is not achievable on conventional computers in polynomial time, parallel computing has allowed for multiple solutions to be tested simultaneously. This is an area where research continues and new algorithms as shown in Sections 20 and 14 lend themselves well to GPU parallel processing systems.

2. Structure of RSA numbers

Consider RSA100 challenge number

$$\begin{aligned} RSA - 100 &= 1522605027922533360535618378132637429718068114961380 \\ &\quad 6886579084945801229632589528976540003506920061 39 \\ &= 37975227936943673922808872755445627854565536638199 \\ &\quad \times 40094690950920881030683735292761468389214899724061 \end{aligned}$$

RSA100 is a 100 binary bit number made up of two 50 binary bit prime numbers. The motivation in breaking this composite number allows us to find the Euler's totient number φ_n. Once this is known, using the public key $P_U = (N, e)$, it is possible to derive the private key $P_R = (N, d)$, and hence all cypher-text encrypted (e) messages can thus be decrypted back to plain text, using (d).

3. A simple RSA encryption/decryption example

Using two primes P_1 and P_2 to generate a composite number N,

$$N = P_1 P_2 = (1462001 \times 1462009) = 2137458620009$$

Totient φ (Euler's totient function)

Calculate totient $\varphi_n = (P_1 - 1)\ (P_2 - 1) = (1462001 - 1)\ (1462009 - 1) = 2137455696000$

Arbitrarily choose a public key such that e is an integer, not a factor of *mod N*, and $1 < e < \varphi$, $e = 13$

The public key is made up of N and e, such that $P_U = (N, e) = (2137458620009, 13)$. A private key is made up of N and d, such that $P_R = (N, d) = (2137458620009, d)$.

d, is determined using the extended Euclidean algorithm.

$e\,d \bmod \varphi_n = 113\,d \bmod 2137455696000 = 1 \Rightarrow \quad d = 1973036027077.$

Therefore, private key, $P_R = (N_1, d) = (2137458620009, 1973036027077)$.

Encrypt a message m, into cipher text C, with public key P_U. Let the message m = 1461989. $C = m^e \text{mod}\, N = 146198913^{13} \text{mod}\, (2137458620009) =$ 1912018123454. To recover the original message, decrypt using Private Key, P_R= (N, d) = (1912018123454, 1973036027077) $m = C^d \text{mod}$ $N = 1912018123454^{1973036027077} \text{mod}(2137458620009) = 1461989$.

From this simple example, consider the following: How can we use a known public key P_U = (N,e) to decrypt the original message? To decrypt the message, the private key is used: $P_R = (N, d)$. How can d, be discovered? d is derived using Euler's totient function [φ_n = $(P_1 - 1)$ $(P_2 - 1)$], and the extended Euclidean algorithm $ed \ mod \ \varphi_n = 1$. However when a public key is transmitted, the totient φ_n and the two primes P_1 and P_2 remain secret. If φ_n, P_1 or P_2 can be determined, the private key will be compromised and the cypher-text will no longer be secure.

When the totient φ_n is known, d can be determined through the normal key generation processes, so the determination of the two primes (P_1, P_2) is not required to recover the message from the cypher-text. The following proof is provided for completeness and shows how the two primes P_1, P_2 can be recovered if the composite N and the totient φ_n are known.

4. If the composite N and the totient φ_n are known, the original primes can be recovered

The quadratic formula can be used to find P_1 and P_2

$\varphi_n = (P_1 - 1)(P_2 - 1), \quad N = P_1, P_2$. General quadratic form: $ax^2 + bx + c = 0 =>$ $x = \frac{-b \pm \sqrt{b^2 - 4ac}}{2a}$

$$\varphi_n = (P_1 - 1)\ (P_2 - 1) = P_1 P_2 - P_1 - P_2 + 1 \text{ recalling } N = P_1 P_2 \Longrightarrow \varphi_n = N - P_1 - P_2 + 1$$

Express primes in terms of N, φ_n $P_1 = N - \varphi_n - P_2 + 1$, $P_2 = N - \varphi_n - P_1 + 1 N = P_1 P_2$ substitute for $P_2 \Longrightarrow N = P_1 (N - \varphi_n - P_1 + 1) = P_1 N - P_1 \varphi_n - P_1^2 + P_1$

$$P_1^2 + P_1 (\varphi_n - N - 1) + N = 0 \ ax^2 + bx + c = 0 : a = 1, b = (\varphi_n - N - 1), c = N, x = \frac{-b \pm \sqrt{b^2 - 4ac}}{2a}$$

$$P_1, P_2 = \frac{-(\boldsymbol{\varphi_n} - N - 1) \pm \sqrt{(\boldsymbol{\varphi_n} - N - 1)^2 - 4(1)N}}{2(1)} = \frac{-(\boldsymbol{\varphi_n} - N - 1) \pm \sqrt{(\boldsymbol{\varphi_n} - N - 1)^2 - 4N}}{2}$$

When N and φ_n are known: N = 2137458620009, φ_n = 2137455696000

$$P_1, P_2 = \frac{2924010 \pm \sqrt{8549834480100 - 8549834480036}}{2} = \frac{2924010 \pm \sqrt{64}}{2} = 1462005 \pm 4$$

$$P_1, P_2 = (1462001, 1462009)$$

Using the quadratic formula, P_1 and P_2 can be recovered if the composite N and the totient φ_n are known.

5. Fermat's factorization method

$N = a^2 - b^2 = (a - b)(a + b)$ is the difference of two squares.

$$P_1 = a - b, P_2 = a + b, P_1 + P_2 = 2a, P_2 - P_1 = 2b; a = \frac{P_2 + P_1}{2}, b = \frac{P_2 - P_1}{2}$$

$$N = a^2 - b^2 = \left(\frac{P_2 + P_1}{2}\right)^2 - \left(\frac{P_2 - P_1}{2}\right)^2 = \frac{1}{4}\left((P_2 + P_1)^2 - (P_2 - P_1)^2\right) = P_1 P_2$$

As the first trial for a, $a_1 = \sqrt{N}$, then check if $\Delta a_1 = a_1^2 - N$ is a square number.

There are only 22 combinations of which the last two digits are a square number. The other 78 can be eliminated.

If Δa_1 is not a square number, then $a_2 : a_2 = a_1 + 1$.

Now $\Delta a_2 = a_2^2 - N \Longrightarrow (a_1 + 1)^2 - N = a_1^2 - N + 2a_1 + 1 = \Delta a_1 + 2a_1 + 1$

$$\Delta a_3 = a_3^2 - N \Longrightarrow (a_2 + 1)^2 - N = a_2^2 - N + 2a_2 + 1 = \Delta a_2 + 2(a_1 + 1) + 1 = \Delta a_2 + 2a_1 + 3$$

$$\Delta a_4 = a_4^2 - N \Longrightarrow (a_3 + 1)^2 - N = a_3^2 - N + 2a_3 + 1 = \Delta a_3 + 2(a_1 + 2) + 1 = \Delta a_3 + 2a_1 + 5$$

so the subsequent differences are obtained by adding two.

Consider the example $N = 2137458620009$.

$$a_1 = \sqrt{N},\ a_1 = \sqrt{2137458620009} \Rightarrow a_1 = 1462005$$

Check if $\Delta a_1 = a_1^2 - N$ is a square number.

$$\Delta a_1 = a_1^2 - N = 1462005^2 - 2137458620009 = 2137458620025 - 2137458620009 = 16 = 4^2$$

$$N = 1462005^2 - 4^2 = (1462005 - 4)(1462005 + 4) = (1462001)(1462009)$$

Maurice Kraitchik, a Belgian mathematician, considered only values of a and $b : a^2 \equiv b^2 \ mod\ N$.

$$a^2 \equiv b^2 \ mod\ N \Longrightarrow \Delta\ 1462005^2 \ mod\ 2137458620009 \equiv 16$$

6. Euler's factorization method

Gaussian primes are of the form $4x - 1$, and primes of the form $4x + 1$ are Pythagorean. Fermat's Christmas theorem on sum of two squares states that an odd prime can be expressed as $P = x^2 + y^2$ iff $P \equiv 1\ mod\ 4$.

Gaussian primes are of the form $P \equiv 3\ mod\ 4$ and are not representable as the sum of two squares.

Consider a composite number N: $N = P_1 P_2$ and P_1: $P_1 = a^2 + b^2$, P_2: $P_2 = c^2 + d^2$.

$$N = P_1 P_2 = (a^2 + b^2)(c^2 + d^2) = (\mathrm{ac})^2 + (\mathrm{bc})^2 + (\mathrm{ad})^2 + (\mathrm{bd})^2$$

$$\textbf{\textit{let}}\quad \mathbf{A}^2 = (\mathbf{ac})^2 + (\boldsymbol{ad})^2, \mathbf{B}^2 = (\boldsymbol{bc})^2 + (\boldsymbol{bd})^2, \mathbf{C}^2 = (\mathbf{ac})^2 + (\boldsymbol{bc})^2, \mathbf{D}^2 = (\boldsymbol{ad})^2 + (\boldsymbol{bd})^2$$

$$N = P_1 P_2 = (\mathrm{a}^2 + \mathrm{b}^2)(\mathrm{c}^2 + \mathrm{d}^2) = (\mathrm{ac})^2 + (bc)^2 + (ad)^2 + (bd)^2 = A^2 + B^2 = C^2 + D^2$$

$$N = A^2 + B^2 = C^2 + D^2 \Rightarrow A^2 - C^2 = D^2 - B^2$$

$$A^2 - C^2 = D^2 - B^2 \Rightarrow (A - C)(A + C) = (D - B)(D + B)$$

$$P_1 = \left(\frac{gcd(A-C, D-B)}{2}\right)^2 + \left(\frac{gcd(A+C, D+B)}{2}\right)^2,$$

$$P_2 = \left(\frac{gcd(A+C, D-B)}{2}\right)^2 + \left(\frac{gcd(A-C, D+B)}{2}\right)^2$$

Consider the example $\boldsymbol{N}$ = 2137458620009; find the factorization values of P_1 and P_2.

Using the sum of squares, $N = 2137458620009 = 324403^2 + 1425560^2 = 643603^2 + 1312720^2$.

Combining the even and odds: $1425560^2 - 1312720^2 = 643603^2 - 324403^2$.

$$A^2 - C^2 = D^2 - B^2 \Rightarrow (A - C)(A + C) = (D - B)(D + B) = (968006)\ (319200) = (2738280)\ (112840)$$

Using the greatest common divisor (gcd):

$$\frac{gcd(A-C, D-B)}{2} = \frac{gcd(968006, 2738280)}{2} = 1201, \quad \frac{gcd(A+C, D+B)}{2} = \frac{gcd(319200, 112840)}{2} = 140$$
$$\frac{gcd(A+C, D-B)}{2} = \frac{gcd(319200, 2738280)}{2} = 1140, \quad \frac{gcd(A-C, D+B)}{2} = \frac{gcd(968006, 112840)}{2} = 403$$
$$P_1 = \left(\frac{gcd(A-C,D-B)}{2}\right)^2 + \left(\frac{gcd(A+C,D+B)}{2}\right)^2 = 1201^2 + 140^2 = 1462001$$
$$P_2 = \left(\frac{gcd(A+C,D-B)}{2}\right)^2 + \left(\frac{gcd(A-C,D+B)}{2}\right)^2 = 1140^2 + 403^2 = 1462009$$

7. Wiener attack

Wiener's theorem. Let $N = P_1P_2$ and $P_1 < P_2 < 2P_1$ and a private key $P_R = (N, d)$ and a public key $P_U = (N, e)$. Let $d < \frac{1}{3}N^{\frac{1}{4}}$, given a public key $P_U = (N, e)$, with $e\,d \equiv 1\, mod\ \ \varphi_n$. The attacker can efficiently recover d [2]. The attack uses the continued fraction method to expose the private key d, when d is small. It assumes $\frac{e}{N} \approx \frac{k}{d} \Rightarrow \varphi_n = \frac{ed-1}{k}$. Consider a public key $P_U = (N, e) :\ P_U = (2137458620009, 1973036027077)$

Continued fraction $\frac{1973036027077}{2137458620009} = [0; 1, 11, 1, 4684, 1, 125, 1, 10, 1, 2, 1, 1, 1, 1, 2, 3, 7, 1, 17] =$

$$\cfrac{1}{1+\cfrac{1}{11+\cfrac{1}{1+\cfrac{1}{4684+\cfrac{1}{1+\cfrac{1}{125+\cfrac{1}{1+\cfrac{1}{10+\cfrac{1}{1+\cfrac{1}{2+\cfrac{1}{1+\cfrac{1}{1+\cfrac{1}{1+\cfrac{1}{1+\cfrac{1}{2+\cfrac{1}{3+\cfrac{1}{7+\cfrac{1}{1+\cfrac{1}{17+\cfrac{1}{\cdots}}}}}}}}}}}}}}}}}}}}$$

$$\frac{e}{N} \approx \frac{k}{d} : \frac{e}{N} = \frac{1973036027077}{2137458620009} = \cfrac{1}{1 + \cfrac{1}{11 + 1 * \frac{1}{1}}} = \frac{12}{13} = \frac{k}{d}$$

$$\varphi_{\text{n}} = \frac{ed - 1}{k} = \frac{1973036027077 * 13 - 1}{12} = \frac{25649468352000}{12} = 2137455696000$$

As per Section 2, if the composite N and the totient φ_n are known, the original primes P_1 and P_2 can be recovered.

8. Sum of squares

Overmars [3] showed that all Pythagorean triples could be represented as $N = n^2 + (n + 2m - 1)^2$. If the composite number N, is constructed using two Pythagorean primes ($4x + 1$) then two representations as the sum of two squares can be found. Euler's Factorization Method (Section 4) can be applied. Finding these two representations is non-trivial and CPU-intensive. The equation $N(m,n) = n^2 + (n + 2m - 1)^2$ provides a course search using increments of n and fine convergence using m. In this way n is incremented and m is decremented about N to find the two solutions along the diagonal of a field of $N(m,n) \approx N$.

Consider the example, $N = 2137458620009$.

$$N(m_1,n_1) = n_1^2 + (n_1 + 2m_1 - 1)^2 = 324403^2 + (324403 + 2(550579) + 1)^2 = 324403^2 + 1425560^2$$
$$N(m_2,n_2) = n_2^2 + (n_2 + 2m_2 - 1)^2 = 643603^2 + (643603 + 2(334559) + 1)^2 = 643603^2 + 1312720^2$$
$$N_1(324403, 550579) = N_2(643603, 334559) = 2137458620009$$

For completeness N can be represented as two Pythagorean triangles as shown [3] $\Delta(m,n)=\Delta(a,b,c)$.

$$a(m,n) = 2n(n + 2m - 1),\ \ b(m,n) = (2m - 1)(2n + 2m - 1),\ \ c(m.n) = n^2 + (n + 2m - 1)^2$$
$$\Delta(m_1,n_1) = \Delta(a_1,b_1,c_1) : \Delta\ (324403, 550579) = \Delta(28197495801360, 8357740887191, 29410042540009)$$
$$\Delta(m_2,n_2) = \Delta(a_2,b_2,c_2) : \Delta(643603, 334559) = \Delta(1689741060320, 1309008976791, 29410042540009)$$

Once the two sum of two squares has been found, Euler's factorization method (Section 4), can be used to find the prime constructions of $N : N = P_1P_2$.

If the composite number (N) is constructed using Pythagorean primes $(4x + 1)$, then a solution exists as two sums of two squares and Euler's factorization method can be applied.

9. Gaussian and Pythagorean primes

As shown in Section 4, if Pythagorean primes $(4x + 1 \equiv 4x - 3)$ are used to construct the composite number (N), a solution exists as two sums of two squares. However, if N is constructed using Gaussian primes $(4x - 1 \equiv 4x + 3)$, then Euler's sum of two squares method cannot be used. Is there a test that we can use to see if the composite has been constructed using Pythagorean primes? (**Table 1**)

Consider the following composite constructions:

i. $N = (4x + 1)(4y + 1)$ using Pythagorean primes

ii. $N = (4x - 1)(4y - 1)$ using Gaussian primes

iii. $N = (4x + 1)(4y - 1)$ using a mix of Pythagorean and Gaussian primes

i. Pythagorean prime construction
$N = (4x + 1)(4y + 1) = 16xy + 4(x + y) + 1$ Two sum of two squares representations exist and Euler's factorization can be used. $1 \equiv P\ mod\ 4$. $9 \equiv P\ mod\ 16$. See Section 4. $793 = 13 * 61 = 3^2 + 28^2 = 8^2 + 27^2$

ii. Gaussian prime construction
$N = (4x - 1)(4y - 1) = 16xy - 4(x + y) + 1 \equiv 4m - 3 \equiv 4n + 1$ Sums of three squares exist. $1 \equiv P\ mod\ 4$. $9 \equiv P\ mod\ 16$.

	$4x-1$	$4x+1$	$x, y = 3, 15$	11	13
$4y-1$	$16xy-4(x+y)+1$	$16xy-4(x-y)-1$	59	649	767
$4y+1$	$16xy-4(y-x)-1$	$16xy+4(x+y)+1$	61	671	793

Table 1.
Possible composite constructs using Pythagorean and Gaussian primes.

$649 = 11 * 59 = 1^2 + 18^2 + 18^2 = 3^2 + 8^2 + 24^2 = 6^2 + 17^2 + 18^2 = 8^2 + 12^2 + 21^2 = 10^2 + 15^2 + 18^2 = 12^2 + 12^2 + 19^2$ Legendre's three-square theorem can test the composite: $N = x^2 + y^2 + z^2$ *true if* $N \neq 4^a(8b+7)$ $a, b \in \mathbb{Z}$,

iii. Mixed Pythagorean-Gaussian prime construction
$N = (4x+1)(4y-1) = 16xy - 4(x-y) - 1$,
$N = (4x-1)(4y+1) = 16xy + 4(x-y) - 1$. Sums of four squares exist.
$3 \equiv P \, mod \, 4$. $13 * 59 = 767$

$$
\begin{aligned}
1^2+1^2+6^2+27^2 &= 1^2+1^2++18^2+21^2 = 1^2+3^2+9^2+26^2 = 1^2+6^2+17^2+21^2 \\
&= 1^2+9^2+18^2+19^2 = 1^2+10^2+15^2+21^2 = 2^2+3^2+5^2+27^2 = 2^2+3^2+15^2+23^2 \\
&= 3^2+6^2+19^2+19^2 = 3^2+7^2+15^2+22^2 = 3^2+11^2+14^2+21^2 = 5^2+6^2+9^2+25^2 \\
&= 6^2+9^2+11^2+23^2 = 6^2+9^2+17^2+19^2 = 6^2+11^2+13^2+21^2 \\
&= 7^2+9^2+14^2+21^2 = 7^2+13^2+15^2+18^2 = 9^2+9^2+11^2+22^2 \\
&= 9^2+10^2+15^2+19^2 = 11^2+14^2+15^2+15^2
\end{aligned}
$$

In summary, a composite whose construction is based upon both Pythagorean and Gaussian primes can easily be identified when $P \, mod \, 4 \equiv 3$ is true. However, sums of four squares exist and Euler's factorization cannot be used. When $P \, mod \, 4 \equiv 1$ is true, the composite could be constructed using Pythagorean primes or Gaussian primes. Use the Legendre test to further discriminate. When the Pythagorean construct is confirmed, the two sums of two squares can be found, and Euler's factorization can be used. If the composite construction is both Pythagorean and Gaussian, sums of three squares exist and Euler's factorization cannot be used.

10. Overmars factorization method

Another classification of the composite number uses a different construct for primes and seeks to define the composite number as follows: Let $N = P_1 P_2$ and test $N : (N \pm 1) mod 4 = 0$. Two cases are considered in the classification, and this determines the constructs of the primes used. Note the sign of ± 1 determines the case used, and the test is both simple and concise [4].

Case (1) $\oplus\ominus$ $(N+1) mod 4 = 0, \quad P_1 = 2(m-n)+1, \quad P_2 = 2(m+n)-1$

1. Let $m_0 \geq \frac{\sqrt{N}}{2}, m \in \mathbb{N}^+$

2. Let $n_0 = \frac{\sqrt{4m_0^2 - N + 1}}{2}, \quad n \in \mathbb{N}^+?, \quad n \notin \mathbb{N}^+ \Rightarrow m_x = m_0 + 1$

3. Let $n = \frac{\sqrt{4m_x^2 - N + 1}}{2}, \quad n \notin \mathbb{N}^+, \mathrm{m_x} = \mathrm{m_x} + 1 \Rightarrow n : n \in \mathbb{N}^+$

4. $P_1 = 2(m-n)+1, P_2 = 2(m+n)-1$

Case (2) $\ominus\ominus(N-1)mod4=0,\quad P_1=2(m-n)-1,\quad P_2=2(m+n)-1$

1. Let $m_0 \geq \frac{\sqrt{N}+1}{2}, m \in \mathbb{N}^+$

2. Let $n_0 = \frac{\sqrt{(2m_0-1)^2-N}}{2},\quad n \in \mathbb{N}^+?,\quad n \notin \mathbb{N}^+ \Rightarrow m_x = m_0 + 1$

3. Let $n = \frac{\sqrt{(2m_x-1)^2-N}}{2},\quad n \notin \mathbb{N}^+, \mathrm{m_x} = \mathrm{m_x} + 1 \Rightarrow n : n \in \mathbb{N}^+$

4. $P_1 = 2(m-n)-1, P_2 = 2(m+n)-1$

Example $N = 5959$

1. Test $(N \pm 1)mod4 = 0 : (5959+1)\ mod\ 4 = 0 \Rightarrow case\ (1)\oplus\ominus$

2. $m_0 \geq \frac{\sqrt{N}}{2} \Rightarrow m_0 = \frac{\sqrt{5959}}{2} \Rightarrow m_0 = 39, n = 6.09, n \notin \mathbb{N}^+$

3. $m_1 = m_0 + 1 = 39 + 1 = 40$

4. $n = \frac{\sqrt{4m_1^2-N+1}}{2} \Rightarrow n_1 = \frac{\sqrt{4(40)^2-5959+1}}{2} = 11, n_1 \in \mathbb{N}^+$

5. $P_1 = 2(m-n)+1 \Rightarrow P_1 = 2(40-11)+1 = 59, P_2 = 2(m+n)-1 \Rightarrow P\_2 = 2(40+11)-1 = 101$

$$N = P_1P_2 = 59\ x\ 101 = 5959$$

This method is reasonable for small composites but becomes computationally unfeasible for large composites.

11. Extensions of the Overmars factorization method

Case (1) $\oplus\ominus(N+1)mod\ a^2 = 0,\quad P_1 = a(m-n)+1,\quad P_2 = a(m+n)-1$

$$N = [a(m-n)+1][a(m+n)-1] = a^2(m^2-n^2) + 2an - 1$$

$$N = (am)^2 - \left[(an)^2 - 2an + 1\right] = (am)^2 - (an-1)^2$$

Case (2) $\ominus\oplus(N+1)mod\ a^2 = 0,\quad P_1 = a(m-n)-1,\quad P_2 = a(m+n)+1$

$$N = [a(m-n)-1][a(m+n)+1] = a^2(m^2-n^2) - 2an - 1$$

$$N = (am)^2 - \left[(an)^2 + 2an + 1\right] = (am)^2 - (an+1)^2$$

Case (1, 2) $\frac{N+1}{a} = a(m^2-n^2) \pm 2n \quad a : a\ is\ a\ factor\ of\ N+1$

$$n = \frac{\sqrt{(am)^2 - N} \pm 1}{a}, m \geq \frac{\sqrt{N}}{a} m = \sqrt{\frac{N + (an \pm 1)^2}{a^2}},$$

Case (3) $\ominus\ominus(N-1)mod\ a^2 = 0,\quad P_1 = a(m-n)-1,\quad P_2 = a(m+n)-1$

$$N = [a(m-n)-1][a(m+n)-1] = a^2(m^2-n^2) - 2am + 1$$
$$N = (am)^2 - 2am + 1 - (an)^2 = (am-1)^2 - (an)^2$$

Case (4) $\oplus\oplus (N-1) mod\ a^2 = 0, \quad P_1 = a(m-n)+1, \quad P_2 = a(m+n)+1$

$$N = [a(m-n)+1][a(m+n)+1] = a^2(m^2-n^2) + 2am + 1$$
$$N = (am)^2 + 2am + 1 - (an)^2 = (am+1)^2 - (an)^2$$

Case (3, 4) $\frac{N-1}{a} = a(m^2-n^2) \pm 2m\ a : a\ is\ a\ factor\ of\ N-1$

$$n = \sqrt{\frac{(am \pm 1)^2 - N}{a^2}}, m \geq \frac{\sqrt{N} \mp 1}{a}, m = \frac{\sqrt{N + (an)^2} \pm 1}{a}$$

a: $a = \gcd(m, n)$ for all cases. Choosing the largest value of a ensures a rapid convergence to the solution. This is illustrated by example.

Consider $N = 211276133$

$$\text{Factors of } (N+1) \Rightarrow 211276133 + 1 = (2)(3^3)(881)(4441) \quad \textit{possible values for a}$$
$$\text{Factors of } (N-1) \Rightarrow 211276133 - 1 = (2^2)(52819033) \quad \textit{possible values for a}$$

$$\text{Case (3) } \ominus\ominus\ (N-1) mod\ a^2 \Rightarrow (211276133 - 1) mod 4 = 0 \Rightarrow a = 2$$

$$[2(m-n)-1][2(m+n)-1] = 211276133, m = 10247, n = 7223 \Rightarrow \gcd(10247, 7223) = 1$$
$$P_1 = 2(10247 - 7223) - 1 = 6047, \quad P_2 = 2(10247 + 7223) - 1 = 34939$$

$$\text{Case (2) } \ominus\oplus\ (N+1) mod\ a^2 \Rightarrow (211276133 + 1) mod 9 = 0 \Rightarrow a = 3$$

$$[3(m-n)-1][3(m+n)-1] \quad = 211276133, m = 6831, n = 4815 \Rightarrow \gcd(6831, 4815) = 9$$
$$[27(m-n)-1][27(m+n)-1] = 211276133, \quad m = 759, n = 535 \Rightarrow \gcd(759, 535) = 1$$
$$P_1 = 27(759 - 535) - 1 = 6047, \quad P_2 = 27(759 + 535) + 1 = 34939$$

Consider $N = 5959$ (Section 8)

$$\text{Factors of } (N-1) \Rightarrow 5959 - 1 = (2)(3^2)(331) \quad \textit{possible values for a}$$
$$P_1 = 3(m-n) - 1, \quad P_2 = 3(m+n) - 1, \quad m = 27, \quad n = 7, \quad \gcd(27, 7) = 1$$
$$\text{Factors of } (N+1) \Rightarrow 5959 + 1 = (2^3)(5)(149) \quad \textit{possible values for a}$$
$$P_1 = 20(m-n) + 1, \quad P_2 = 20(m+n) - 1, \quad m = 4, \quad n = 1, \quad \gcd(4, 1) = 1$$

Consider RSA100

$$P_1 = 37975227936943673922808872755445627854565536638199$$
$$P_2 = 40094690950920881030683735292761468389214899724061$$
$$P_1 = (2)(3167)(3613)(1659412543822590349622856694449324700910569) + 1$$
$$P_1 = (2^3)(3)(5^2)(109)(409)(20839813)(60236089)(49147216823)(23011759155976667) - 1$$
$$P_2 = (2^2)(5)(41)(2119363)(602799725049211)(38273186726790856290328531) + 1$$
$$P_2 = (2)(3)(11)(59)(1029653080403720622256901265864444886804031773) - 1$$

$$
\begin{aligned}
N &= P_1P_2 \\
&= \left[(2^3)(3)(5^2)(109)(409)(20839813)(60236089)(49147216823)(23011759155976667) - 1\right] \\
&\quad * \left[(2^2)(5)(41)(2119363)(602799725049211)(38273186726790856290328531) + 1\right] \\
&\quad \textit{factors of } N+1 = (2^2)(5)(7)(13^2)(63421)(83694613) \\
&\qquad (12123888348222649495900709321006776111308 9 \\
&\qquad 3465646351221267386320068406978173999673) \\
&\quad \textit{factors of } N-1 = (2)(3^2)(210974974123) \\
&\qquad (400944086233670527306310281636760087998315 \\
&\qquad 35156737766028636341028404902787982077857676 7)
\end{aligned}
$$

$N + 1$ is the better candidate, as it has more factors to try. So cases (1,2) are considered.

Case (2) $N = [a(m-n)-1][a(m+n)+1] = a^2(m^2-n^2) - 2an - 1\frac{N+1}{a} = a(m^2-n^2) - 2n\ Try\ a: a = (2)(5): \frac{N+1}{a} = a(m^2-n^2) - 2n,$
$\frac{N+1}{10} = 10(m^2-n^2) - 2n = \frac{N+1}{20} = 5(m^2-n^2) - n$
$m \geq \frac{\sqrt{N}}{a} = 3902057185540126551228957333948437101890500690019$

$$
\begin{aligned}
\frac{N+1}{a} &= (1522605027922533360535618378132637429718068114961380688 6 \\
&\quad 579084945801229632589528976540003506920061 39) + 1/20 \\
&= 761302513961266680267809189066318714859034057480690 34 \\
&\quad 43289542472900614816294764488270001753460030 7
\end{aligned}
$$

$$
\begin{aligned}
a = 10 \Rightarrow m &= 3903495944393227747674630402410354812189021818113, \\
n &= 1059731506988603553937431268657920267324681542 93\ \gcd(m,n) = 1 \\
P_1 = 10(m-n)+1 &= 37975227936943673922808872755445627854565536638199, \\
P_2 = 10(m+n)-1 &= 40094690950920881030683735292761468389214899724061
\end{aligned}
$$

When a is small, this method becomes computationally unfeasible.

12. Overmars factorization using smooth factors

Consider the construction of primes (Sections 8 and 9), $P = a(m \pm n) \pm 1$. More generally, $P: P = a(m \pm n) \pm x$ Consider $N = P_1P_2 \Rightarrow 8079781 = 1249 \times 6469$ (**Table 2**).

Case (1) $\oplus\ominus(N + x^2) mod\ a^2 = 0, \quad P_1 = a(m-n) + x, \quad P_2 = a(m+n) - x$

$$N = [a(m-n)+x][a(m+n)-x] = a^2(m^2-n^2) + 2anx - x^2$$

$$N = (am)^2 - \left[(an)^2 - 2anx + 1\right] = (am)^2 - (an-x)^2$$

Case (2) $\ominus\oplus(N + x^2) mod\ a^2 = 0, \quad P_1 = a(m-n) - x, \quad P_2 = a(m+n) + x$

$$N = [a(m-n)-1][a(m+n)+1] = a^2(m^2-n^2) - 2anx - x^2$$

$$N = (am)^2 - \left[(an)^2 + 2anx + 1\right] = (am)^2 - (an+x)^2$$

x	$N-x^2$	$\pm x$	a	m	n	gcd(m,n)	Smoothness
1	2^2 3 5 311 433	⊖⊖	10	386	261	1	5-smooth
3	2^2 479 4217	⊖⊖	2	1931	1305	1	
5	2^2 3 673313	⊖⊖	6	644	435	1	
7	2^2 3^2 103 2179	⊕⊕	18	214	145	1	3-smooth
11	**2^2 3^2 5 44887**	⊖⊖	**90**	**43**	**29**	**1**	**5-smooth**
13	2^2 3 211 3191	⊕⊕	6	641	435	1	
17	2^2 3 673291	⊖⊖	6	646	435	1	
19	2^2 3 5 17 89^2	⊕⊕	30	128	87	1	5-smooth
23	2^2 3 673271	⊖⊖	6	647	435	1	
29	2^2 3^4 5 4987	⊖⊖	18	216	145	1	5-smooth

Table 2.
$N - x^2$.

Case (1,2) $\frac{N+x^2}{a} = a(m^2 - n^2) \pm 2nx \quad a : a\ is\ a\ factor\ of\ N + x^2$

$$n = \frac{\sqrt{(am)^2 - N} \pm x}{a}, m \geq \frac{\sqrt{N + (a \mp x)^2}}{a}, m = \sqrt{\frac{N + (an \pm x)^2}{a^2}}$$

Case (3) $\ominus\ominus(N - x^2) mod\ a^2 = 0, \quad P_1 = a(m - n) - x, \quad P_2 = a(m + n) - x$

$$N = [a(m-n) - x][a(m+n) - x] = a^2(m^2 - n^2) - 2amx + x^2$$
$$N = (am)^2 - 2amx + x^2 - (an)^2 = (am - x)^2 - (an)^2$$

Case (4) $\oplus\oplus(N - x^2) mod\ a^2 = 0, \quad P_1 = a(m - n) + x, \quad P_2 = a(m + n) + x$

$$N = [a(m-n) + x][a(m+n) + x] = a^2(m^2 - n^2) + 2amx + x^2$$
$$N = (am)^2 + 2amx + x^2 - (an)^2 = (am + x)^2 - (an)^2$$

Case (3,4) $\frac{N-x^2}{a} = a(m^2 - n^2) \pm 2mx \quad a : a\ is\ a\ factor\ of\ N - x^2$

$$n = \sqrt{\frac{(am \pm x)^2 - N}{a^2}}, m \geq \frac{\sqrt{N} \mp x^2}{a}, m = \frac{\sqrt{N + (an)^2} \pm x^2}{a}$$
$$N = [90(43 - 29) - 11][90(43 + 29) - 11] = 1249 \times 6469$$

When a smooth x can be found, larger a values allow for faster convergence to a solution. The selection of x and a is somewhat arbitrary and prime constructs are a modification of Fermat's $a^2 - b^2$. Smooth factors of $N \pm x^2$ produce larger a values and convergence faster to a solution.

13. Primes

The current state of the art in prime number generation is Atkin's sieve [5, 6].

The algorithm completely ignores any numbers with remainder mod 60 that is divisible by 2, 3 or 5, since numbers with a mod 60 remainder divisible by one of these three primes are themselves divisible by that prime. Atkin stated three theorems given below:

1. All numbers n with mod 60 remainder 1, 13, 17, 29, 37, 41, 49 or 53 are mod 4 $\equiv$ 1. These numbers are prime if the number of solutions to $4x^2 + y^2 = n$ is odd and the number is squarefree.

2. All numbers n with mod 60 remainder 7, 19, 31 or 43 have a mod 6 $\equiv$ 1. These numbers are prime if and only if the number of solutions to $3x^2 + y^2 = n$ is odd and the number is squarefree.

3. All numbers n with mod 60 remainder 11, 23, 47 or 59 have a mod 12 $\equiv$ 11. These numbers are prime if and only if the number of solutions to $3x^2 - y^2 = n$ is odd and the number is squarefree.

None of the primes are divisible by 2, 3 or 5 and are not divisible by their squares (2^2, 3^2, and 5^2). For a thorough analysis of "primes of the Form $x^2 + ny^2$" the reader is referred to a text by Cox [7].

The often overlooked works of Dubner, who is credited with the term "primorial" [8] are now considered [9, 10]. The primorial is a factorial of primes: $1\# = 2$, $2\# = 2x3 = 6$, $3\# = 2x3x5 = 30$, $4\# = \#3x7 = 210$ and so on. $0\# = 1$. The primorial is by definition squarefree.

The nth primorial is the product of n primes, where $\pi(n)$ is the prime counting function.

$$n\# = \prod_{i=1}^{\pi(n)} p_i = p_{\pi(n)}\#$$

Using this structure, Dubner was able to create series of primes in a particular primorial.

It can be shown that the structure of primes is palindromic in the primorials [11].

For example, in **Figure 1**, take the discrete derivative of the numbers in the third primorial, 3#. The following palindromic sequence can be added to #3 = 30 and subtracted from #4 = 210 to determine all of the primes in that primorial:

30 + 1,	10,	2,	4,	2,	4,	6,	2,	6,	4,	2,	4,	6,	6,	2,	6,	4,	2,	6,	4,	6,	8,	4,	2
210 − 1,	10,	2,	4,	2,	4,	6,	2,	6,	4,	2,	4,	6,	6,	2,	6,	4,	2,	6,	4,	6,	8,	4,	2

This describes the second table in **Figure 1**. All of the primes in the third primorial can be found using 24 ***small*** numbers. Mod 7 is used to sieve and eliminate composite multiples of 7. Mod 11 and 13 are used to highlight further composites, but these are kept and used to generate primes in the next primorial.

Modulo testing: $P \bmod m = 0,\ P_k < m < \sqrt{(k+1)\#}$

For $k = 3$, $P_k : P_3 = 5$, $P_{k+1} : P_4 = 7$, $\#3 = 30$, $\#4 = 210$, $\sqrt{210} \approx 14$, $m = 7, 11, 13$, eliminate $P_{k+1} = 7$

As shown in **Figure 2**, 24 small numbers are used to derive 482 new values. This uses 10 modulo tests to identify composites and 1 modulo test to eliminate factors of 11 (**Figure 3**).

$P_n\#$, $\Delta P_{n-1}\#$ Current primorial and the difference between primes from the previous. Simple array descriptor provides rich prime fields of higher densities. Small numbers describe primes of higher magnitude. Large arrays of primes can be stored in much less memory.

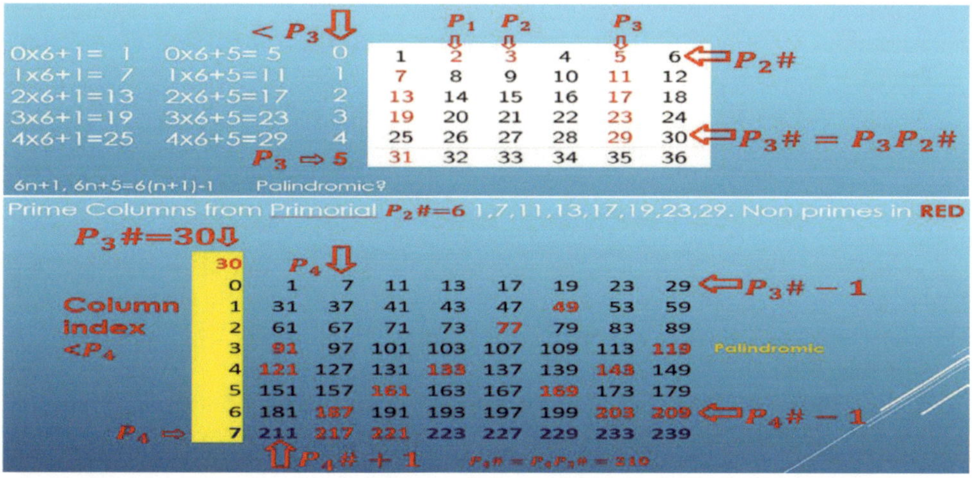

Figure 1.
Creating primes using primorials.

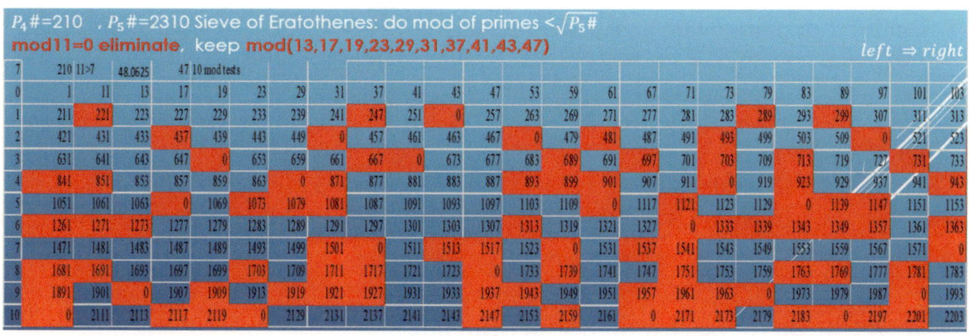

Figure 2.
Primes in the 4th primorial.

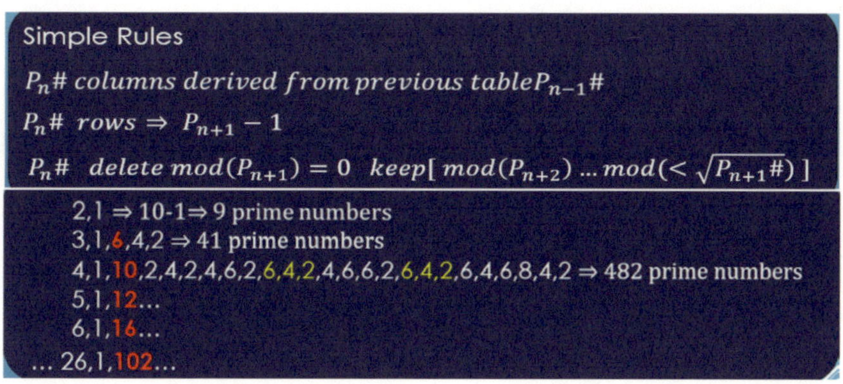

Figure 3.
Gaps between primes of each successive primorial.

14. Number systems

Conventional numbering systems consist of a base (or radix).

The primorial number system is said to be 'primoradic'; having a primorial base. The primorial number system is a mixed radix numeral system adapted to the numbering of the primorials (**Table 3**).

n	...	7	6	5	4	3	2	1
p_n	n...	17	13	11	7	5	3	2
$n\#$	...	510510	30030	2310	210	30	6	2
highest	$P_{n+1}-1$	18	16	12	10	6	4	1

Table 3.
Primorial radix number system.

General properties of mixed radix number systems apply to the base primorial system. The primorial number system OEIS A000040 is denoted by a subscript "$\prod$".

Consider the following example:

Primorial to decimal, Base$_{\prod}$ to Base$_{10}$

$3\ 4\ 1\ 0\ 1_{\prod}$ stands for $3_4 4_3 1_2 0_1 1_0$, whose value is

$$= 3\times p_4\# + 4\times p_3\# + 1\times p_2\# + 0\times p_1\# + 1\times p_0\# = 3\times \mathbf{210} + 4\times \mathbf{30} + 1\times \mathbf{6} + 0\times \mathbf{2} + 1\times \mathbf{1}$$

$$= ((((3\times 7+4)\times 5+1)\times 3+0)\times 2+1)\times 1 = 757_{10}.$$

Decimal to primorial, Base$_{10}$ into Base$_{\prod}$

757_{10} into a primorial representation by successive divisions:

757 ÷ 2 = 231, remainder 1

378 ÷ 3 = 126, remainder 0

126 ÷ 5 = 25, remainder 1

25 ÷ 7 = 3, remainder 4

3 ÷ 11 = 3, remainder 3 => $3\ 4\ 1\ 0\ 1_{\prod}$

15. RSA100 factorization using primorials

$$N = (P_1)(P_2) = (aP_k\# + c)(aP_k\# + d) = (aP_k\#)^2 + (c+d)aP_k\# + cd$$

$$P_k\#^2 \le N \quad 1522605027922533360535618378132637429718068114961380688657908\because$$
$$4945801229632589528976540003506920 06139/p_{31}\#^2$$

$$(aP_k\#)^2 \le N \quad 1522605027922533360535618378132637429718068114961380688657908\because$$
$$494580122963258952897654000350692006139/(9p_{31}\#^2)$$

$$N = (aP_k\# + c)(aP_k\# + d) = (aP_k\# + cP_{k-1}\# + e)(aP_k\# + dP_{k-1}\# + f)$$

$$P_k\# = P_k(P_{k-1}\#)$$

$$N = (aP_k(P_{k-1}\#) + cP_{k-1}\# + e)(aP_k(P_{k-1}\#) + dP_{k-1}\# + f)$$
$$= ((aP_k + c)P_{k-1}\# + e)((aP_k + d)P_{k-1}\# + f)$$

$$N = (aP_k + c)(aP_k + d)(P_{k-1}\#)^2 + (f(aP_k + c) + e(aP_k + d))(P_{k-1}\#) + ef$$

$$(aP_k + c)(aP_k + d)(P_{k-1}\#)^2 \le N \Rightarrow (aP_k + c)(aP_k + d) = \frac{N - Nmod(P_{k-1}\#)^2}{(P_{k-1}\#)^2}$$

$$N = 1523830x^2 + 2740604600516696743786326304074090349972 6862x$$
$$+ 1223137822471921778127070785059156467154889 7759$$

$\mathbf{1523830 = 2 \times 5 \times 7 \times 11 \times 1979 = (770)(1979){=}(1234{-}464)(1234{+}745)}$
Not symmetrical about square root [12]

$\mathbf{1522868 = 2^2 \times 317 \times 1201 = (1201)(1268) = (1234 - 33)(1234 + 34)}$
Symmetrical about square root.

$$\boldsymbol{N = (aP_k + c)(aP_k + d)(P_{k-1}\#)^2 + (f(aP_k + c) + e(aP_k + d))(P_{k-1}\#) + ef}$$

$$\boldsymbol{(aP_k + c)(aP_k + d)(P_{k-1}\#)^2 \leq N \Rightarrow (aP_k + c)(aP_k + d) = \frac{N - Nmod(P_{k-1}\#)^2}{(P_{k-1}\#)^2}}$$

$$152164293549261753976557910666413674840137961591 4\ddots$$

$$3121693153860418832346277226920287113789343979 66\ddots$$

$$800/p_{30}\#^2$$

Consider each congruency and look for a factorization that is symmetrical about the square root.

In this case 1234 + 34 =1268, 1234 – 33 = 1201.

$$N = (aP_k + c)(aP_k + d)(P_{k-1}\#)^2 + (f(aP_k + c) + e(aP_k + d))(P_{k-1}\#) + ef$$

$$30431475913593577738588710930551227419722971658953x+$$

$$15181665958090166488552341928111599882352701906734540563 1\ddots$$

$$4011835670903453420391527341879178 69,$$

$$N = ((aP_k + c)P_{k-1}\# + e)((aP_k + d)P_{k-1}\# + f)$$

$$\mathbf{k = 31,\ \ P_{31} = 127,\ \ (aP_k + c) = 1201,\ \ (aP_k + d) = 12}$$

$$a = 9,\ \ c = 58,\ \ d = 125,\ \ P_{31} = 127$$

$$\boldsymbol{N = (9P_{31}\# + 58P_{30}\# + e)(9P_{31}\# + 125P_{30}\# + f)}$$

$$\boldsymbol{N = (1201)(1268)P_{30}^2 + (1201f + 1268e)P_{30} + ef}$$

$$\boldsymbol{N = (a^2 + m)P_{31}^2 + (a(c + d) + n)P_{31} + cd}$$

$$\boldsymbol{a^2 + m = \frac{N - NmodP_k^2\#}{P_k^2\#} = 94 \qquad \Rightarrow a = 9,\ \ m = 13}$$

$$\boldsymbol{a^2P_{k^\#}^2 + [a(c + d) + mP_k\#]P_k\# + (nP_k\# + cd)}$$

$$\boldsymbol{P_k\# = P_k(P_{k-1}\#) \Rightarrow N = (1201)(1268)P_{30}^2\# + (1201f + 1268e)P_{30}{}^\# + ef}$$

$$\boldsymbol{N = (9P_{31}\# + 58P_{30}\# + e)(9P_{31}\# + 125P_{30}\# + f)}$$

Repeat these steps for $\boldsymbol{P_{29}\#}$ and so on... **(Table 4)**

$$\boldsymbol{N = (9P_{31}\# + 58P_{30}\# + 41P_{29}\# + g)(9P_{31}\# + 125P_{30}\# + 46P_{29}\# + h)}$$

k	31	30	29	28	27	26	25	24	23	22	21	20	19	18	17	16	...	1
P_k	127	113	109	107	103	101	97	89	83	79	73	71	67	61	59	53		2
P_1	9	58	41	32	43	101	13	14	60	50	54	33	3	32	12	12		1
P_2	9	125	46	106	75	95	71	79	21	3	19	58	23	32	30	13		1

Table 4.
P_1 and P_2 as base Primorial numbers.

$$N = 1522868x^2+$$
$$304314758135937773858871093055122741972297165895 3x+$$
$$151816659580901664885523419281115998823527019067345405631\because.$$
$$401183567090345342039152734187917869.$$
$$N = (1268x + 131416668713543553156137150841043477425966207 41)$$
$$(1201x + 115523138021269692464799993016892001426375632 09), x = p_{30}\#)$$
$$\boldsymbol{N} = (\boldsymbol{9P_{31}}\# + \boldsymbol{58P_{30}}\# + \boldsymbol{e})(\boldsymbol{9P_{31}}\# + \boldsymbol{125P_{30}}\# + \boldsymbol{f})$$
$$\boldsymbol{N} = (9\mathbf{P_{31}}\# + \mathbf{58P_{30}}\# + 115523138021269692464799993016892001426375632 09) *$$
$$(\mathbf{9P_{31}}\# + \mathbf{125P_{30}}\# + 131416668713543553156137150841043477425966207 41)$$
$$\boldsymbol{N} = (\boldsymbol{9P_{31}}\# + \boldsymbol{58P_{30}}\# + \boldsymbol{41P_{29}}\# + \boldsymbol{g})(\boldsymbol{9P_{31}}\# + \boldsymbol{125P_{30}}\# + \boldsymbol{46P_{29}}\# + \boldsymbol{h})$$
$$\boldsymbol{N} = (\boldsymbol{9P_{31}}\# + \boldsymbol{58P_{30}}\# + \boldsymbol{41P_{29}}\# + 831789325949168631706766649344199459626767 79) *$$
$$(\mathbf{9P_{31}}\# + \mathbf{125P_{30}}\# + \boldsymbol{46P_{29}}\# + 273857017733028251413011637989228497546748161)$$

The conversion to a decimal from the base primorial (Section 12) provides $\boldsymbol{P_1}$ and $\boldsymbol{P_2}$

$$\boldsymbol{P_1} = (37975227936943673922808872755445627854565536638199)_{10}$$
$$\boldsymbol{P_2} = (40094690950920881030683735292761468389214899724061)_{10}$$

16. Lenstra-Lenstra-Lavász lattice reduction (LLL)

The (LLL) forms the basis of the Coppersmith attack (Section 15), and a brief explanation is given here with further reading and references for the reader. The Lenstra-Lenstra-Lavász (LLL) lattice basis reduction algorithm [13] calculates an LLL-reduced, short, nearly orthogonal lattice basis, in time $O(d^5 n \log^3 B)$, where B is the largest length of b_i under the Euclidean norm, given a basis $B = \{b_1, b_2, \ldots, b_d\}$ with n-dimensional integer coordinates, for a lattice L (a discrete subgroup of R^n) with $d \leq n$ and giving polynomial-time factorization of polynomials with rational coefficients.

A thorough explanation is given by Bosma [14], and a summary of the example contained in the reference is given below.

INPUT: Let lattice basis $b_1, b_2, b_3 \in Z^3$ be given by the columns of $\begin{bmatrix} 1 & -1 & 3 \\ 1 & 0 & 5 \\ 1 & 2 & 6 \end{bmatrix}$

OUTPUT: LLL-reduced basis $\begin{bmatrix} 0 & 1 & -1 \\ 1 & 0 & 0 \\ 0 & 1 & 2 \end{bmatrix}$

Using the Lenstra-Lenstra-Lavász lattice reduction (LLL), the short vectors in a lattice can be found. This is used by the Coppersmith attack. Coppersmith's algorithm uses the LLL to construct polynomials with small coefficients that all have the same root modulo. When a linear combination is found to meet inequality conditions, standard factorization methods can find the solutions over integers.

17. Coppersmith attack

When $\boldsymbol{d}$ is small $\left(\textbf{and } \boldsymbol{e} \textbf{ is large, via the Euler totient rule}\right)$, the Wiener attack (Section 5) can be used. Conversely, when $\boldsymbol{d}$ is large, $\boldsymbol{e}$ is small. Particular applications of the Coppersmith method for attacking RSA include cases when the public exponent e is small or when partial knowledge of the secret key is available (Section 13) [15].

A small public exponent $\boldsymbol{e}$, reduces the encryption time. Common choices for $\boldsymbol{e}$ are 3, 17 and $\mathbf{65537}\left(\mathbf{2^{16}}+\mathbf{1}\right)$ [16]. These are Fermat primes $\boldsymbol{F_x} : \boldsymbol{F_x} = \mathbf{2^{2^x}} + \mathbf{1}$ and are chosen because the modular exponent derivation is faster. The Coppersmith method reduces the solving of modular polynomial equations to solving polynomial equations over integers.

Let $\boldsymbol{F}(\boldsymbol{x}) = \boldsymbol{x}^{\boldsymbol{n}} + \boldsymbol{a}_{\boldsymbol{n}-1}\boldsymbol{x}^{\boldsymbol{n}} - \mathbf{1} + \ldots + \boldsymbol{a}_1\boldsymbol{x} + \boldsymbol{a}_0$ and $\boldsymbol{F}(\boldsymbol{x}_0) \equiv \mathbf{0} \ \boldsymbol{mod} \ \boldsymbol{M}$ for an integer $|\boldsymbol{x}_0| < \boldsymbol{M}^{\frac{1}{n}}$. Coppersmith can find the integer solution for $\boldsymbol{x}_0$ by finding a different polynomial $\boldsymbol{f}$ related to $\boldsymbol{F}$ that has the root $\boldsymbol{x}_0 \ \boldsymbol{mod} \ \boldsymbol{M}$ but only has small coefficients. The small coefficients are constructed using the LLL (Section 14). Given $\boldsymbol{F}$, the LLL constructs polynomials $\boldsymbol{p}_1(\boldsymbol{x}), \boldsymbol{p}_2(\boldsymbol{x}), \ldots \boldsymbol{p}_{\boldsymbol{n}}(\boldsymbol{x})$ that all have same root $\boldsymbol{x}_0 \boldsymbol{mod} \ \boldsymbol{M}^{\boldsymbol{a}}, \boldsymbol{a} \in \mathbb{Z}$. $\boldsymbol{a}$ depends on the degree of $\boldsymbol{F}$ and the size of $\boldsymbol{x}_0$. Any linear combination has the same root $\boldsymbol{x}_0 \boldsymbol{mod} \ \boldsymbol{M}^{\boldsymbol{a}}$.

The next step is to use LLL to construct a linear combination $\boldsymbol{f}(\boldsymbol{x}) = \sum \boldsymbol{c}_i \boldsymbol{p}_{\boldsymbol{i}}(\boldsymbol{x})$ of the $\boldsymbol{p}_{\boldsymbol{i}}(\boldsymbol{x})$ so that the inequality $|\boldsymbol{f}(\boldsymbol{x}_0)| < \boldsymbol{M}^{\boldsymbol{a}}$ holds. Then standard factorization provides the zeroes of $\boldsymbol{f}(\boldsymbol{x})$ over $\mathbb{Z}$.

Let N be an integer and $f \in \mathbb{Z}[x]$ be a monic polynomial of degree d, over integers such that $x^d + c_{n-1}x^{d-1} + \ldots + c_2x^2 + c_1x + c_0$. Set $X = N^{\frac{1}{d} - \in}$ for $\frac{1}{d} > \in > 0$. Given (N, f) then all integers $x_0 < X : f(x_0) \equiv 0 \ mod \ N$ can now be found. All roots of $f \ mod \ N$, smaller than $X = N^{\frac{1}{d}}$ can be found.

18. Pohlig-Hellman

The Pohlig-Hellman [17] algorithm is a method to compute a discrete logarithm (which is a difficult problem) on a multiplicative group. The order of which is a smooth number (also called ***friable***), meaning its order can be factorized into small primes. A positive integer is called B-smooth if none of its prime factors is greater than B. For example, 1620 has prime factorization $2^2 \times 3^4 \times 5$; therefore 1620 is 5-smooth because none of its prime factors are greater than 5. This is similar to that of the Overmars factorization method (Section 10). The Pohlig-Hellman [17] algorithm applies to groups whose order is a prime power. The basic idea is to iteratively compute the p-adic digits of the logarithm by repeatedly "shifting out" all but one unknown digit in the exponent and computing that digit by elementary methods. This is a similar idea to Section 13.

INPUT: A cyclic group $\boldsymbol{G}$ of order $\boldsymbol{n}$ with a generator $\boldsymbol{g}$, an element $\boldsymbol{h} \in \boldsymbol{G}$, and a prime factorization $\boldsymbol{n} = \prod_{i=1}^{r} \boldsymbol{p}_i^{e_i}$ OUTPUT: The unique integer $\boldsymbol{x} \in \{\mathbf{0}, \ldots, \boldsymbol{n} - \mathbf{1}\} : \boldsymbol{g}^{\boldsymbol{x}} = \boldsymbol{h}$

Example: Let $\boldsymbol{p} = \mathbf{41}, \boldsymbol{\alpha} = 7, \ \boldsymbol{\beta} = \mathbf{12}$ solve $12 = 7^x \ \boldsymbol{mod} \ 41$

1. Find the prime factors of $\boldsymbol{p} - \mathbf{1} \ \Rightarrow \ \mathbf{41} - \mathbf{1} = \mathbf{40} = \mathbf{2^3 5} \Rightarrow \boldsymbol{g_s} = \mathbf{2}, \mathbf{5}$. Find one $\boldsymbol{x}$ for each $\boldsymbol{g}$.

2. For $\boldsymbol{g} = \mathbf{2}, \quad \boldsymbol{x} = \mathbf{2^0}\boldsymbol{x}_0 + \mathbf{2^1}\boldsymbol{x}_1 + \mathbf{2^2}\boldsymbol{x}_2 \ 2^3 \Rightarrow \boldsymbol{cubic} \rightarrow \boldsymbol{three \ terms}$

i. $x_0 : \beta^{\frac{p-1}{g_0}} = \alpha^{\frac{p-1}{g}X_0} \Rightarrow 12^{\frac{40}{2}} = \left(7^{\frac{40}{2}}\right)^{x_0} - 1\, mod\, 41 = (-1)^{x_0} mod\ 41\ test\ for\ x_0 : x_0 = 0, 1, 2, \ldots$

$-1\, mod\ 41 \not\equiv (-1)^0\ mod\ 41 - 1\, mod\ 41 \not\equiv (-1)^1 mod\ 41\quad hence\ x_0 = 1$

ii. $x_1 : \beta_1 = \beta_0\, \alpha^{-(x_0)} = 12(7)^{-(1)} = 31\, mod\ 41$

$\beta_1^{\frac{p-1}{g_1}} = \alpha^{\frac{p-1}{g}X_1},\ g_1 = 2^2 31^{\frac{40}{4}} = \left(7^{\frac{40}{2}}\right)^{x_1} \Rightarrow 31^{10} = \left(7^{20}\right)^{x_1}\quad 31^{10} \Rightarrow (1\, mod 41)\ hence\ x_1 = 0$

iii. $x_2 : \beta_2 = \beta_1\, \alpha^{-(x_1)} = (31)\left(7^{-(0)}\right) = 31\, mod\ 41$

$\beta_2^{\frac{p-1}{g_2}} = \alpha^{\frac{p-1}{g}X_2}, g_2 = 2^3\ 31^{\frac{40}{8}} = \left(7^{\frac{40}{2}}\right)^{x_2} \Rightarrow 31^5 = \left(7^{20}\right)^{x_2}\quad -1\, mod\ 41 = -1^{\frac{1}{2}}\, mod\ 41\ hence\ x_2 = 1$

Recall: $X = 2^0 x_0 + 2^1 x_1 + 2^2 x_2\ \ so\ \ X = 1.1 + 2.0 + 4.1 = 5$
$x = 5\, mod\ 2^3 = 5\, mod\ 8$. Now we need another x from the other g

3. For $g = 5, x = 5^0 x_0\ only\ one\ 5, only\ one\ term$.

i.$x_0 : \beta^{\frac{p-1}{g_0}} = \alpha^{\frac{p-1}{g}X_0} \Rightarrow 12^{\frac{40}{5}} = \left(7^{\frac{40}{5}}\right)^{x_0} \Rightarrow 12^8 = \left(7^8\right)^{x_0} \Rightarrow 18 \equiv 37^{x_0}\ mod\ 41$

$x_0 \neq 0, 1\ try\ x_0 = 2\ \ 18 \not\equiv 37^2\ mod\ 41\ \ 18 \equiv 37^3\ mod\ 41\ \ hence\ x = \ 5^0 x_0 = (1)(3) = 3$

$Hence\ x = 3\, mod\ 5, \qquad so\ x = 5\, mod\ 8\ and\ x = 3\, mod\ 5$

By the Chinese remainder theorem, $x = 13\, mod\ 40\ \ since\ the\ exponents\ are\ p - 1 = 41 - 1 = 40\ \ hence\ 12 \equiv 7^{13}\ mod 41$. So the solution to $12 = 7^x$ $mod\ 41 \Rightarrow x = 13$.

19. Shor's algorithm

Shor's algorithm [18], factors composite numbers, $N = P_1 P_2$, consisting of two primes in polynomial time using quantum computing techniques. The algorithm evaluates the period of $a^x\ mod\ n$ where $\mathbf{gcd}(a, n) = \mathbf{1}$. This is inefficient using sequential computing on a conventional computer. When run on a quantum computer, a congruence of squares with probability 0.5 occurs in polynomial time. For two co-prime sinusoids of period $\mathbf{P_1}$ and $\mathbf{P_2}$, at what point do they zero-cross each other? The phase of each sinusoid at any given point is observed, and if they are

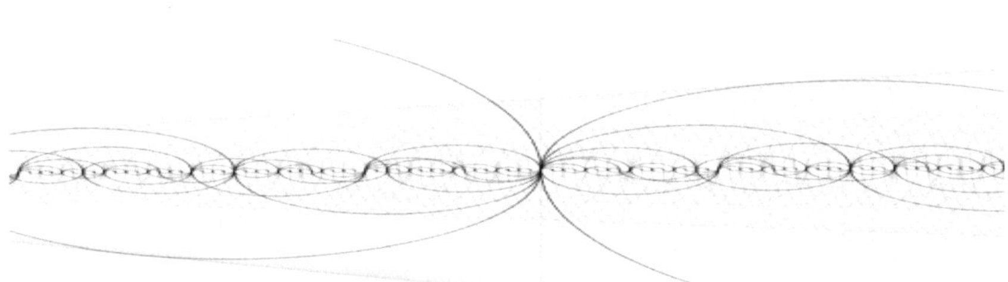

Figure 4.
N as a composite of two Sinusoids P_1 and P_2 [19].

factors of N then the phase of $\mathbf{P_1}$ and $\mathbf{P_2}$ is zero. Shor's algorithm tests the phase of $P_1 = P_2 = N = 0$ (**Figure 4**).

Phase estimation is well suited to quantum computers and hence this factorization technique produces solutions in polynomial time. For further information on quantum phase estimation, the reader is directed to WIKI [20]. The impact of this type of attack is discussed in detail by Mosca [21].

1. Choose $a < N$

2. Find the period r of $a^n \; mod \; N$ (using Quantum computing)

3. Check $r \; is \; even : a^{\frac{r}{2}}+1 \equiv 0 \; mod \; N$

4. $P_1 = \gcd\left(a^{\frac{r}{2}} - 1, \;\; N\right), P_2 = \gcd\left(a^{\frac{r}{2}} + 1, N\right)$

Consider $N = 35,$

1. $a : a < N, \; choose \; a = 8$

2. Find the period r of $a^n \; mod \; N$

   a. $8^1 mod \; 35 = 8$

   b. $8^2 mod \; 35 = 29$

   c. $8^3 mod \; 35 = 22$

   d. $8^4 mod \; 35 = 1$

   e. $8^5 mod \; 35 = 8 \Rightarrow period \; r = 4$

3. $r : r \; even, \; r = 4 \; is \; even$

4. $P_1 = \gcd\left(a^{\frac{r}{2}} - 1, N\right) = \gcd\left(8^{\frac{4}{2}} - 1, 35\right) = \gcd(63, 35) = 7$
   $P_2 = \gcd\left(a^{\frac{r}{2}} + 1, N\right) = \gcd(65, 35){=}5$

Euler's factorization (Section 6) cannot be used because 7 has no sum of squares nor does 35.

Fermat's factorization (Section 5)

$$N = (a - b)(a + b) = a^2 - b^2 = 36 - 1{=}6^2 - 1^2{=}(6 - 1)(6{+}1){=}(5)(7){=}35$$

Overmars factorization (Section 10)

$$N = [a(m - n) + 1][a(m + n) + 1]{=}[2(4{-}2){+}1][2(4{+}2){+}1{=}[5][7]$$

Overmars triangles (Section 8) Δ(m,n) = Δ(a,b,c): Δ(3,1)=Δ (12,35,37)Recalling $b(m, n) = (2m - 1)(2n + 2m - 1) \Rightarrow b(3, 1) = (5)(7)$

20. Attacking public key infrastructure

Public infrastructure cryptographic hardware uses a library ***RSALib.*** This is found in both NIST FIPS 140-2 and CC EAL 5+. These are certified devices for use in identity cards, passports, Trusted Platform Modules, PGP and tokens for authentication and software signing. This is in use in tens of millions of devices worldwide. Nemec et al. [22] have identified a vulnerability that allows for the factorization of 1024 and 2048 bit keys in less than 3 CPU months.

RSALib primes are of the form $\boldsymbol{p = k\ \ M + (65537^{a} mod\, M)}$.

These can be fingerprinted using the discrete logarithm $\log_{65537} \boldsymbol{N\ mod\ M}$.

$$N = P_1P_2 = (k * M + 65537^{a} mod\, M)\left(l * M + 65537^{b} mod\, M\right) \Rightarrow N \equiv 65537^{a+b} \equiv 65537^{c}\ mod\ M$$

The public modulus $\boldsymbol{N}$ is generated by 65537 in the multiplicative group $\mathbb{Z}_{M}$. The public modulus of *RSALib* can thus be fingerprinted with the discrete logarithm $\boldsymbol{c} = \log_{65537} \boldsymbol{N\ mod\ M}$. This can be factorized using Pohlig-Hellman (Section 16). The group $\boldsymbol{G = 65537}$ is smooth $|\boldsymbol{G}| = \boldsymbol{2^4 * 3^4 * 5^2 * 7 * 11 * 13 * 17 * 23 * 29 * 37 * 41 * 53 * 83}$ for RSA_{512} keys. The smoothness of G is due to the smoothness of M being Primorial.

Factorization is achieved using the Coppersmith algorithm with a known $\boldsymbol{p\ mod\ M : 65537^{a} mod\, M}$. Nemec *et al* used the Howgrave-Graham[23] implementation of the Coppersmith's algorithm to find a small solution $\boldsymbol{x_0}$ of:

$$\boldsymbol{f(x) = x + (M^{p-1} mod\, N)\ \left(65537^{a'} mod\, M'\right)\quad (mod\, N)}$$

A summary of ***RSALib*** vulnerability and its impact is now given and the reader is directed to Memec et al. [22] for further detail. eIDs used in passports for citizens are affected. Code signing is vulnerable. Twenty-four percent of TPMs used in laptops are affected (sample size 41). A third of PGP, used in email systems could be factorizable. There was no observable impact on TLS/HTTPS. One hundred percent of SCADA systems sampled were affected (sample 15). E-health and EMV payment cards were also likely to be susceptible.

Mitigating the impact of the ***RSALib*** vulnerability requires changing the algorithm. This requires a firmware replacement which is not possible in already deployed devices such as smartcards and TPMs whose code is stored in read-only memory. Key lengths not of 512, 1024, 2048 and 4096, such as RSA_{3936} appear to be resilient. The use of key pairs outside of vulnerable devices could be deployed using another library. Changes to ***RSALib*** are required so that proveable safe primes are constructed not using the vulnerability.

21. Overmars factorization, bringing it together

Section 11 considered the following cases. The following discussion generalizes these cases and provides the structure for algorthmic solutions to be found. The palindromic nature of primes (Section 12) can be exploited further to explore solutions in a particular Primorial range. Recall;

$$\text{Case } (1\oplus\ominus, 2\ominus\oplus)\ \boldsymbol{(N + x^2) mod\ a^2 = 0,\quad P_1 = a(m-n) \pm x,\quad P_2 = a(m+n) \mp x}$$

$$\boldsymbol{N = [a(m-n) \pm x][a(m+n) \mp x] = a^2(m^2 - n^2) \mp 2anx - x^2 = (am)^2 - (an \mp x)^2}$$

$$\boldsymbol{\frac{N + x^2}{a} = a\left(m^2 - n^2\right) \pm 2nx \quad a : a\ is\ a\ smooth\ factor\ of\ N + x^2}$$

$$\boldsymbol{n} = \frac{\sqrt{(\boldsymbol{am})^2 - \boldsymbol{N}} \pm \boldsymbol{x}}{\boldsymbol{a}}, \boldsymbol{m} : \frac{\sqrt{\boldsymbol{N} + (\boldsymbol{a} \mp \boldsymbol{x})^2}}{\boldsymbol{a}} \leq \boldsymbol{m} < \infty \boldsymbol{m} = \frac{\sqrt{+(\boldsymbol{an} \mp \boldsymbol{x})^2}}{\boldsymbol{a}}$$

$$\boldsymbol{P_1} = \boldsymbol{a}(\boldsymbol{m} - \boldsymbol{n}) \mp \boldsymbol{x} = \boldsymbol{am} - \sqrt{(\boldsymbol{am})^2 - \boldsymbol{N}}\boldsymbol{N}\ \boldsymbol{mod}\left[\boldsymbol{am} - \sqrt{(\boldsymbol{am})^2 - \boldsymbol{N}}\right] \equiv 0$$

Case $(3\ominus\ominus, 4\oplus\oplus)$ $(N - x^2) mod\, a^2 = 0, \quad P_1 = a(m-n) \mp x, \quad P_2 = a(m+n) \mp x$

$$N = [a(m-n) \mp x][a(m+n) \mp x] = a^2(m^2 - n^2) \mp 2amx + x^2 = (am \mp x)^2 - (an)^2$$

$$\frac{N - x^2}{a} = a(m^2 - n^2) \mp 2mx \quad a : a \text{ is a smooth factor of } N - x^2$$

$$n = \frac{\sqrt{(am \mp x)^2 - N}}{a}, m : \frac{\sqrt{N + a^2} \pm x^2}{a} \leq m < \infty, \quad m = \frac{\sqrt{N + (an)^2} \pm x^2}{a}$$

$$P_1 = a(m-n) \mp x = am \mp x - \sqrt{(am \mp x)^2 - N}N\ mod\left[(am \mp x) - \sqrt{(am \mp x)^2 - N}\right] \equiv 0$$

Now we need to develop the methodology for finding (selecting) $\boldsymbol{a}$ and $\boldsymbol{x}$. This brings together the concepts of primorials [9], Smooth [24], small factors [17], factorization (Fermat), modulo testing as per Atkin's Sieve [5] and the structure of primes (Sections 12 and 18), to find as large an $\boldsymbol{a}$ as possible so that Overmars Factorization [4] converges more rapidly to a solution.

Recall the following (Section 12). Primes are of the form $\boldsymbol{P = 4x \pm 1}$ **and** $\boldsymbol{P = 6x \pm 1}$. Composite numbers, constructed from these primes: $\boldsymbol{N = P_1 P_2}$, are a combination of Pythagorean and Gaussian primes. The following test $(\boldsymbol{N \pm 1})\boldsymbol{mod\ 4 \equiv 0}$ can be used to determine which combination of primes was used to construct the composite. If $(\boldsymbol{N + 1})\boldsymbol{mod\ 4 \equiv 0}$ is true a mix of Pythagorean and Gaussian primes was used. If $(\boldsymbol{N - 1})\boldsymbol{mod\ 4 \equiv 0}$ is true then the composite consists of only Gaussian or only Pythagorean primes. The Sieve of Atkin [5] uses $\boldsymbol{mod 12 \equiv 0}$ and $\boldsymbol{mod\ 60 \equiv 0}$. This is now applied as per Overmars [4] in the following manner, if $\boldsymbol{mod\ 12 \equiv 0}$ is true then $\boldsymbol{a = 6}$, if $\boldsymbol{mod\ 60 \equiv 0}$ is true let $\boldsymbol{a = 30}$. The ideas of Atkin are further extended in both directions: $\boldsymbol{mod\ 4 \equiv 0 \Rightarrow a = 2,\quad mod\ 420 \equiv 0 \Rightarrow a = 210,\quad mod\ 4620 \equiv 0 \Rightarrow a = 2310,}$ $\boldsymbol{mod\ 60060 \equiv 0 \Rightarrow a = 30030}$...

This is Primorial, $\boldsymbol{P_k\# : P_k\#,\ \ k^{th}}$ ***Primorial*** is"*Smooth*". The general form (Section 19) is now given: Case $(1\oplus\ominus, 2\ominus\oplus)$ $\boldsymbol{\frac{N+x^2}{a} = a(m^2 - n^2) \pm 2nx,}$ $\boldsymbol{(N + x^2)mod\ a \equiv 0,\quad a : a = 2P_k\#,\quad x : 1 \leq x \leq \frac{\sqrt{N}}{a}}$ Case $(3\ominus\ominus, 4\oplus\oplus)$ $\boldsymbol{\frac{N-x^2}{a} = a(m^2 - n^2) \mp 2mx, (N - x^2)mod\ a \equiv 0, a : a = 2P_k\#,\quad x : 1 \leq x \leq \frac{\sqrt{N}}{a}}$

If $\boldsymbol{a} : \boldsymbol{a} = 2\boldsymbol{P_k}\#$ can be choosen, then we search $\boldsymbol{x}$ in the primes to find solutions to $\boldsymbol{(N \pm x^2)mod(2P_k\#) \equiv 0}$ A solution is found for $\boldsymbol{P_1(m)}$, when $\boldsymbol{P_1 \in \mathbb{Z}}$. Case $(1\oplus\ominus, 2\ominus\oplus)$ $\boldsymbol{N\ mod\ [P_1] \equiv 0,\ P_1 : P_1 = am - \sqrt{(am)^2 - N}}$ Case $(3\ominus\ominus, 4\oplus\oplus)$ $\boldsymbol{N\ mod\ [P_1] \equiv 0, P_1 : P_1 = am \mp x - \sqrt{(am \mp x)^2 - N}}$

Consider Section 11 example, $\boldsymbol{N = P_1P_2 \Rightarrow 8079781 = 1249 * 6469}$

Integer solutions $x = \sqrt{N - 2bP_k\#}$. From **Table 5**, determining which x value should be used is not clear. Whilst $x = 1$ should work, no solutions will be found if $a : a = 30$. From **Table 5** only when $x = 11$ or 19 do we find solutions. Ranking the possible solutions in terms of factors 29 (8) would be first, 19 (7) second and 11 (6) third.

Based upon low order factors the rankings would be 29 $(2^2\, 3^4)$ first and 11 $(2^2\, 3^2)$ second. Setting $a = 30, x = 29$ will not find solutions for m, n. Setting $a = 30, x = 11 \Rightarrow m = 129, n = 57, \gcd(129, 57) = 3,$ so the optimal value for

x	mod60	mod180	mod1620	$N-x^2$	$\pm x$	b	a	m	n	gcd(m,n)	Smoothness
1	0			$2^2\ 3\ 5\ 311\ 433$	⊖⊖		10	386	261	1	5-smooth
1	0			$2^2\ 3\ 5\ 311\ 433$	⊕⊕		6	643	435	1	5-smooth
11	**0**	**0**		$\mathbf{2^2\ 3^2\ 5\ 44887}$	⊖⊖	**3**	**90**	**43**	**29**	**1**	**5-smooth**
19	0			$2^2\ 3\ 5\ 17\ 89^2$	⊕⊕	1	30	128	87	1	5-smooth
29	0	0	0	$2^2\ 3^4\ 5\ 4987$	⊖⊖		18	216	145	1	5-smooth

Table 5.
Smooth candidates of the factors of $N - x^2$.

$a = 90$. $P_1 = 30m - 11 - \sqrt{(30m-11)^2 - N}$. Look for solutions to $(30m-11)^2 - N$ which are a perfect square. In this case, $m = 129 \Rightarrow (30*129-11)^2 - 8079781 = 6812100 = 2610^2$.

Recall that the starting value for $m : \frac{\sqrt{N+a^2 \pm x^2}}{a} \leq m < \frac{N-1}{2a} \Rightarrow 99 \leq m < 134663$, 30 iterations.

Whilst this is quite a good result the first failure needs also to be taken into account. This would be bound by the Primorial and

P_1: $1 < P_1 < \sqrt{N} : am - \sqrt{(am)^2 - N} = 1 \Rightarrow m < \frac{N+1}{2a}$

Here $m : \frac{\sqrt{N+a^2 \pm x^2}}{a} \leq m < \frac{N+1}{2a} \leq 123 \leq m < 134663 \Rightarrow 134540$ iterations.

This can be further bound by the Primorial. In the case of RSA numbers, the binary bits available to represent a particular prime number range can also be used to *bound* the range (**Table 6**).

Consider $N = 23852269081$.

In this case, solutions using modulo testing generate good candidates to solve for (m, n), however for $a = 30030$, three of the candidates have no solution. Using sequential programing, each possible candidate is considered one after another, until the maximum m value. However, using parallel programing techniques on GPUs (such as nVIDIA P100s), all of the candidates can be tested simultaneously and the processes are all terminated when one of the processes finds a solution. This is very efficient and effective in finding P_1, P_2. Once these are known, along with the public key $P_u = (N, e)$, using Euler's totient, the private key $P_R = (N, d)$ can be determined. Once the private key is known the cypher-text is no longer secure.

x	Modulo testing				$N-x^2$	a	m	n	gcd(m,n)	Smoothness
	60	**420**	**4620**	**60060**						
1	0				$2^3\ 3^2\ 5\ 101\ 461\ 1423$	30				5-smooth
11	0				$2^5\ 3\ 5\ 13\ 97\ 157\ 251$	30	5524	2002	2	5-smooth
19	0	0			$2^4\ 3^3\ 5\ 7\ 1577531$	210	789	286	1	7-smooth
61	0	0	0		$2^4\ 3\ 5\ 7\ 11^3\ 10667$	2310				11-smooth
401	0	0	0	0	$2^3\ 3\ 5\ 7^2 11\ 13\ 19\ 1493$	30030				13-smooth
1601	0	0	0	0	$2^3\ 3^3 5\ 711\ 13^2\ 1697$	30030				13-smooth
45281	0	0	0	0	$2^3\ 3\ 5\ 7\ 11\ 13\ 181501$	30030				13-smooth
45589	0	0	0	0	$2^5\ 3\ 5\ 7\ 11\ 13\ 45317$	30030	4	2	2	13-smooth

Table 6.
Smooth candidates of the factors of $N - x^2$.

22. Conclusion

In short RSA is secure and difficult to factorise. Conventional sequential computing machines, running in polynomial time, take an infeasible amount of CPU cycles to find factorization solutions to RSA keys. Quantum computing holds great promise and Shor's algorithm [18] demonstrates how this can be achieved. However, quantum computing is realistically still some way off. Opportunities exist using conventional computing (sequential and parallel) with better mathematical techniques. Section 18 showed how implementation vulnerabilities are introduced when "clever" low cost (CPU cycles) are implemented. The case in point showed methods for signature identification, upon which tailored targeted attacks could be launched against infrastruture FIPS140-2 devices, such as cryptographic routers. These sorts of attacks can be deployed in polynomial time using sequential programing techniques. Section 20, Overmars shows how factorization can be implemented using parellel processing techniques.

There is still much to be done and areas of further interest are a better understanding of the structure of primes. This will lead to faster prime number generating algorithms and hence faster solutions to the factorization problem. This will also lead to the generation of more robust primes that are less susceptible to factorization methods. An example of this is the use of non-Pythagorean primes. Section 5 showed how Euler's factorization could be used to attack such composite numbers. Hence a simple method to thwart this would be to use a mix of Pythagorean and Gaussian primes. Section 6 showed how small $\boldsymbol{d}$ values in the RSA private key $\boldsymbol{P_R} = (\boldsymbol{N}, \boldsymbol{d})$ could be attacked using Wiener's method. Small $\boldsymbol{e}$ values in the public key $\boldsymbol{P_U} = (\boldsymbol{N}, \boldsymbol{e})$ can be attacked using a combination of LLL, Coppersmith and Pohlig-Hellman (Sections 15–17). All of these attacks can be mitigated by choosing $\boldsymbol{d}$ **and** $\boldsymbol{e}$ carefully and ensuring that both are sufficiently large.

Development of quantum computing is continuing at break-neck speed, however useful machines are yet to appear. Parallel computing however is here and now and whilst factorizing RSA keys is not achievable on conventional computers in polynomial time, parallel computing has allowed for multiple solutions to be tested simultaneously. This is an area where research continues and new algorithms such as shown in Sections 20 and 14 lend themselves well to GPU parallel processing systems.

"There are known knowns. These are things we know that we know. There are known unknowns. That is to say, there are things that we know we don't know. But there are also unknown unknowns. There are things we don't know we don't know" [25].

Author details

Anthony Overmars
Curtin University, Perth, Australia

*Address all correspondence to: 3@crykey.com

References

[1] Available from: https://www.marketsandmarkets.com/Market-Reports/network-encryption-market-187543224.html [Retrieved: 17 January 2019]

[2] Boneh D. Twenty years of attacks on the RS cryptosystems. Notices for the American Mathematical Society (AMS). 1999;**46**(2)

[3] Overmars A, Ntogramatzidis L, Venkatraman S. A new approach to generate all pythagorean triples. AIMS Mathematics. 2019;**4**(2):242-253. DOI: 10.3934/math.2019.2.242

[4] Overmars A, Venkatraman S. A fast factorisation of semi-primes using sum of squares. Computers & Mathematics with Applications. 2019;**24**(2):62. https://doi.org/10.3390/mca24020062

[5] Atkin AOL, Bernstein DJ. Prime sieves using binary quadratic forms. Mathematics of Computation. 2004;**73**: 1023-1030

[6] Sieve of Atkin. Wikipedia. Available from: https://en.wikipedia.org/wiki/Sieve_of_Atkin

[7] Cox DA. Primes of the Form $x^2 + ny^2$. 2nd ed. John Wiley & Sons; 2013. ISBN: 978-1-118-39018-4

[8] Primorial. Wikipedia. Available from: https://en.wikipedia.org/wiki/Primorial

[9] Dubner H. Factorial and primorial primes. Journal of Recreational Mathematics. 1987;**19**(3):197-203

[10] Dubner H. A new primorial prime. Journal of Recreational Mathematics. 1989;**21**(4):276

[11] Overmars A. The palindromic structure of primes in the primorials. TBA; 2019

[12] Overmars A. RSA100 factorisation using primorials. TBA; 2019

[13] Lenstra AK, Lenstra HW Jr, Lovász L. Factoring polynomials with rational coefficients. Mathematische Annalen. 1982;**261**(4):515-534

[14] Bosma W. Chapter 4 LLL. In: Lecture Notes. 2010. pp. 86-109. Available from: http://www.math.ru.nl/~bosma/onderwijs/voorjaar07/compalg7.pdf [Retrieved: 17 January 2019]

[15] Coppersmith D. Finding a small root of a bivariate integer equation; factoring with high bits known. Lecture Notes in Computer Science. 1996;**1070**:178-189

[16] Salah IK, Darwish A, Oqeili S. Mathematical Attacks on RSA cryptosystems. Journal of Computer Science. 2006;**2**(8):665-671

[17] Pohlig SC, Hellman ME. An improved algorithm for computing logarithms over GF(p) and its cryptographic significance. IEEE Transactions on Information Theory. 1978;**IT-24**(1):106-110

[18] Shor PW. Polynomial-time algorithms for prime factorization and discrete logarithms on a quantum computer. 1995. Available from: https://arxiv.org/abs/quant-ph/9508027

[19] Davidson M. Prime numbers visualized as periodic waveforms. 2012. Available from: https://cycling74.com/articles/prime-numbers-visualized-as-periodic-waveforms [Retrieved: 31/01/2019]

[20] WIKI. Quantum phase estimation algorithm. Available from: https://en.wikipedia.org/wiki/Quantum_phase_estimation_algorithm

[21] Mosca M. A resource estimation framework for quantum attacks against

cryptographic functions—Part 2 (RSA and ECC). 2017. Available from: https://globalriskinstitute.org/publications/resource-estimation-framework-quantum-attacks-cryptographic-functions-part-2-rsa-ecc/

[22] Nemec M, Sys M, Svenda P, Klinec D, Matyas V. The return of Coppersmith's attack: Practical factorization of widely used RSA moduli. In: CCS'17, Session H1: Crypto Attacks; October 30-November 3, 2017, Dallas, TX, USA. 2017. pp. 1631-1648

[23] Howgrave-Graham N. Finding small roots of univariate modular equations revisited. In: Proceedings of the 6th IMA International Conference on Cryptography and Coding. Springer-Verlag; 1997. pp. 131-142

[24] Schumaker R. The formulas for the distribution of the 3-smooth, 5-smooth, 7-smooth and all other smooth numbers. 2016. Available from: https://arxiv.org/abs/1608.06928

[25] Rumsfeld D. 2002. Available from: https://en.wikipedia.org/wiki/There_are_known_knowns

Chapter 3

A Survey of Fast Scalar Multiplication on Elliptic Curve Cryptography for Lightweight Embedded Devices

Youssou Faye, Hervé Guyennet and Ibrahima Niang

Abstract

Elliptic curve cryptography (ECC) is one of the most famous asymmetric cryptographic schemes which offers the same level of security with much shorter keys than the other widely used asymmetric cryptographic algorithm, Rivest, Shamir, and Adleman (RSA). In ECC, the main and most heavily used operation is the scalar multiplication kP, where the scalar value k is a private integer and must be secured. Various methods for fast scalar multiplication are based on the binary/ternary representation of the scalar. In this chapter, we present various methods to make fast scalar multiplication on ECC over prime field for lightweight embedded devices like wireless sensor network (WSN) and Internet of Things (IoT).

Keywords: elliptic curve cryptography, fast scalar multiplication, wireless sensor network, IoT

1. Introduction

Nowadays WSNs become a part of the Internet; the integration of WSNs into the Internet of Things (IoT) must involve new security issues. Symmetric cryptography can be the best solution in a constrained platform and embedded devices such as sensor. For a large number of nodes, the asymmetric key cryptography is the widely used algorithm because of its scalability. Elliptic curve cryptography (ECC) is one of the most famous asymmetric cryptographic schemes, which offers the same level of security with much shorter keys than the other widely used asymmetric cryptographic algorithm, Rivest, Shamir, and Adleman (RSA) [1]. Scalar multiplication is denoted by kP (where P is a point on an elliptic curve and k represents a scalar). The scalar multiplication is the recurrent and most heavily used operation in ECC because it is used for key generation, encryption/decryption of data, and signing/verification of digital signatures. The mathematics of an elliptic curve implies three arithmetic levels: scalar arithmetic, point arithmetic, and field arithmetic [2]. To make fast computation of scalar multiplication, which is the major computation involved in ECC, many works are devoted to the point arithmetic and scalar arithmetic. Point operations mean point addition and doubling, tripling, or quadrupling (or similar operation). In the framework of this chapter, we will concisely examine various researchers on the scalar arithmetic level.

The discussion on this chapter proceeds as follows: In Section 2, we start with the background on ECC over prime fields. Section 3 gives works on fast scalar multiplication on scalar arithmetic, followed by Section 4 which describes works on parallelization of scalar multiplication on scalar arithmetic. The conclusion and perspectives are given in the last section.

2. Overview on ECC over finite prime fields

2.1 Preliminaries

In this section, we give a brief overview on ECC over finite prime fields. By definition, an elliptic curve E over finite field F (of order n) denoted by $E(F)$ can be described by the Weierstrass Eq. [3]:

$$\boldsymbol{E}: \boldsymbol{y}^2 = \boldsymbol{x}^3 + \boldsymbol{ax} + \boldsymbol{b} \tag{1}$$

where a and $b \in F_p$ and Fp is a prime field. Most important finite fields used to date to implement cryptosystem have been binary, prime, and extension fields. In this chapter, we work in the context of prime field F_p, where $p > 3$ and $p = q^r$, with $r = 1$ and q a prime number called the characteristic of Fp.

Before it can be used for cryptography, the necessary condition is the discriminant of polynomial:

$$\boldsymbol{F}(\boldsymbol{x}) = \boldsymbol{x}^3 + \boldsymbol{ax} + \boldsymbol{b}, \boldsymbol{\Delta} = 4a^3 + 27b^2 \neq 0 \tag{2}$$

The set of pairs (x, y) solves (1), where $x,y \in Fp$ and the point at infinity (denoted ∞) forms an abelian group. The scalar multiplication directly depends on two basic operations over points on an elliptic curve: point doubling (2P) and point addition (P + Q) where P and Q are two different points on the elliptic curve. If $P = (x_p, y_p)$ and $Q = (x_q, y_q)$, two points ($\neq \infty$) on the elliptic curve over F_p denoted by $E(F_p)$, then point addition $P + Q = (x_{pq}, y_{pq})$ or point doubling $2P = P + Q = (x_{pq}, y_{pq})$ if P = Q can be calculated as

$$\begin{cases} x_{pq} = \lambda^2 - x_p - x_q \\ y_{pq} = \lambda(x_p - x_{p+q}) - y_p \end{cases} \tag{3}$$

$$\begin{cases} \lambda = \dfrac{y_q - y_p}{x_q - x_p} \; if\ P \neq Q \\ \lambda = \dfrac{3x_p^2 + a}{2y_p} \; if\ P = Q \end{cases} \tag{4}$$

The negative of point $P = (xp,yp)$ is point -P (xp,-yp), where P and -P are two points on the elliptic curve (**Figure 1**).

2.2 Encryption/decryption with ECC

The security of ECC relies on the difficulty of solving the elliptic curve discrete log problem (ECDLP). Let E be an elliptic curve over finite field F and P ∈ E(F), given a multiple Q of P, the elliptic curve discrete log problem is to find d ∈ F such that dP = Q. For example, if $P = (2, 2)$ and $Q = (0, 6)$, then 3P = Q, so d=3 is a solution to the discrete logarithm problem. Three operations are very much required to formulate a valid cryptosystem in ECC: key generation, encryption, and decryption.

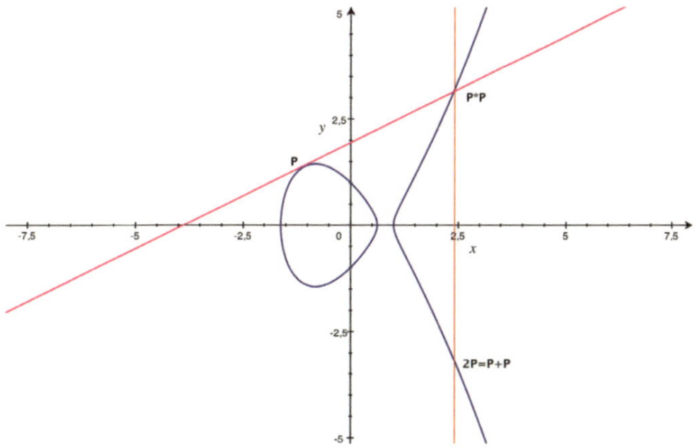

Figure 1.
Point addition in ECC.

2.2.1 Key generation with ECC

Public and private keys are associated with public parameters *(p, E, P, n)* where P is the generator point, with order n. n is always equal to the order of the elliptic curve group E and *nP=* . The private key d is randomly selected in the interval [1, n − 1], and the corresponding public key is *Q=dP*. The ECDLP consists in determining d from public parameters *(p, E, P, n)*.

Algorithm 1. Keys generation

Input: p, E, P, n // public parameters generated
Output: Public key (Q) and private key d generated
begin
1. Select randomly d in interval [1, n-1]
2. Compute Q=dP
3. Return(Q, d)
end

2.2.2 Encryption with ECC

For encryption, the message m is mapped to a valid point *M* on the curve and is encrypted by point addition with kQ where *k* is a random positive integer chosen by the sender and *Q* = *dP* represents the public key of receiver. The random *k* makes sure that even for a same message, the cipher text generated is different each time. The sender then sends the pair of cipher point $C_2=M+kQ$ and $C_1=kP$ to the receiver. The receiver, upon receiving the cipher point pair C_1 and C_2, computes $dC_1=d(k)P=k(dP)= kQ$ by its own private key d and subtracts the result from the second point: $m=C_2 -kQ$.

Algorithm 2. Encryption.

Input: (p, E, P, n), Q and m //public parameters,public key and plaintext message m
Output: (C_1,C_2) // encrypted text
begin
1. Mapping message m to a point M ∈ E(Fp)
2. Select k ∈[1, n-1]
3. Compute C_1=kP
4. Compute C_2=M+kQ
5. Return(C_1, C_2)
end

2.2.3 Decryption with ECC

Algorithm 3. Decryption.

Input: (p, E, P, n), d, C_1, C_2 //public parameters, private key encrypted message
Output: m// plaintext message
Begin
1. Compute M =C_2 - dC_1,
2. Reverse mapping to retrieve m from M
3. Return (m)
end

The process of mapping a plaintext message m to point M on the curve is important in ECC. There are several mapping schemes that are used to map a plaintext message to a point on the elliptic curve [3–7]. A good mapping scheme must follow several guidelines:

- Mapped points should be on the elliptic curve. If G is the mapping function, $G(m) \longrightarrow (x,y) \in Ep(a,b)$.
- Mapping should always be invertible so that the receiver after decryption can reverse map the points to original plain text: $m = G^{-1}(x,y)$.
- Message mapping in ECC also plays a significant role as it decides how vulnerable the encrypted message is to attacks.
- A good message mapping scheme must reduce the use of unnecessary bandwidth.
- A good mapping scheme should not take much time to map the message to points on the map.

There are several mapping schemes using different approaches: maps each character in the plaintext to a point on the elliptic, maps each sequence of characters in the plaintext to a point on the elliptic, maps the full plaintext to a point on the elliptic, etc. For example, as in [8], if we use 192 bit key length, the National Institute of Standards and Technology (NIST) recommended elliptic curve with the following parameters:

a=−3.
b =245,515,554,600,894,381,774,029,391,519,745,178,476 9,108,058,161,191,238,065.
Prime *p* = 6,277,101,735,386,680,763,835,789,423,176,059,013,767,194,773, 182,842,284,081.
Point *P* ={60,204,628,237,568,865,675,821,348,058,752,611,191,669,876,636, 884,684,818,174,050,332,293,622,031,404,857,552,280,219,410,364,023,488, 927,386,650,641}.
d = 28,186,466,892,849,679,686,038,856,807,396,267,537,577,176,687, 436,853,369.
Q ={2,803,000,786,541,617,331,377,384,897,435,095,499,124,748,881,890,727, 495,642, 4,269,718,021,105,944,287,201,929,298,168,253,040,958,383,009, 157,463,900,739}.

A plaintext message "**National Institute of Technology**" is taken as input.

1. Encryption process

   - Convert the text to ASCII values.
   - Partition the ASCII value as group size of 11 ASCII values.
   - Its equivalent ASCII values are {78,97,116, 105, 111, 110, 97, 108, 32, 73, 110},{115, 116, 105, 116, 117, 116, 101, 32, 111, 102, 32}, and{84, 101, 99,104,110, 111, 108, 111, 103,121, 44}.
   - Each group is converted into big integers using FromDigits function (in Mathematica) with base 65,536. The values for "National Institute" corresponding to the two first groups are as follows: {113,999,290,923, 567,984,853,125,612,857,907,836,245,105,850,253,422} and {168,075, 275,215,227,115,988,112,137,860,778,550,742,826, 363,519,008}.
   - A sends National Institute to B and computes scalar multiplication $kP = C_1$ = {95,058,406,573,787,743,380,879,387,493 754,072,690,640,209,963, 862,157,133, 5,437,547,807,282,051,947,615, 392,556,992,837,333,921,930, 872,121,480,709,807}.
   - A computes point addition $M+kQ = C_2$ ={5,357,129,649,847,875,387,947, 498,550,298,509,562,929,834,704 857,479,081,282,775,001,499,802, 163,650,458,076,998,673,808,830,204,345,207,458,648,302,309}, {6,179,418,438,352,156,963, 426,038,838,668,574,778,107,168,582, 785,759,775,636,5,950,440,184,023,478,909,084,289,343,254, 612,149,604,486,787,772,222,099,923}.

2. Decryption process

   - B receives C1 =kP and C2=M+kQ values.
   - Using the private key d, B performs scalar multiplication dC1.
   - Convert the subtraction operation to addition format: −dC1 = −kQ = 3,141,192 528,502,843,791,482,798,499,504,492,303,369,782,687,173, 663,895,377, − 2,544,834 938,121,667,890,493,126,265,872,103,594, 828,330,153,127,462,384,491}.
   - B performs point addition operation with -kQ: M = {113,999,290,923,567,984,853 125,612,857,907,836,245,105,850, 253,422, 16,807,527,521,522,711,598,811,213,786,077 8,550,742,826,363, 519,008}, {122,768,389,944,749,391,054,808,248,629,988,098,406, 227,392,397,356, 46,769,769,584,977,140,992,804,375,150,062, 379,259,053,557,678,135}.
   - Convert each bloc into ASCII values using IntegerDigits function (in Mathematica) with base 65,536, and retrieve ASCII values.

3. Fast scalar multiplication on scalar arithmetic

On a scalar arithmetic level, the double-and-add (DA) technique is the traditional binary algorithm, which is used and based on point operation, namely, doubling of a point and addition of points. Well-known algorithms, such as nonadjacent form (NAF), window NAF, and sliding window [3, 9, 10], can reduce effectively the number of point operations. Some other algorithms, such as double-base chains, have been developed to compute faster scalar multiplication by using binary and ternary representation [11–15]. Algorithms, based on the aforementioned algorithms, optimize faster scalar multiplication [16–18]. Optimization is done by some approaches, which also use the binary representation of the scalar k [19–21]. For other solutions, optimization is based on selecting a set of elliptic curves for cryptography (Weierstrass curve, twisted Edwards curve) on which scalar multiplication is faster than the recent implementation record on the corresponding NIST curve.

3.1 Double-and-add algorithm

The double-and-add technique is the traditional binary algorithm, which is based on point operations, namely, doubling of a point and addition of points. The double-and-add algorithm is an additive representation of the algorithms used for exponentiation. As shown on Algorithm 4, the scalar is represented in binary on l bits: $\sum_{i=0}^{l-1} k_i 2^i$, where $k_i \in \{0, 1\}$. The binary method i=0 scans the bits of scalar $[k]P = \underbrace{(P + P + P + \ldots\ldots + P)}_{k\ times}$ either from left to right or right to left. A doubling operation is done for each scanned bit k_i of k, followed by a point addition if the scanned bit is non-zero $(k_i \neq 0)$.

Algorithm 4. Double-and-add LSB/MSB.

```
Input: k=(k_{l-1},..........., k_1,k_0)_2, P ∈ E (Fp)
Output: Q=[k]P
Begin
| Q ← ∞
  for i ← 0 to l − 1 do                // begin scanning bits from right-to-left.
  |  if k_i = 1 then
  |   |Q ← Q + P
  |      end                           // an addition operation is performed
  | P ← 2P
  |      end                           // a doubling operation is performed
|    return (Q)
end
```

For a given scalar k, the number of point doubling operation is *(l-1)*, and those of point addition operation is equal to the number of non-zero bits (denoted by hamming weight h) -1. The cost of multiplication depends on the length of the binary representation of k and the number of Harming weight (the number of 1's) of scalar in this representation. The average Harming weight on all scalar k of length l bits is approximately *l/2*. Thus, in an average, binary Algorithm 4 requires *(l-1) doublings and (l-1)/2 additions*.

For example, k = 379 = $(101111011)_2$, l=9, and the number of non-zero bits h is equal to 7. So computation 379P requires 8 doublings and 5 additions.

The *double-and-add* method can be generalized by using fixed or variable size windows. The scalar k is divided into m blocks of w bit(s) (w an integer of variable size), for each block corresponds to a number V_i.

As in DA where bits are scanned one by one, and if the scanned bit is equal to 0, $Q=2^1Q$ (point doubling) is performed; if not (scanned bit equal to 1 > 0), $Q=2^1Q$ (point doubling) and $Q=Q + 1P$ (point addition) are performed. In window algorithm where blocks are scanned one by one, and if the value of the block is equal to 0, we perform $Q=2^wQ$; if not (values of blocks w bits performed =Vi), we performed $Q=2^wQ$ and $Q=Q+V_iP$ as shown in Algorithm 5.

For example, k = 379 = $(101111011)_2$ partitioned into blocks $\underbrace{1011}_{w=4}\ \underbrace{110}_{w=3}\ \underbrace{11}_{w=2}$, so, V_i is, respectively, equal to 3, 6, and 11 corresponding, respectively, to precomputed points 3P, 6P, and 11P. Thus, for this example, the scalar multiplication from block *(m-1)* to block 0 can be done as follows: [11]P→2^3. [11]P(3 repeated doublings) + [6]P(addition) → 2^2, and [94]P(2 repeated doublings) + [3]P (addition) → [379]P. Thus, five point doubling operations and two point addition operations are calculated.

Algorithm 5. Windows algorithm.

```
Input: k = ( k_{l-1}k_{l-2}k_{l-3}k_{l-4} , ....., k_5k_4k_3 , k_2k_1k_0 )_2, P ∈ E (Fp)
             \_____ block (m-1) _____/         \_block 1_/ \_block 0_/
Output: Q=[k]P
Begin
    Q ← ∞
    for i ← m − 1 to l − 1 do
        Q = 2^w Q                    // begin scanning block by block.
        if V_i > 0 then              // compute repeated point doublings w times
        |Q ← Q + V_iP                // compute addition with precomputed point V_iP
            end
        end
    return (Q)
end
```

However, this algorithm involves precomputed points whose number depends on the size of the blocks. If the blocks have a fixed-size w bits, the number of precomputed points is $(2^w - 2)$ where -2 represents the blocks for V_i= 0 or 1. If the blocks have variable size, as, for example, with three blocks of $w1$ bits, $w2$ bits, and $w3$ bits, the number of precomputed points p is $(2^w - 2)$. It should be noted that using the window method reduces the computation time and increases the memory storage and calculation time of precomputed points. If the size of the blocks increases, the number of precomputed points increases exponentially, and the number of performed operations decreases. Thus, the selection of the window size implies the computation time. A compromise is needed between the size of the blocks and the computation time related to precomputed points. According to NIST recommendations, the best window length is w=4. To reduce the number of precomputed points, the sliding window method of variable size with maximum digits equal to w can be used. For this method, the values Vi of blocks are odd; consecutive zeroes are taken into account. Therefore, a window starts and ends with a non-zero number.

For example, scalar k = 379 = $(101111011)_2$ is partitioned into blocks $\underbrace{1}_{w=4}\ \underbrace{1111}_{w=3}\ \underbrace{11}_{w=2}$, so, V_i values are, respectively, 1, 15, and 3 corresponding, respectively, to precomputed points 1P, 15P, and 3P. The scalar multiplication from block *(m-1)* to block 0 can be performed as follows: P → [2]P(1 point doubling) → 24[62] P(4 repeated point doublings) + [15]P(point additions)→ 2.[47]P(1 point doubling) → 22[94]P(2 repeated point doublings)+ [3]P(point addition) → [379]P. The result is eight point doublings and two additions.

Optimization can be done by finding a representation with a minimum zero bits in order to reduce the number of addition operations: this is the objective of the solutions described in the next section.

3.2 Nonadjacent form

Like addition, point subtraction on an elliptic curve is also effective especially when it comes to computing easily the opposite of a point on which we only change a coordinate: *P (x, y)* to *-P(x,-y)*. We can use a signed representation of bits of the integer k. One of the particularly interesting representations is the nonadjacent form which uses $\{-1, 0, 1\}$: $\sum_{i=0}^{l-1} k_i 2^i$, where $ki \in \{-1, 0, 1\}$. To compute scalar multiplication *[k]P* by NAF, digits on NAF representation of scalar k are scanned from most significant digit to last significant digit. For each digit, a point doubling operation is performed, and point addition is computed when the digit is equal to 1 or a point subtraction when the digit is equal to -1. The advantage of this representation is that it possesses the following properties:

1. *k* has a unique NAF denoted NAF (k).

2. NAF(k) has the fewest non-zero digits of any signed digit representation of k.

3. The length of NAF(k) is at most one more than the length of binary k.

For example, for k = 255_2 = $(11111111)_2$ where the density of non-zero digits is maximum, the computation of 255P implies seven point additions. But if we transform it into 256P -P which is equal to (10000000–1)P, only one addition is needed. Thus, the NAF(k) $= (10000000\overline{1})_2$where $\overline{1}$ representes -1. The NAF(k) can be generated by dividing successively k by 2. If k is odd, the rest r $\in \{-1, 1\}$ is chosen so that the quotient *(k-r)/2* is even. Thus, the next digit of NAF representation will be equal to 0.

Algorithm 6. Computing NAF for scalar *k*.

```
Input: k = the scalar k (integer)
Output: NAF(k),
Begin
        i ← 0
        while(k ≥ 1)do
        if(k_i odd)then
          k_i ← 2 − (kmod4);
          k = k_i;
        end
        else
          k_i ← 0
        end
        k_i = k/2;
        i ← i + 1;
        end
  return (k_{i−1}, k_i, ............k_1, k_0)
end
```

Based on DA algorithm from left to right, Algorithm 6 computes scalar multiplication by using NAF(k).

Thus, the average density of non-zero digits (-1 or 1) for all NAF (*k*) with length *(l-1)* digits is approximately *(l-1)/3*. The average computation of Algorithm 7 is *(l-1)* point doublings and *(l-1)/3* point additions. However, it requires a scalar conversion time from k to NAF(k) (see Algorithm 6). The NAF method can be generally used for a set of digits $\left(C_{2^w} = \left\{-2^{w-1}, \ldots..2^{w-1}\right\}\right)$ to represent the scalar k. That's equivalent to split it into fixed – size windows w. For example,

Algorithm 7. NAF method.

```
Input: NAF(k), P ∈ E (Fp)
Output: Q= [k]P
Begin
    Q ← ∞                         //scan from most significant digit to less significant
    for(i ← l − 1 to 0)do
        Q ← 2Q                    // compute point doubling
        if(k_i = 1)then           // compute point addition
            |Q ← Q + P
        end
        if (k_i = −1) then        //compute point substraction
            |Q ← Q − P
        end
    end
    return (Q)
end
```

$(C_{2^3} = \{-4, -3, -2, -1, 0, 1, 2, 3, 4\}$.We can define NAFw(k) as follows :
$NAF(k)_w = \sum_{i=0}^{l} k_i 2^i P$, with $|k_i| < 2^{w-1}$.

For example, if the scalar k = 379 = $(101111011)_2$, so $NAF_2(k)$, $NAF_3(k)$, and $NAF_4(k)$ can be computed (with $-1 = \overline{1}$):

1. $NAF_2(k)$=(1 0 $\overline{1}$ 0 0 0 0 $\overline{1}$ 0 $\overline{1}$)

2. $NAF_3(k)$=(3 0 0 0 0 $\overline{1}$ 0 0 3)

3. $NAF_4(k)$ =(3 0 0 0 0 0 0 $\overline{5}$)

Algorithm 8 presents DA method using NAF of scalar k on fixed-size windows.

Algorithm 8. NAF method with fixed size windows.

```
Input: NAF(k), P ∈ E (Fp), precomputed points [j]P for j ={1, 3,..., (2^(w−1)-1)}
Output: Q= [k]P
Begin
    Q ← ∞                         //begin scanning from most significant digit to last
    for(i ← l − 1 to 0)do         significant digit.
        Q ← 2Q                    // compute point doubling
        if (k_i ≠ 0) then
            if (k_i > 0) then
                |Q ← Q + [k_i]P;  // compute point addition
            end
            else
                |Q ← Q − [k_i]P;
            end                   //compute point substraction
        end
    end
    return (Q)
end
```

The average density of non-zero digits for all NAF (k) with length l digits is approximately $l/(w+1)$. Thus, Algorithm 8 performs on average $(l-1)$ point doublings and $l/(1+w)$ point additions. However, this method generates precomputed points $[j]P$ for j=1, 3, . . ., $2^{w-1}-1$. Despite the cost of precomputed points (1 point doubling + (2^{w-2} -1) point additions), the usage of $NAF_w(k)$ with windows remains more interesting than the one without window.

A last generalization of this method is to use $NAF_w(k)$ with variable window size (or sliding) lengths with a maximum number of digits. These windows begin and end with a non-zero. If we take the example of $NAF_2(k)$ =($1\,0\,\bar{1}\,0\,0\,0\,0\,\bar{1}\,0\,\bar{1}$) with sliding windows having a maximum length of three digits, these windows begin and end with non-zero digits. We thus obtain

$$NAF_2(k) = \underline{1\,0\,\bar{1}}\,0\,0\,0\,0\,\underline{\bar{1}\,0\,\bar{1}}$$

The precomputed points are [3]P and [5]P; the scalar multiplication is as follows: [3]P → [6]P(point doublings) → [12]P(point doublings) → [24]P(point doublings) → [48]P(point doublings) → [96]P(point doublings) → [192]P(point doublings) → [384]P(point doublings) → [379]P(point subtraction of -[5]P). Thus, we perform 8 point operations, against 12 in the case where the windows are fixed.

3.3 Mutual opposite form (MOF) algorithm

More recent mechanisms like the mutual opposite form (MOF) [22] and the complementary recoding algorithm [23] used signed representation digits $\{-1, 0, 1\}$.

In MOF, the representation of the scalar k is obtained by subtracting each k_{i-1} bit from that of k_i. The most significant bit is 1 and the least significant digit is -1. Its output is comparable to that of NAF.

For example, if the scalar k = 379 = $(101111011)_2$, then MOF (k) = $1\,\bar{1}\,1\,0\,0\,0\,\bar{1}\,1\,0\,\bar{1}$ can be calculated. The conversion is simpler than that of NAF because it only requires subtraction operations. In addition MOF can scan bits or digits from left to right or vice versa, which is more flexible.

3.4 One's complementary recoding algorithm (CR1)

In one's complementary recoding method, the representation of the scalar k is obtained through its complement $\bar{k}$: $\sum_{i=0}^{l-1} k_i 2^i = 2^l - \bar{k} - 1$. The $\bar{k}$ complement is obtained by inverting each bit of the k scalar. For example, if the scalar k $= 379 = (101111011)_2$, then it can be computed : $k = 2^9 - \bar{k} - 1 =$ $(1000000000–010000100 - 1)_2 = (10\bar{1}0000\bar{1}00–1)_2$. Thus, we can see that the density of the non-zero bits is reduced from 7 to 4. However, if the number of 1 in the original k scalar is greater than $l/2$, the method is not more interesting because the goal is to have the least 1 in the final representation.

3.5 Double-base number system

In the methods discussed above, the scalar is represented in a single base; the double-base numbering system (DBNS) offers a representation in two bases [11]. The scalar k is represented as a sum of combined powers of 2 and 3: k=$\sum_{i=1}^{l} k_i 2^{a_i} 3^{b_i}$, where $k_i \in \{-1, 1\}$ and a_i, $b_i \geq 0$. The direct usage of this system can induce a high computational cost: $\sum_{bi}$triples, $\sum_{ai}$doublings. Significant improvement can reduce costs by reusing all intermediate calculations. We keep the initial representation of k with the additional constraint that the exponents form two decreasing sequences: $a_{max} \geq a_1 \geq a_2 \geq .... a_{the}$ and $b_{max} \geq b_1 \geq b_2 \geq .....a_{the}$. This formulation makes it possible to calculate only a_{max} doublings, b_{max} triplements, and *(lt - 1)* additions. For example, $752= 2^3{\times}3^4 + 2^2{\times}3^3{-}2^2$.

The scalar multiplication is as follows: $2^2\ (3^3\ (2 \times 3P + P)\ {-P})$. Thus, the cost of scalar multiplication is *4 triplements + 3 doublings + 2 additions*. This approach has been generalized using a slightly larger number space requiring pre-calculated points [24]. In this case the values of k_i are prime numbers other than 3: {±1, ±5, ±7, ±11}.

3.6 Comparison

If memory storage is available, the precomputed points can be used to decrease the computation time. The window method or block can be used differently on signed representations such as NAF, MOF, complement coding, or unsigned representations such as double-and-add. If we are interested in sliding window representation, the number of precomputed points varies according to the methods. Take the example of variable windows size (sliding) having a maximum number of five digits.

For the double-and-add method, we will have all the odd combinations of the maximum of 5 bits, that is, which begin and end with a 1. We will thus have at most 15 precomputed points: [3]P, [5]P, [7]P, [9]P, [11]P, [13]P, [15]P, [17]P, [19]P, [21]P, [23]P, [25]P, [27]P, [29]P, and [31]P.

For wNAF method, the blocks are processed through variable windows size (or sliding) having a maximum number of five digits. These windows begin and end with a non-zero digit. As a result, the value V_i of each block of the scalar k is odd and is less than 2^w. There are no two consecutive non-zero digits, so the number of zeros is at least equal to the number of zero digits in the −1 block. The maximum number of precomputed points required is (2^{w-2}) - 1. If the maximum length of the window is 5 bits, the largest corresponding precomputed point is $\underbrace{10101}_{w=5} = 21P$, and possible combinations for precomputed points are the following:

w=3bits	w=4bits	w=5bits	w=5bits
1 0 1=5P	1 0 0 1= 9P	1 0 1 0 1= 21P	$\bar{1}$ 0 $\bar{1}$ 0 $\bar{1}$=-21P
1 0 $\bar{1}$=3P	1 0 0$\bar{1}$ = 7P	1 0 1 0 $\bar{1}$= 19P	$\bar{1}$ 0 $\bar{1}$ 0 1=-19P
$\bar{1}$ 0 1=-3P	$\bar{1}$ 0 0 1= -7P	1 0 0 0 1= 17P	$\bar{1}$ 0 0 0 $\bar{1}$=-17P
$\bar{1}$ 0 $\bar{1}$=-5P	$\bar{1}$ 0 0 $\bar{1}$= -9P	1 0 0 0$\bar{1}$ = 15P	$\bar{1}$ 0 0 0 1=-16P
		1 0 $\bar{1}$ 0 1= 13P	$\bar{1}$ 0 1 0 $\bar{1}$=-13P
		1 0 $\bar{1}$ 0 $\bar{1}$= 11P	$\bar{1}$ 0 1 0 1=-13P

Note that the negative points are the symmetrical positive points, they are neither stored nor computed, and they are obtained almost free. For windows with a maximum size of 5 bits, the number of precomputed points is 10.

MOF uses a signed representation just like NAF, but there can be two consecutive non-zero digits. For windows with a maximum of 5 bit length, the derivation of the computed points is done by subtracting each bit k_{i-1} from the block with that of k_i.

For example, for some values (16–31) of 5-bit blocks, we have:

10000. .10000 $1\bar{1}000 \rightarrow P$	10001. .10001 $1\bar{1}001\bar{1} \rightarrow 9P$	10010. .10010 $1\bar{1}01\bar{1}0 \rightarrow 9P$	10011. .10011 $1\bar{1}010\bar{1} \rightarrow 5P$
10100. .10100 $1\bar{1}1\bar{1}00 \rightarrow 5P$	10101. .10101 $1\bar{1}1\bar{1}1\bar{1} \rightarrow 11P$	10110. .10110 $1\bar{1}10\bar{1}0 \rightarrow 11P$	10111. .10111 $1\bar{1}100\bar{1} \rightarrow 3P$
11000. .11000 $10\bar{1}000 \rightarrow 3P$	11001. .11001 $10\bar{1}1\bar{1}0 \rightarrow 13P$	11010. .11010 $10\bar{1}01\bar{1} \rightarrow 13P$	11011. .11011 $10\bar{1}10\bar{1} \rightarrow 7P$
11100. .11100 $100\bar{1}00 \rightarrow 7P$	11101. .11101 $100\bar{1}1\bar{1} \rightarrow 15P$	11110. .11110 $1000\bar{1}0 \rightarrow 15P$	11111. .11111 $10000\bar{1} \rightarrow P$

The remaining combinations give the same negative values. Thus, the number of precomputed points is 7: [3]P, [5]P, [7]P, [9]P, [11]P, [13]P, and [15]P.

Complement recoding uses the same representation of MOF, but for the derivation of precomputed points, it takes all combinations of up to 5 bits, beginning and ending with a non-zero number, i.e., $(2^{w-1} - 1) = 15$ precomputed points: [3]P, [5]P, [7]P, [9]P, [11]P, [13]P, [15]P, [17]P, [19]P, [21]P, [23]P, [25]P, [27]P, [29]P, and [31]P. **Table 1** presents a comparison between different methods.

3.7 Scalar reduction method

We have developed a scalar reduction (SR) algorithm; its main advantage is that it can be easily applied to almost all existing fast scalar multiplication methods described in previous sections. This scalar reduction scheme is an improvement based on the negative of a point. Through this, it makes a specific reduction of the scalar in a selected interval. Using negation is a well-known trick in cryptanalysis as well as in cryptography for computation of scalar multiplication with addition-subtraction chains [25, 26]. This scheme replaces point *kP* by an equivalent representation of another point *tP* in the scalar multiplication operation where k and t are scalars and $k > t$. This technique is applied in the interval $[\lfloor n/2 \rfloor + 1, n-1]$, where $\lfloor n/2 \rfloor$ is the integer part function of n/2. As the negative of a point is obtained almost free, we have used it to make fast computation. Given point $P=(x_p, y_p)$ in affine coordinates, the negative of point $kP=(x_{kp}, y_{kp})$ can be computed as $kP=(x_{kp}, y_{kp})$, and then change the sign on the y-coordinate (y_{kp}). Thus, by *kP* the scalar reduction technique gets equivalent point tP through Eq. (5).

Methods	Cost	Precomputed points	W = 5	Directions
DA	$(l-1)D+\frac{(l-1)}{2}A$	0	....	⇆
NAF	$(l-1)D+\frac{(l-1)}{3}A$	0	....	→
MOF	$(l-1)D+\frac{(l-1)}{2}A$	0	....	⇆
RC1	$<(l-1)D+\frac{(l-1)}{3}A$	0	....	⇆
wNAF	$(l-1)D+\frac{l}{w+1}A$	$< 2^{w-1}-1$	10	→
wMOF	$(l-1)D+\frac{l}{w+1}A$	$<= 2^{w-1}-1$	7	⇆
wRC1	$<(l-1)D+\frac{l}{w+1}A$	$2^{w-1}-1$	15	⇆

Table 1.
Cost for computation and memory storage.

$$\begin{cases} 1.\ \text{If}\ \ k \in]\lfloor n \rfloor, n-1[,\ kP = tP\ \text{where}\ t = (k-n) \\ \\ 2.\ \text{If}\ \ k \in]0 \left\lfloor \frac{n}{2} \right\rfloor, [,\ kP = tP\ \text{where}\ t = k \end{cases} \tag{5}$$

For example, p =23 is a prime number, just to better explain this technique, but in reality p is much bigger than this. For an elliptic E over F23 defined by $E(F_{23})$, $y^2=x^3+x+1$, then # $E(F_{23})$=28, $E(F_{23})$ is a cyclic group, and P(0, 1) is a generator point. SR makes an equivalent representation on the set of points in $[\lfloor n/2 \rfloor+1, n-1]$, so that computing points 16P, 22P, and 27P can be, respectively, replaced by -12P, -7P, and -P. In this case, the computation of 27P is replaced by the calculation of -P and is almost free. For WSN or IoT embedded devices, replacing the calculation of kP by tP using Eq. (5.1) in $[\lfloor n \rfloor+1, n-1]$ can significantly accelerate scalar multiplication. From Eq. (6), all scalars can be scanned: In the interval $[\lfloor n \rfloor+1, n-1]$, for this example we have the following equivalence representations.

- [15]P = [13]P + 2([1]P)
- [16]P = [12]P + 2([2]P)
- [17]P = [11]P + 2([3]P)
- ....= ....+..........
- ....= ....+..........
- [26]P = [2]P + 2([12]P)
- [27]P = [1]P + 2([13]P)

It can be inferred that $\sum_{k=\lfloor n/2 \rfloor+1}^{n-1} kP = \sum_{k=1}^{\lfloor n/2 \rfloor-1} kP + 2\sum_{1}^{\lfloor n/2 \rfloor-1} kP$. Thus

$$\sum_{k=1}^{n-1} kP = 2 \sum_{k=1}^{\lfloor n/2 \rfloor-1} kP + \left\lfloor \frac{n}{2} \right\rfloor P + \sum_{1=1}^{\lfloor n/2 \rfloor-1} kP \tag{6}$$

In SR technique, [15]P, [16]P, ..., [26]P, [27]P] can be replaced, respectively, by [−13]P, [−12]P,........., [−2]P, [−1]P in interval $[\lfloor n \rfloor+1, n-1]$. The expression $\sum_{k=\lfloor n/2 \rfloor+1}^{n-1} kP$ can be replaced by

$$\sum_{k=1}^{n-1} kP = 2 \sum_{k=1}^{\lfloor n/2 \rfloor-1} kP + \sum_{k=1}^{\lfloor n/2 \rfloor-1} |k|P + \left\lfloor \frac{n}{2} \right\rfloor P \tag{7}$$

The complexity of scalar multiplication can be determined by the bit length of k which is equal to $\lfloor log_2(k) \rfloor+1$, or $\log_2(k)$ if $k=2^x$, where x is an integer. In binary representation, $log_2(k)$ can be replaced in scalar reduction technique by

$$\log_2\left(k - 2\left(k - \frac{n}{2}\right)\right) = \log_2 k + \log_2\left(1 + \frac{n-2k}{k}\right) \tag{8}$$

Thus, the gain α in bit length is $\alpha = \left| \log_2\left(1 + \frac{n-2k}{k}\right) \right| = \left| \log_2\left(\frac{|t|}{k}\right) \right|$. (9)

NAF	SR	DA	Gain	$\frac{n}{6}$	$\frac{n}{3}$	$\frac{n}{2}$	$\frac{2n}{3}$	$\frac{5n}{6}$	n-1
		√		6579	6572	7604	6555	6931	7471
√				6282	6326	5317	6239	6698	5114
	√			6578	6573	7600	6416	6600	27
√	√			6279	6325	5320	6100	6556	27
	√	√	$\alpha_{(sr/da)}$				2.12%	4.77%	99.63%
√	√		$\alpha_{(sr/naf)}$					1.46%	99.47%
√	√	√	$\alpha_{(sr\text{-}naf/da)}$				6.94%	5.41%	99.63%

SR, scalar reduction.

Table 2.
Running times (ms) using affine coordinates.

SR technique is tested in affine coordinates. The scalars are in binary and NAF form combined with the scalar reduction scheme. The gain rate depends on the value of k. For comparison, if $(\alpha_{rs/da})$, $(\alpha_{rs/naf})$, and $(\alpha_{rs-naf/da})$ define, respectively, the gain rate of the scalar reduction (SR) method compared to double-and-add (DA), NAF and SR combined with NAF are compared to DA. The results are given in **Table 2**.

4. Parallelization of scalar multiplication on scalar arithmetic

Parallel computing is another choice for accelerating computation and balancing workload. For distributed system, a task can be divided into smaller ones which are then carried out simultaneously by different processors. The parallel computing for accelerating computation of scalar multiplication is a very hot research topic in cryptography. It can be also achieved through one or more arithmetic levels: on the formulas of operations such as addition and doubling, between the operations themselves, or on the scalar by partitioning it. In most current works, various solutions have been proposed in literature, but in this chapter we present works based on scalar arithmetic.

4.1 Efficient elliptic curve exponentiation

The efficient elliptic curve exponentiation based on point precomputation is proposed in [24]. To calculate Q = kP where Q and P are 2 points represented in Jacobian coordinates and k is a positive integer of 160 bits, a precomputed table which consists of 62 points is prepared.

$A[s] = \sum_{j=0}^{4} a_s, j^{2^{32j}} G3$ and $B[s] = \sum_{j=0}^{4} a_s, j^{2^{16+32j}} G3$ where $1 \le s \le 31$ and $a_s,0 \ldots, a_s,0$ is a binary representation of $s = \sum_{j=0}^{4} a_{s,j} 2^j$. Then calculation of kP is done by Algorithm 9.

Since this method is based on precomputation, a precomputed table is prepared, and the exponentiation loop can be performed separately by different processors.

4.2 Parallel scalar multiplication on two processors

In [27], two processors and a circular buffer are used to perform parallel scalar multiplication. A buffer acts as a communication channel between the two

Algorithm 9. Elliptic curve exponentiation based on precomputation.

Input: Data k = $\sum_{i=0}^{l-1} k_i 2^i P$
Output: kP,
Begin

for $0 \le j \le 15$ **do**

$u_i = \sum_{i=0}^{4} \mathbf{k}_{32i+j} + 2^i$

$v_i = \sum_{i=0}^{4} \mathbf{k}_{32i+16+j} + 2^i$

$A[0] = \infty$

$B[0] = \infty$

$T = \infty$

end

for i from 15 to 0 **do**

$T \leftarrow 2T$

$T \leftarrow 2T + A[u_i] + B[v_i]$

end

Return T

end

processors to reduce the average time of the scalar multiplication. As in the producer-consumer problem, the first processor initially reads P and then keeps scanning k_i and computing point doubling. It writes 2^iP into the buffer whenever a non-zero k_i is detected. The second processor reads 2^iP from the buffer and performs additions. The computation is terminated when there is no more 2^iP in the buffer.

4.3 Parallelization by partitioning the scalar

For other schemes, this technique of parallelization consists in partitioning the scalar k (represented on l bits) into *m* fixed-size blocks on SIMD architectures [28]. This partitioning generates precomputed points that need to be calculated and stored prior to starting parallel calculations.

Recent work [29], inspired by [30], uses this technique in *m* blocks of length *v* bits in wireless sensor networks. The scalar is represented on *l* bits and is divided into m blocks B_i of length $vb = l/m$ according to *m* sensors chosen to participate in the computation.

$$kP = B_0 2^{0v} P + B_1 2^{1v} P + B_2 2^{2v} P + \ldots\ldots\ldots + B_{m-1} 2^{(m-1)v} P \tag{10}$$

where $B_i = \sum_{iv}^{iv+v-1} l_i 2^j P$ with l_j the bit on position *j* on the binary sequence of length *l*.

This partitioning generates precomputed points $Pi = 2^{ib}P$. For example, consider a scalar *k* of 160 bits and point *P*; we want to compute *kP* on four sensors. The scalar *k* is broken down into four blocks of 40 bits:

$$kP = \underbrace{(B_{0.0}B_{0.1}\ldots\ldots B_{0.39})_2.2^0P}_{blockB_0} + \underbrace{(B_{1.40}B_{1.41}\ldots\ldots B_{1.79})_2.2^{40}P}_{blockB_1} + \underbrace{(B_{2.80}B_{2.81}\ldots\ldots B_{2.119})_2 2^{80}P}_{blockB_2} + \underbrace{(B_{3.120}B_{3.121}\ldots\ldots B_{3.159})_2 2^{159}P}_{blockB_3}$$

Precomputed points are 2^{40}P, 2^{80}P, and 2^{120}P. Note that all parallelism techniques based on scalar partitioning generate pre-calculated points, which must first be calculated and stored, thus leading to additional memory and energy consumption.

In [31], a parallel computation of *kP* between N sensor nodes is presented by partitioning the scalar k to *m* blocks of length $v = k/N$ bits, and each block is computed by one sensor node. A distributed algorithm (double-and-add, NAF, etc.) composed of m blocks is also proposed, and each block mi of the distributed algorithm operates on one block mi of the scalar. **Algorithms 10** and **11** show, respectively, block i for double-and-add and NAF algorithms.

Algorithm 10. Double-And-Add for node *i*

Input: $d=(d_{v-1},.........., d_1,d_0)_2$, $P \in E\ (Fp)$
Output: $Q=[d]P$
Begin
$Q \leftarrow \infty$
for $j \leftarrow 0\ to\ v-1$ **do** // begin scanning bits from right-to-left.
if $d_j = 1$ **then**
$Q \leftarrow Q + 2^{vi}P$
end //$2^{vi}P$ is the pre-computed point
$P \leftarrow 2P$
end
return (Q)
end

Algorithm 11. NAF method for *i.*

Input: $NAF(d)= (d_{v-1},.........., d_1,d_0)$, $P \in E\ (Fp)$
Output: $Q= [d]P$
Begin
$Q \leftarrow \infty$
for $j \leftarrow 0\ to\ v-1$ **do** // begin scan from right to left step by step
$P \leftarrow 2Q$
if $(d_j = 1)$ **then** // compute point doubling
$Q \leftarrow Q + 2^{vi}P$ // $2^{vi}P$ is the pre-computed point
end
if $(d_j = -1)$ **then**
$Q \leftarrow Q - 2^{vi}P$
end
end
return (Q)
end

So as not to compromise security when partitioning scalar, the reliability and efficiency are taken into account. They demonstrate that after partitioning the scalar k to m blocks of length *v*, the node which leads calculation keeps one of the *m* blocks into its local memory and distributes *(m-1)*blocks to others nodes. In this case, a possibility is to send the *(m-1)* blocks securely by symmetric encryption. If blocks are sent randomly without encryption, the intruder, after gaining *(m-1)* blocks of the m blocks, must perform $(m!2^v)P$ to find the private scalar *k*. Moreover, if the intruder gains the *(m-1)* results sent by other nodes, security is not compromised; it has to deal against the ECDLP. So, it is as difficult to find *k* from kP

DOI: http://dx.doi.org/10.5772/intechopen.86584

as k from the $(m\text{-}1)$ points derived from calculation of scalar multiplication on $(m\text{-}1)$ blocks. For each block d_iP, it needs to find d_i. And then after, it also needs to perform $(m!2^v)P$ before getting scalar k.

4.4 Performance measurement

The predominance of scalar multiplication in all operations makes the performance of the cryptosystem relatively based on this scalar operation. Theoretically, the efficiency of the formula using Jacobian coordinates can be determined by the number of multiplication (M) and of square (S) operations which compose it. Operations like addition, subtraction denoted by A, and multiplication with a constant are negligible when faced with square and multiplication of two variables. It is widely accepted that the cost of square is equivalent to 0.6–1 of the cost of multiplication [32–34]. Hence, for a scalar multiplication with a scalar of length of n bits, we can determine the ratio $(r{=}S/M)$ from which each approach justifies better performance.

5. Conclusion

To perform fast computation of scalar multiplication, which is the major computation involved in ECC, much research has been devoted to the point arithmetic level and the scalar arithmetic. In this chapter, we have presented only works on scalar arithmetic level. All the methods studied are almost based on scanning bits or digits of the scalar with a scan step. In the comparative studies, we found that calculations can be faster if the number of bits scanned is higher. However, scanning a number of bits greater than 1 results in precomputed points that need to be computed or stored before. In future works, we can explore mechanisms for accelerating calculation of precomputed points in order to avoid storing them. Like computing point doubling formula, we can consider effective point operation formulas which should allow to increase the scan step.

Author details

Youssou Faye[1*], Hervé Guyennet[2] and Ibrahima Niang[3]

1 University Assane Seck, Senegal

2 University of Franche Comte, Femto-St, France

3 University Cheikh Anta Diop, Senegal

*Address all correspondence to: yfaye@univ-zig.sn

References

[1] Robshaw MJB, Yin YL. Elliptic Curve Cryptosystems, An RSA Laboratories Technical Note. Revised June 27, 1997.

[2] Hakerson D, Menezes A, Vanston S. Guide to elliptic curve cryptography. In: Meloni N, Hasan MA, editors. Elliptic Curve Scalar Multiplication Combining Yaos Algorithm and Double Bases. CHES 2009. NY: Springer-Verlag; 2004. pp. 304-316

[3] Hankerson D, Menezes A, Vanstone S. Guide to Elliptic Curve Cryptography. London: Springer; 2004. pp. 95-123

[4] Muthukuru J, Sathyanarayana B. Fixed and variable size text based message mapping technique using ECC. Global Journal of Computer Science and Technology. 2012

[5] Trappe W. Introduction to Cryptography with Coding Theory. Pearson Education India; 2006

[6] Padma BH, Chandravathi D, Roja PP. Encoding and decoding of a message in the implementation of elliptic curve cryptography using Koblitz method. International Journal on Computer Science and Engineering. 2010;**2**(5): 1904-1907

[7] Sengupta A, Ray UK. Message mapping and reverse mapping in elliptic curve cryptosystem. Security and Communication Networks. 2016;**9**(18): 5363-5375

[8] Singh LD, Singh KM. Implementation of text encryption using elliptic curve cryptography. Procedia Computer Science. 2015;**54**: 73-82

[9] Gordon DM. A survey of fast exponentiation methods. Journal of Algorithms. 1998:129-146

[10] Khleborodov D. Fast elliptic curve point multiplication based on window non-adjacent form method. Applied Mathematics and Computation. 2018; **334**:41-59

[11] Dimitrov V, Imbert L, Mishra PK. Efficient and secure elliptic curve point multiplication using double-base chains. In: Advances in Cryptology, ASIACRYPT05, LNCS, Vol. 3788, Springer-Verlag. 2005. pp. 59-78

[12] Ciet M, Joye M, Lauter K, Montgomery PL. Trading inversions for multiplications in elliptic curve cryptography. Designs, Codes, and Cryptography. 2006;**39**:189-206

[13] Meloni N, Hasan MA. Elliptic curve scalar multiplication combining yaos algorithm and double bases. In: CHES 2009. 2009. pp. 304-316

[14] Al Musa S, Xu G. Fast Scalar Multiplication for Elliptic Curves over Prime Fields by Efficiently Computable Formulas. 2018. Available from: https://eprint.iacr.org/2018/964.pdf

[15] Al Musa S. Multi-Base Chains for Faster Elliptic Curve Cryptography. 2018. Available from: https://dc.uwm.edu/etd/1970

[16] Tian M, Wang Y, Xu S. An efficient elliptic curves scalar multiplication algorithm suitable for wireles network. In: Second International Conference on Networks Security, Wireless Communication and trusted Computing. IEEE Computer Society; 2010. pp. 95-98

[17] Imai V, Masato E. Faster multi-scalar multiplication based on optimal double-base chains. In: World Congress on Internet Security (WorldCIS-2012). IEEE; 2012. pp. 93-98

[18] Khleborodov D. Fast elliptic curve point multiplication based on binary and binary non-adjacent scalar form methods. Advances in Computational Mathematics. 2018:1-19

[19] Tian M, Wang J, Wang Y, Xu S. An efficient elliptic curve scalar multiplication algorithm suitable for wireless network. In: 2010 Second International Conference on Networks Security, Wireless Communications and Trusted Computing; Wuhan, China. April 2010. pp. 95-98

[20] Suppakitpaisarn V, Imai H, Masato E. Fastest multi-scalar multiplication based on optimal double-base chains. In: 2012 World Congress on Internet Security (WorldCIS), Guelph, Ontario, Canada: IEEE. June 2012. pp. 93-98

[21] Faye Y, Guyennet H, Niang I, Shou Y. Fast scalar multiplication on elliptic curve cryptography in selected intervals suitable for wireless sensor networks. In: Cyberspace Safety and Security. Zhangjiajie, China: Springer International Publishing; 2013. pp. 171-182

[22] Standard Specifications for Public Key Cryptography. IEEE Standard 1363; 2000

[23] Okeya K. Signed binary representations revisited. In: Proceedings of CRYPTO04. 2004. pp. 123-139

[24] Doche C, Imbert L. Extended double-base number system with applications to elliptic curve cryptography. In: International Conference on Cryptology in India. Berlin, Heidelberg: Springer; 2006. pp. 335-348

[25] Bernstein DJ, Lange T, Schwabe P. On the correct use of the negation map in the Pollard rho method. In: International Workshop on Public Key Cryptography. Taormia, Italy: Springer Berlin; 2011. pp. 128-146

[26] Morain F, Olivos J. Speeding up the computations on an elliptic curve using addition-subtraction chains. Theoretical Informatics and Applications Informatique theorique et Applications. 1990;**24**(6):531-543

[27] Ansari B, Wu H. Parallel scalar multiplication for elliptic curve cryptosystems. In: 2005 International Conference on Communications, Circuits and Systems, 2005. Proceedings. Vol. 1. IEEE. May 2005. pp. 71-73

[28] Wu K, Li D, Li H, Chen T, Yu F. Partitioned computation to accelerate scalar multiplication for elliptic curve cryptosystems. In: 2009 15th International Conference on Parallel and Distributed Systems (ICPADS); IEEE. December 2009. pp. 551-555

[29] Shou Y, Guyennet H, Lehsaini M. Parallel scalar multiplication on elliptic curves in wireless sensor networks. In: 14th International Conference on Distributed Computing and Networking (ICDCN), LNCS, Vol. 7730, 2013, Bombay, India. 2013. pp. 300-314

[30] Lim C, Lee P. More flexible exponentiation with pre-computation. In: Advances in Cryptology—CRYPTO94, LNCS, Vol. 839, Springer-Verlag. 1994. pp. 95-107

[31] Faye Y, Guyennet H, Yanbo S, Niang I. Accelerated precomputation points based scalar reduction on elliptic curve cryptography for wireless sensor networks. International Journal of Communication Systems. 2017;**30**(16): e3327

[32] Bernstein D, Hankerson D, López J, Menezes A. Software implementation of

the NIST elliptic curves over prime fields. In: Cryptographers Track at the RSA Conference; Springer. 2001. pp. 250-265

[33] Großschädl J, Avanzi RM, Savaş E, Tillich S. Energy-efficient software implementation of long integer modular arithmetic. In: International Workshop on Cryptographic Hardware and Embedded Systems; Springer. 2005. pp. 75-90

[34] Lim CH, Hwang HS. Fast Implementation of Elliptic Curve Arithmetic in GF (p n); 2000

Chapter 4

Numerical Problem Encryption for High-Performance Computing Applications

Riccardo Bernardini

Abstract

Recent years witnessed the diffusion of cloud-based services. Cloud services have the interesting advantage that they can provide resources (CPU, disk space, etc.) that would be too expensive to deploy and maintain in-house. A major drawback of cloud-based services is the problem of handling private data and—possibly—intellectual property to a third party. With some service (e.g., data storage), cryptography can provide a solution; however, there are some services that are more difficult to protect. An example of such services is the renting of CPU to carry out numerical computation such as differential equation solving. In this chapter, we discuss the problem of encrypting *numerical problems* so that their solution can be safely outsourced. The idea is to transform (*encrypt*) a given numerical problem into a different one whose solution can be mapped back to the solution of the original problem if the *key* used at the encryption stage is known.

Keywords: HPC, numerical analysis, security, cloud

1. Introduction

The rise of *cloud computing* has made it possible for SMEs to procure, on a pay-per-use basis, resources that until few years ago they had to acquire themselves. Although cloud computing offers interesting opportunities, it has some drawbacks too. One important drawback is the lack of *data privacy*: as soon as the SME hands its data to the cloud provider, there is the risk that the data could be exposed to third parties. Privacy protection in cloud services is indeed one of the key challenges highlighted by the *Public Consultation on Cloud Computing and Software* [1].

In some cases, the SME can take some simple countermeasures to mitigate privacy risks. For example, the SME can send to the provider an encrypted version of the data in the case of storage service (see **Figure 1a**). This is possible since the cloud provider can store the data just as a "binary blob" without the need to understand them.

However, there are some services where simple solutions are not feasible, for example, the procurement of high-performance computing (HPC) resources on the cloud. It is a fact that many potential users are not eager to employ cloud HPC services because of the risk of data disclosure. In fact, simple data encryption mechanisms are not sufficient to deal with security and privacy protection in data centric environments, and even "the right to be forgotten" does not cover indirect security and privacy aspects [2].

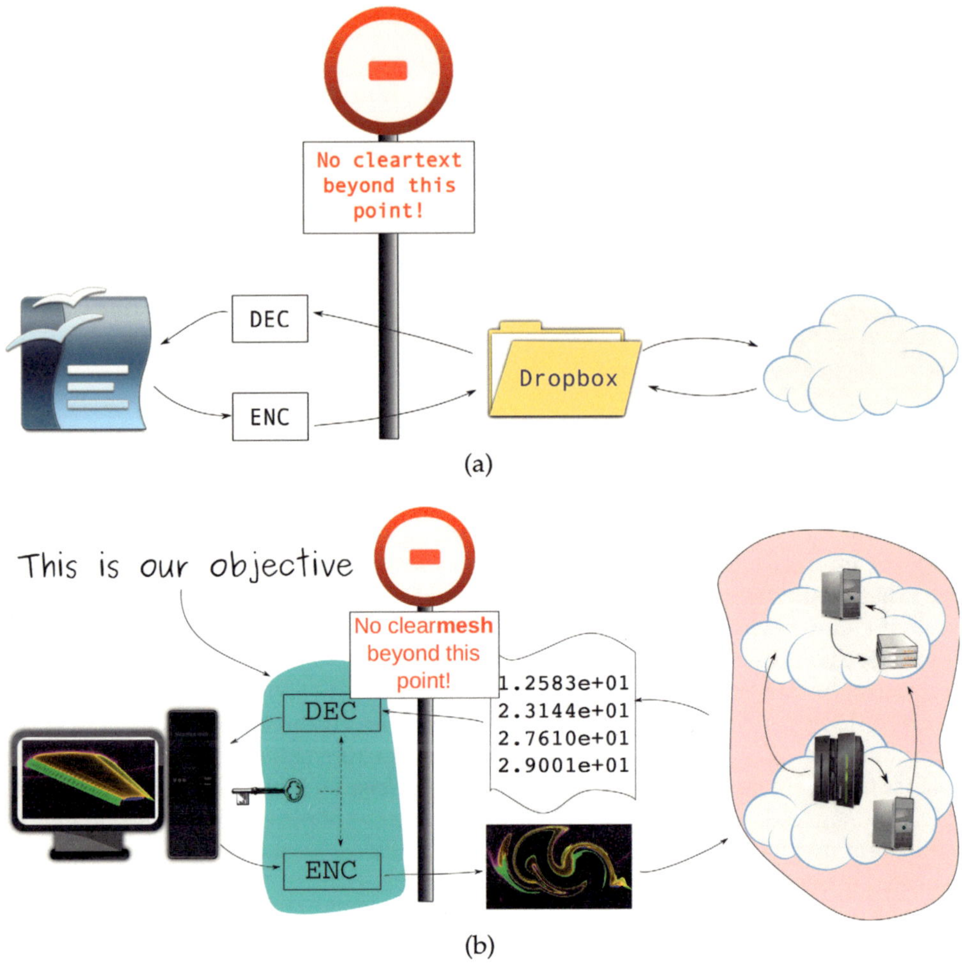

Figure 1.
(a) Using safely storage on networks and (b) renting safely CPU on network.

Ideally, we would like a solution reminiscent of what is done for storage: encrypt the computation before sending it to the cloud and decrypt what we receive from the cloud. **Figure 1b** shows a graphical representation of this idea: on the left hand side, we see a user that needs to compute the airflow around a new wing in an aerodynamic application. In order to outsource that aerodynamic problem, the user processes it with a secret key in the block ENC with the aim of transforming it into a *different numerical* problem that is uploaded to the cloud. A number of HPC providers collaborating on the cloud may be needed to solve this computation-intensive problem. The encrypted solution is then synthesized and sent back to the user (wing designer) that processes it with DEC in order to get the final answer. Standard cryptography techniques (e.g., RSA, AES, etc.) in this context provide only limited result. The question is if the user uploads their data in encrypted form to the cloud, how can the cloud process it?

At a first glance, this seems an unsolvable problem, but recent developments in the field of theoretical cryptography can address this apparent paradox using a set of secure techniques belonging to the family of secure multiparty computation (SMPC). Some efficient SMPC solutions, such as additive homomorphic encryption or garbled circuit, allow evaluating particular functions on encrypted data, but unfortunately they require interaction with the user, often making the cooperation more expensive than the direct solution. On the other hand, fully homomorphic encryption (FHE) allows evaluating functions on encrypted binary data, without decrypting it nor interacting with the client. This implies that the cloud can compute any function of the data uploaded by the user (without learning anything about the plain-text data) and return the encrypted answer.

Even more recent developments in the field of cryptography show that even cryptographic obfuscation can be achieved (under strong but plausible assumptions): using obfuscation, one can upload a piece of software to the cloud, which now can be run on any input data without learning anything about the proprietary code—think of a researcher who find a new algorithm to diagnose some diseases. Now the researcher can sell diagnosis as an external service on a cloud provider, without fearing that the cloud can steal or leak his proprietary methods.

While SMPC and FHE provide wonderful theoretical results, they will have little or no practical impact in the way users work with the cloud. The computational overhead introduced by FHE is huge, and an obfuscated version of even a simple function (a point function with few bit inputs) requires gigabytes of memory.

2. The setup

2.1 The basic setup

Figure 2 shows a more detailed setup with two possible scenarios. We have, with reference to **Figure 2a**, an original problem that we will call the *engineering problem*; for example, determine drag and lift of a new innovative wing profile or the electronic configuration of a new molecule. The first step in the solution of the engineering problem is its transformation into a *numerical problem* (typically a linear system or an eigenvalue problem) that is solved by means of a well-known numerical algorithm in order to obtain a *numerical solution*. The final step is to use the numerical solution to obtain the *engineering solution*, that is, the values that are of interest for us (e.g., drag and lift in the wing problem). It is worth to discuss in some details the three steps.

2.1.1 From the engineering problem to the numerical problem

Many engineering problems require the solution of differential equations that when discretized give rise, usually, to a linear system or an eigenvalue problem. The matrices obtained with the discretization can be quite large but (usually) sparse. Note that instead the engineering problem has usually a relatively compact description; in the example at hand, it would be a description of the geometry of the wing (by means of 3D model format) together with a description of the air flow [3–5]; in the case of the molecule, it could be a description of the configuration of the molecule (e.g., by means of its structural formula).

Although intuitively one can imagine that the solution of the numerical problem is the heaviest part, even the discretization step can be nontrivial. For example, some discretization technique—e.g., the popular finite element method (FEM)—requires to partition the space using a grid whose generation can be fairly complex [6]. Finally, it is worth observing that with large problems, not only the required CPU time can be a problem but also the amount of memory required that can become readily prohibitive because of the "dimension curse." Indeed many engineering problems involve at least four dimensions: one for time and three for space. This suggests that working with very sparse matrices (and preserving their sparse

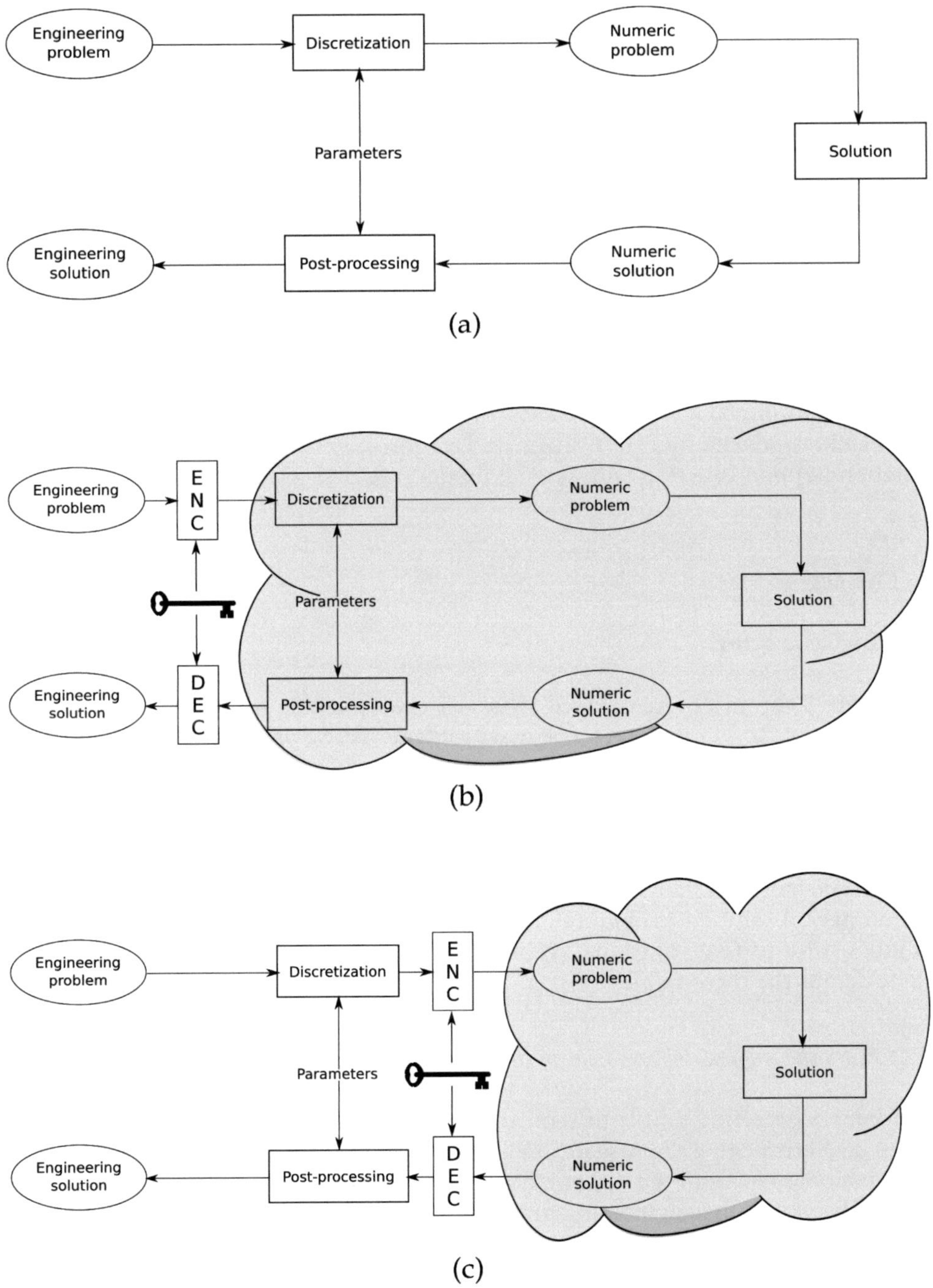

Figure 2.
(a) Typical scenario: an engineering problem is converted to a numeric problem that is solved to derive the desired engineering solution, (b) outsourcing by encrypting the engineering problem and (c) outsourcing by encrypting the numerical problem.

structure) is of utmost importance. This will be important in the following when talking about some proposals found in the literature.

Finally, it is worth observing that there is a good degree of arbitrary in the discretization step: if a grid is used, it is not uniquely determined; in finite difference method (FDM), the ordering used to map the grid points to matrix coordinates is arbitrary; in methods based on function space discretization (e.g., Galerkin-like methods), there is a wide freedom in the choice of basis functions. This implies that while it is known how to go from an engineering problem to its numerical counterpart, it is not clear how (or "if") it is possible to go in the other direction. This is important in our context since we can expect that the opponent will be interested in the engineering problem rather than in the numerical one.

2.1.2 Numerical solution

In this step the numerical problem (typically, a linear system or an eigenvalue problem) is solved to give the numerical solution (typically, a vector). If the problem is very large, this step can be very CPU-consuming. Algorithms used for the solution typically exploit the very sparse structure of the matrices involved. For example, in the solution of a linear system, usually an iterative procedure is preferred, since the iterative procedure exploits more easily any sparsity (the cost of a product matrix-vector is proportional to the number of non-zero elements), while the inverse of a sparse matrix is not necessarily sparse, requiring much more memory and CPU time to be handled.

This suggests that if the encryption is applied at the numerical problem level (see Section 3 in the following), care must be exercised in order not to spoil the sparsity, although this goes against with the requirement—sometimes stated—of hiding the number of zeros (see Section 4.1.1).

2.1.3 From the numerical solution to the engineering solution

This step usually is not as computationally demanding as the previous ones. It amounts to extract from the numerical solution the values of interest (e.g., drag and lift in the wing example) or producing suitable visualizations of the data (e.g., in the electronic distribution of a molecule example).

3. Encrypting the problem

There are two possibilities, shown in **Figure 2**, of encrypting the problem: in a case (see **Figure 2b**) the original problem is directly encrypted and outsourced, leaving both discretization and numerical solution to the cloud; we will call this solution the *engineering problem encryption* (*EPE*). In the other case (see in **Figure 2c**), the discretization step is done on the client computer, and only the numerical problem (e.g., solution of linear system) is encrypted and outsourced; we will call this solution the *numerical problem encryption* (*NPE*). Pros and cons of the two solutions are as follows.

EPE: From the point of view of the work to be done on the client, this solution is preferable since the possibly large cost of the discretization step is outsourced to the cloud. This solution, however, requires a different encryption technique for every problem (e.g., an encryption technique suitable for aerodynamic problems cannot be used for computational chemistry problems). To the best of our knowledge, there is currently no proposal working at the EPE level.

NPE: On the one hand, this solution requires that the client does the discretization step and the computational cost of this step cannot be negligible; on the other hand, many engineering problems reduce to a just few numerical problems when discretized. This means that a procedure to encrypt, say, a linear system can be applied in many engineering problems that require the solution of differential equations.

Note that in both cases the key remains in the client, similarly to what happens in the case of remote storage. This implies that the client can employ very long keys, maybe as long as the data to be encrypted, since there is not a problem of distributing the key.

3.1 Numerical issues

Since we are interested in numerical problems, the issue of the impact of the encryption/decryption on the precision of the result needs to be taken into account. For example, consider the following protocol, similar to many techniques proposed for protecting a linear system [7–9]:

$$\mathbf{A}\mathbf{x} = \mathbf{b} \tag{1}$$

with $\mathbf{A} \in \mathbb{R}^{n \times n}$ and $\mathbf{x}, \mathbf{b} \in \mathbb{R}^n$. System (1) is protected by randomly generating two permutation matrices $\mathbf{P}, \mathbf{Q} \in \mathbb{R}^{n \times n}$ and a diagonal matrix $\mathbf{D} \in \mathbb{R}^{n \times n}$ and replacing $\mathbf{A}$ and $\mathbf{b}$ with, respectively,

$$\hat{\mathbf{A}} = \mathbf{PAQD} \tag{2}$$

$$\hat{\mathbf{b}} = \mathbf{Pb} \tag{3}$$

and sending the problem

$$\hat{\mathbf{A}}\hat{\mathbf{x}} = \hat{\mathbf{b}} \tag{4}$$

to the cloud. It is immediate to check that the solutions of (1) and (4) are related by

$$\mathbf{x} = \mathbf{QD}\hat{\mathbf{x}} \tag{5}$$

Eq. (5) can be considered as the decryption algorithm. This looks fine, but the value returned for $\hat{\mathbf{x}}$ usually has some error $\boldsymbol{\varepsilon}$. It is immediate to verify that this induces an error $\mathbf{QD}\boldsymbol{\varepsilon}$ on the decrypted value. If $\mathbf{D}$ has some large entries, this will amplify the noise that affects the decrypted value. Moreover, right multiplication by $\mathbf{D}$ can affect the condition number of $\mathbf{A}$, worsening the conditioning of the system. **Figure 3** shows the result of a numerical experiment demonstrating this problem: we generated 5000 symmetric matrices $\mathbf{A}$ and 5000 diagonal matrices $\mathbf{D}$ of sizes ranging from 10×10 to 200×200, and for every iteration, we computed the condition number amplification

$$\rho = \text{cond}(\mathbf{AD})/\text{cond}(\mathbf{A}) \tag{6}$$

where $\text{cond}(\mathbf{A}) = |||\boldsymbol{A}|||_2 |||\mathbf{A}^{-1}|||_2$ is the 2-norm condition number of $\mathbf{A}$. Entries of $\mathbf{A}$ were Gaussian with zero mean and unit variance, while entries of $\mathbf{D}$ have been generated using a variety of distributions: Gaussian as the entries of $\mathbf{A}$, uniform in $[0, 1]$, uniform in $[1/2, 3/2]$, and uniform in [1,2].

The right hand column of **Figure 3** shows the histogram of ρ in logarithmic scale for 100×100 matrices; **Figure 3b** shows the minimum, maximum, and average values of ρ as function of the matrix size. Different rows of **Figure 3** are relative to different ways of generating $\mathbf{D}$. Although from **Figure 3** one can see that sometimes the conditioning can improve ($\rho < 1$), it is clear that there is a non-negligible probability of worsening the condition number of several orders of magnitude, especially if the entries of $\mathbf{D}$ can go near to zero (first two rows of **Figure 3** relative to the cases Gaussian and uniform in [0,1]).

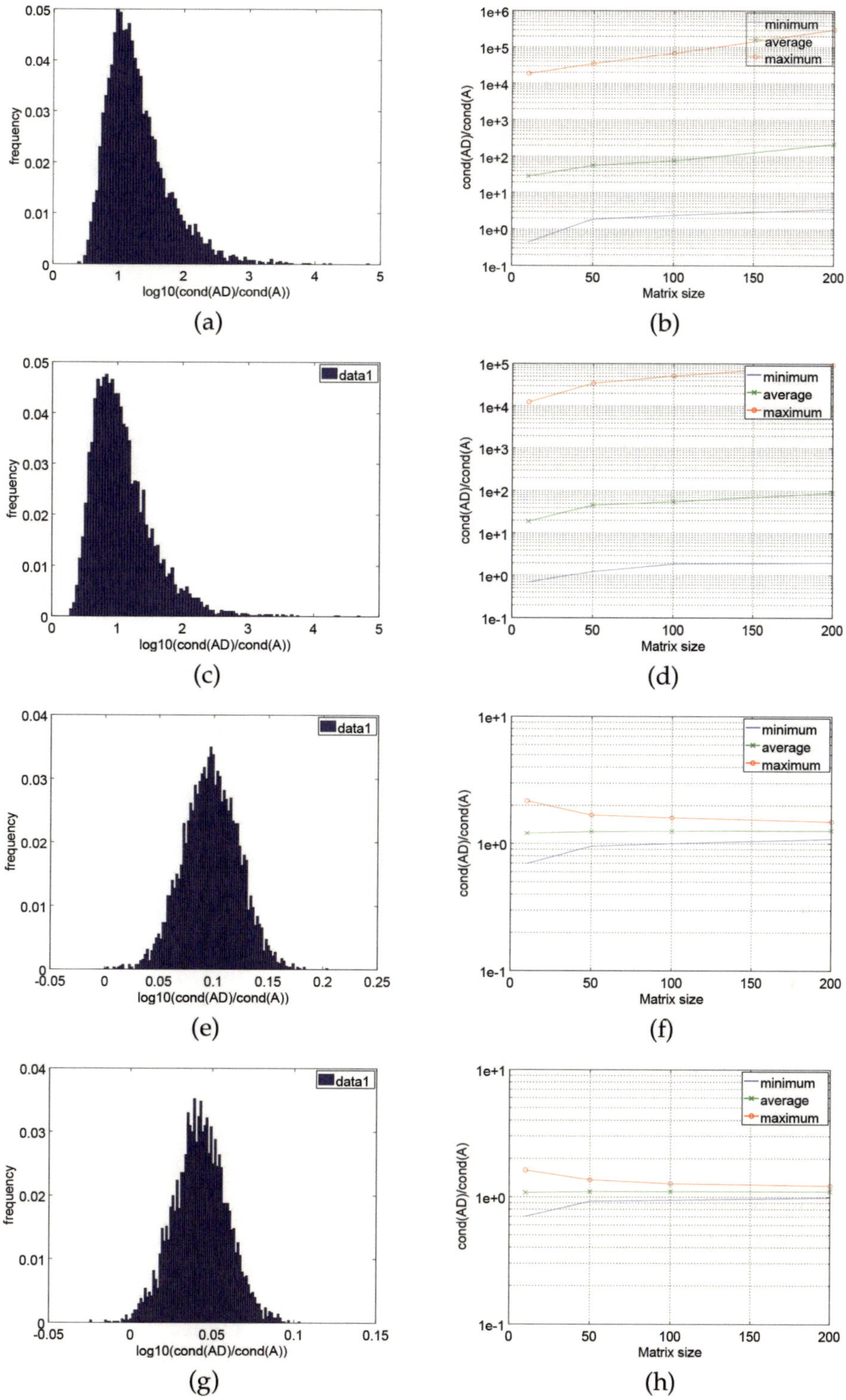

Figure 3.
(a) Histogram of the condition number amplification $\rho = cond(\mathbf{AD})/cond(\mathbf{A})$ in logarithmic scale for 100×100 matrices; matrix entries of both $\mathbf{A}$ and $\mathbf{D}$ are Gaussian with mean zero and unitary variance; (b) minimum, maximum, and average values of ρ as a function of the matrix size; (c) and (d) like (a) and (b), but the entries of $\mathbf{D}$ are uniformly distributed in $[0,1]$; (e) and (f) like (c) and (d), but the entries of $\mathbf{D}$ are uniformly distributed in $[1/2, 3/2]$; (g) and (h) like (c) and (d), but the entries of $\mathbf{D}$ are uniformly distributed in $[1,2]$.

4. The adversary model

In the literature, two kinds of "bad behavior" can be present together or not in a specific opponent:

Honest but curious: In this case all the parties follow correctly the protocol, and the computed result is correct, but the cloud tries to learn the protected secret. Note that it is reasonable to expect that the opponent is interested in the *engineering problem* or the corresponding solution rather than in the numerical counterparts. The numerical problem/solution can be seen as a mean to find out the engineering problem/solution. Note that the freedom that one has in the discretization step can potentially be used to make it more difficult to invert it.

Malicious: The cloud does not follow correctly the protocol and, in particular, could try to "cut some corners" returning results that are not correct. In many cases, this attack can be easily counteracted by checking the result returned by the cloud; this is possible since many problems can be computationally heavy to solve, but it is fairly easy to check if a solution is correct; think, for example, the case of a linear system.

In some cases, even a full check can be quite demanding; in those cases, a random selection of checks to be done can give a fairly good assurance that the result is correct. For example, in the case of a linear system, a random subset of the equations can be checked. The probability of a false positive (an uncorrected result is accepted) decreases exponentially with the number of checks, while the computational cost grows only linearly. Indeed, many check techniques proposed in the literature can be reduced to this idea.

Remark 4.1

It is worth observing that since we are talking about floating point computation, we need to take into account numerical noise that results from computation. For example, if a numerical system is solved with an iterative approach, the returned solution will differ from the "true" solution by a, hopefully, small error. This needs to be taken into account when checking if the solution is correct.

In a typical context the adversary is interested in getting the original problem or the solution. It is worth observing that while in the classical cryptography setup, the opponent recovers completely the message or nothing at all; in this case, there is the possibility that the adversary recovers an approximate version of the problem/ solution. Observe also that the setup of **Figure 2c** makes the problem for the adversary more difficult since after recovering the numerical problem there is the problem of doing the inverse of discretization.

Finally, it is worth observing that the encryption/decryption steps could amplify the numerical noise introduced by the solution algorithm.

4.1 Security criterion

A major difference between traditional cryptography and cryptography of numerical problems is the information that an opponent can gain about the secret. In the most typical case, in a practical application of classical cryptography, two cases are possible: (i) the opponent succeeds in the attack and learns the whole secret and (ii) the attack is unsuccessful and very little, or nothing is learned about the secret; the case where a partial success can be achieved is quite uncommon. Suitable security criterion in this kind of application is information-theoretical criterion (where the adversary has unlimited computational power) or based on computational indistinguishably (where we admit that the computational power of the adversary can grow only polynomially).

In the context of encryption of numerical problems instead, it is possible that the opponent gains some partial or *low-resolution* information. For example, in the case of a new wing, the adversary is interested in learning the profile of the wing; the adversary has a strong *a priori* information about the profile, and only some detail information to integrate such a priori are needed. Depending on the specific encryption technique, it could be possible for the adversary to find said details but only up to a resolution. The ambiguity could be "unsolvable" even with infinite computational power (more or less the equivalent of information-theoretical security), or maybe it could be that the amount of computation required to improve the resolution increases more than the polynomial with the required resolution (this would be the equivalent of classical computational indistinguishably).

There is also the possibility that the encryption technique leaks some *invariant* of the problem. For example, if linear system $\mathbf{Ax} = \mathbf{b}$ is encrypted by applying two orthogonal matrices $\mathbf{U}$, $\mathbf{V}$ as in

$$\underbrace{\mathbf{UAV}}_{\hat{\mathbf{A}}}\underbrace{\mathbf{V}^t\mathbf{x}}_{\hat{\mathbf{x}}} = \underbrace{\mathbf{Ub}}_{\hat{\mathbf{b}}}, \tag{7}$$

matrix $\hat{\mathbf{A}}$ preserves the singular values of $\mathbf{A}$. Is this a problem? Most probably, it depends on the specific underlining engineering problem. As in another example, consider the encryption protocol described in (2). In this case, $\hat{\mathbf{A}}$ preserves not the singular values of $\mathbf{A}$ but its sparsity (i.e., the number of non-zero entries). Again, if this is a problem or not probably depends on the corresponding engineering problem.

To the best of our knowledge, most of the literature consider the classical cryptography criterion of computational indistinguishably, and more research about criterion specific for numerical problem could prove useful.

4.1.1 About sparsity preservation

As said before, many discretization techniques produce matrices that are very sparse. This is very important from the viewpoint of computational efficiency since there are algorithms that are able to exploit the sparseness, working only with the non-zero entries of the matrix. This suggests that the encryption should preserve the sparseness or, at least, not reduce it in a significant way. However, some researchers raise the concern that even the fraction of non-zero entries can be private information. This would suggest that the encryption step should not preserve matrix sparsity.

It is also worth observing that in some application, the number of non-zero entries is known a priori with good precision. For example, in FDM/FEM discretization methods for differential equations, the fraction of non-zero entries depend on the structure of the grid employed which can be considered known with good precision. A quantitative and objective approach to the importance of preserving or hiding the sparsity can be an interesting field for future research activity.

5. Existing techniques

The field of encrypting numerical problems is relatively new, and there is not a huge variety of encryption algorithms proposed; many of them are just variations of some basic scheme. To the best of our knowledge, no algorithm found in the literature tries to encrypt the engineering problem; it rather tackles the numerical problem. Also, it is very difficult to find some discussion about the numerical stability of the proposed scheme.

5.1 Basic techniques

There are few basic techniques used in the literature to encrypt matrices and vectors.

Addition: To matrix $\mathbf{A}$ a matrix $\mathbf{K}$ is added to obtain $\hat{\mathbf{A}} = \mathbf{A} + \mathbf{K}$. This approach is not widely used, probably because sum does not "propagate" nicely in usual linear algebra operations (e.g., linear systems, eigenvalue problems, determinants, singular value decomposition). Moreover, in the case of linear systems, it is not obvious how to choose $\mathbf{K}$ in order to have $\hat{\mathbf{A}}$ invertible.

Product by a diagonal matrix: Matrix $\mathbf{A}$ is multiplied (on the left, on the right, or both) by a diagonal matrix $\mathbf{D}$. The effect on problems like linear systems is quite easy to describe, and it suffices that all the diagonal entries are not zero in order to guarantee the invertibility of $\hat{\mathbf{A}}$, but, as shown in Section 3.1, if $\mathbf{D}$ is randomly chosen, the condition number of $\mathbf{A}$ can increase by several orders of magnitude.

Product by a permutation: Matrix $\mathbf{A}$ is multiplied (on the left, on the right, or both) by a permutation matrix $\mathbf{P}$. This grants that $\text{cond}\left(\hat{\mathbf{A}}\right) = \text{cond}(\mathbf{A})$ (therefore also invertibility is preserved). A product by a permutation requires no floating point multiplications, although the cost of data movement (especially if $\mathbf{A}$ is very large) is not necessarily small. Sparsity is preserved, and this can be seen either as an advantage or as a drawback (see Section 4.1.1). Some characteristic values such as determinant and singular values are preserved.

Product by a unitary matrix: Matrix $\mathbf{A}$ is multiplied (on the left, on the right, or both) by a matrix $\mathbf{R}$ such that $\mathbf{R}^t\mathbf{R} = \mathbf{I}$. This grants that $\text{cond}\left(\hat{\mathbf{A}}\right) = \text{cond}(\mathbf{A})$. Product by $\mathbf{R}$ does not necessarily preserve sparsity. If $\mathbf{R}$ is generated as a sequence of planar rotations, product by $\mathbf{R}$ (stored as sequence of rotation, not as a full matrix) can be more efficient than usual matrix product. Singular values and determinant are preserved.

5.2 Brief literature review

Maybe the numerical problem most frequently addressed is the problem of solving linear systems. Lei et al. [7] proposed a scheme similar to (2) where $\mathbf{A}$ is both left and right multiplied by a diagonal matrix and a permutation. The proposal of Wang et al. [10] is one of the few that proposes to use classical homomorphic encryption together with an iterative algorithm; the approach of Wang et al. requires to use matrices with integer entries (eventually by rescaling the system) and a continuous exchange between the cloud and the user. Chen et al. in [11] pointed out a weakness of [10] and proposed a variation to solve the problem. Another solution based on matrix pre- and post-multiplication is suggested in [8].

A problem similar to linear system is linear regression. Chen et al. in [9] used pre- and post-multiplication approaches with two diagonal matrices. Zhou et al. in [12] pointed out a possible weakness (in the hypothesis of an integer problem). Similar approaches, still based on matrix pre- and post-multiplication, can be found also for matrix product [13, 14], determinant computation [15], and singular value decomposition [16].

6. Conclusions

We analyzed the problem of outsourcing safely numerical and engineering problems to the cloud. It turns out that the field is still in an evolving phase. Many approaches are different instances of pre- and post-multiplication masking techniques; security criterion is a reformulation of criterion from classical cryptography and does not address the peculiarities of numerical problem protections; finally, the problem of how the encryption/decryption impacts on issue such as numerical conditioning of the problem is usually not addressed. Future research directions will aim to cover such still open areas.

Author details

Riccardo Bernardini
University of Udine, Udine, Italy

*Address all correspondence to: riccardo.bernardin@uniud.it

References

[1] Griffin D. Report on the public consultation for H2020 Work Programme 2016–17: Cloud computing and software. Tech. Rep., DG CONNECT E.2. 2014

[2] Jeffery K, Schubert L. Complete computing: Toward information, incentive and intention. Tech. rep., DG CONNECT E.2. 2014

[3] Hsieh A. Direct numerical simulation of complex turbulence [PhD thesis]. University of Colorado; 2017

[4] Alfonsi G. On direct numerical simulation of turbulent flows. Applied Mechanics Reviews. 2011;**64**:0802-0803

[5] Landahl MT, Mollo-Christensen E. Turbulence and Random Processes in Fluid Mechanics. 2nd ed. Cambridge, UK: Cambridge University Press; 1992

[6] Belytschko T, Rabczuk T, Huerta A, Fernández-Méndez S. Meshfree Methods, Ch. 10. Atlanta, GA, USA: American Cancer Society; 2004

[7] Lei X, Liao X, Huang T, Li H, Hu C. Outsourcing large matrix inversion computation to a public cloud. IEEE Transactions on Cloud Computing. 2013;**1**(1):1

[8] Kumar M, Meena J, and Vardhan M, Secure amp;amp; efficient delegation of system of linear equation to a malicious cloud server. In: 2017 4th International Conference on Electronics and Communication Systems (ICECS); Feb 2017. pp. 12-17

[9] Chen F, Xiang T, Lei X, Chen J. Highly efficient linear regression outsourcing to a cloud. IEEE Transactions on Cloud Computing. 2014;**2**:499-508

[10] Wang C, Ren K, Wang J, Wang Q. Harnessing the cloud for securely outsourcing large-scale systems of linear equations. IEEE Transactions on Parallel and Distributed Systems. 2013;**24**: 1172-1181

[11] Chen F, Xiang T, Yang Y. Privacy-preserving and verifiable protocols for scientific computation outsourcing to the cloud. Journal of Parallel and Distributed Computing. 2014;**74**(3): 2141-2151

[12] Zhou L, Zhu Y, Choo K-KR. Efficiently and securely harnessing cloud to solve linear regression and other matrix operations. Future Generation Computer Systems. 2018;**81**: 404-413

[13] Lei X, Liao X, Huang T, Heriniaina F. Achieving security, robust cheating resistance, and high-efficiency for outsourcing large matrix multiplication computation to a malicious cloud. Information Sciences. 2014;**280**:205-217

[14] Kong S, Cai Y, Xue F, Yu H, Ditta A. Cloud outsourcing computing security protocol of matrix multiplication computation based on similarity transformation. International Journal of Wireless and Mobile Computing. 2018; **14**(1):90-96

[15] Lei X, Liao X, Huang T, Li H. Cloud computing service: The case of large matrix determinant computation. IEEE Transactions on Services Computing. 2015;**8**:688-700

[16] Pramkaew C, Ngamsuriyaroj S. Lightweight scheme of secure outsourcing svd of a large matrix on cloud. Journal of Information Security and Applications. 2018;**41**:92-102

Chapter 5

Overlay Security: Quantum-Safe Communication over the Internet Infrastructure

Shlomi Dolev

Abstract

The need for a quantum-safe Internet is emerging, and this is a great opportunity to re-examine the legacy of public key infrastructure. There is a need for perspective on the evolution of cryptography over the years, including the perfect information-theoretical secure schemes and the computationally secure schemes, in particular. There is also a need to examine the evolving Internet infrastructure to identify efficient design and secure cryptographic schemes over the existing Internet infrastructure. A combination of overlay security, blockchain, and Merkle trees with Lamport's signatures offers just such an easily implementable quantum-safe Internet.

Keywords: public key infrastructure, post-quantum cryptography, secret sharing, blockchain, Lamport signatures

1. Introduction

Securing the digital world is essential as critical infrastructures are based on communicating with remote computers. The trust in the computer network is based on having a secure and authenticated communication. The change in social activity, where the big four companies Google, Amazon, Facebook, and Apple (GAFA) influence many aspects in modern society implies the need for secure computer and network infrastructures. The past interest in quantum cryptography has grown significantly in recent years. National Institute of Standards and Technology (NIST) authors wrote an overview on the subjects in 2009 [25], and the activity expanded dramatically, having dedicated conferences on the subject [27]. The most challenging component of Internet security that needs to be considered is the replacement of the existing asymmetric encryption scheme, namely, to replace an RSA [29]. For this there are several candidates: lattice-based cryptography (e.g., shortest vector problem, closest vector problem), code-based cryptography (e.g., McEliece, Niederreiter), and more (see, e.g., [24]). The second challenging task is a replacement for signature scheme; here hash-based Lamport's one-time signature together with the Merkle tree is believed to address that need (see [39] for an overview). The integration of the post-quantum cryptographic ingredients into a complete infrastructure is also challenging (as we detail in the sequel).

We present a design for quantum-safe communication over the existing Internet infrastructure. No hardware changes are required, only software updates over the

IntechOpen

heterogeneous Internet architecture. Different aspects of the solution are presented in the sequel.

2. Quantum computing today

The emergence of quantum computers is a fact [12]; beyond the commercial non-universal commercial quantum computer of several thousand qubits (quantum bits) of D-Wave [10], IBM commercializes 50 qubits quantum computers [18]. The quantum computer race leads to exponential growth in the number of qubits, where in 2018 Intel presented 49 qubits quantum computer [19] and Google announced 72 qubits computers [16]. In addition, several startups including Rigetti announced a 36 qubits quantum computer [28] and a quantum processing unit (QPU) (see also Ion Q [20] and QCI [32]).

Many quantum computers restrict the qubits that participate as inputs for quantum gate operations and employ qubit teleportation to allow quantum gate operations over non-neighboring quantum bits, e.g., [36, 8]. The advance in techniques for producing entangled qubits and teleportation [37, 38] may assist in using several quantum computers to cooperate on a task by teleporting qubits from one to another, thus building a virtual quantum computer with the needed qubits for the task. In particular, for breaking the asymmetric encryption schemes in use almost immediately, much earlier than estimated.

3. Quantum algorithms

Shor's algorithm [35], designed for quantum computers, changed the way modern cryptography and Internet security are captured. New algorithms for quantum computers are frequently invented [31, 4].

Computationally secure cryptography is based on the unproven assumption of the existence of one-way function, a function that can be computed easily but is hard to be inverted. The risk that an algorithm that breaks a considered one-way function will be found always exists, e.g., [1]. Even one-way functions proposed for post-quantum cryptosystems are at risk of the discovery of new efficient inverse algorithms. One famous example of an open problem for decades is the primality test that had no polynomial deterministic algorithm, until just such an algorithm was found [2].

4. Perspective on encryption

The asymmetric encryption schemes, proposed by Merkle [23], Diffie and Hellman [9], and Rivest et al. [29], revolutionized cryptography. The idea to use computational tasks in order to establish a symmetric key started with the suggestion of Merkle to use computation puzzles. Merkle's puzzle scheme started with Alice choosing at random many computation puzzles, possibly hashed random numbers (with tuned lengths) each concatenated with a sequence number, such that Bob is able to randomly choose one of the puzzles and reverse this number in reasonable time. Then, Bob sends a few of the bits of the revealed random number back to Alice, identifying the puzzle Bob decided to solve. Both Alice and Bob will be using the unrevealed bits of the solved puzzle as their symmetric key. Eve on the other hand will not know which of the puzzles was chosen by Bob, will likely have to solve many puzzles before identifying the puzzle randomly chosen by Bob, and revealing the symmetric key they use. Later Diffie and Helman and then Rivest, Shamir and Adelman suggested more efficient schemes based on number theory assumptions.

Asymmetric encryption enabled the creation of a symmetric key among communicating parties over tapped communication links [23, 9] and is even able to identify the intervention of malicious parties in the communication [29]. The identification of such malicious parties was due to the capability of [29] to sign certificates that monolithically associated a public key with the entity identity description to which the public key belongs. The signature was issued by a trusted third party, the certificate authority. This public key infrastructure is the de facto security infrastructure today, securing Internet activity, including military, governmental, social, financial, and, in fact, all activities in the Internet.

Thus, the appearance of quantum computers and fitting quantum algorithms, which may break the basic mathematical foundations of [9, 29], has great implications. Post-quantum cryptosystems [26] are examined, e.g., [15], replacing the believed to be one-way functions that are currently used by other functions, which are also believed to be one-way functions. Provable perfect encryption does exist, namely, encryption based on the classical one-time pad [34], as long as the one-time pad is a true random sequence. True random sequences are possibly produced by the use of quantum effects, e.g., [17].

Another difficulty in using one-time pad is the need to share the one-time pad prior to communication. The one-time pad can be shared prior to communication by physically delivering a copy of the one-time pad. Distribution of a one-time pad to many users may risk the loss or duplication of one copy of the one-time pad, nullifying the secrecy of the encryption.

Quantum key distribution [3] suggests using quantum bits superposition for detecting a tapper in the communication of random bits; however this scheme can only be used in direct links of at most 100 km. Recently, [22, 30] succeeded in using satellites and quantum bits entanglement to share a key over longer distances. This key can be viewed as a short one-time pad, as the rate of the received random bits is limited. One difficulty is the need to mobilize the symmetric key received from the satellite in one satellite receiver to the actual place the key should be used and the fact that the key authenticates the satellite receiver, but may not yield the identification of other users.

5. Overlay security

Occasionally, one needs to send a credit number electronically, sending one email with the first digits of the credit card and then another email with the rest. Still, the email servers and the Internet server providers may act as a man in the middle and tap in, capturing part or all of the digits of the credit card. It is possible to send a random string (one-time pad) via WhatsApp (owned by Facebook) and the bitwise x-or of the credit card with the random string via Gmail. On one hand, this resembles sending entangled bits in two channels. On the other hand, just like content distribution networks (CDN), e.g., Akamai, that uses overlay network of the Internet ISPs as their source for extra reliability and services, *overlay security* uses the accumulated secrecy, authenticity, and identification of the diverse capabilities of the communication channels, applications, and protocols.

The maturity and evolvement of the Internet technology enabled the CDN company to use the Internet infrastructure as a playground for delivering contents at will. In the last decades, more and more communication channels identify, authenticate, and secure the communication between entities. Email, SMS, push notifications, and messengers (WhatsApp, Facebook Messenger, Skype, Snapchat, LINE, LinkedIn, Telegram, Weibo, Slack, etc.) form logical secured channels. Each of the channels, even if they use the same physical channel, implies already built trust in the identification and authentication of the entity communicated through the channel. Moreover, the maintenance and repair of the security of each channel are guaranteed by the channel supplier. Still, each channel may act as a man-in-the-middle accumulating the communications transmitted through the channel servers. The use of a random one-time pad over channels nullifies information accumulated by the server of each channel.

This is the current playground suggested to be used by the overlay security concept, to create a symmetric key based on perfectly secure information-theoretical secure scheme, namely, quantum-safe replacements for asymmetric encryption. In addition, the security of new channels can be obtained inductively by the security of existing channels, employing them to create a random shared key for the new channel.

6. Redundancy and secret sharing

Overlay security uses several channels and random numbers to obtain a high level of confidence in identification, authentication, and secrecy, a level implied by all the used channels. However, if one of the channels, say Android push notification, is not available (possibly in China), then the communication is blocked. Secret sharing [33, 5] schemes imply a tunable threshold for the number of channels needed to reconstruct the secret. Shamir secret sharing is based on polynomials over a finite field, where each participant, in our case channel, receives one point of the polynomial and the secret is the free coefficient of the polynomial. For example, if the polynomial is a random linear function with the secret being the free coefficient, any two participants/channels can reveal the secret, but a single participant/channel has absolutely no information on the secret. Polynomials with greater degrees used over many channels may imply more trust in the aggregated identification, authentication, and secrecy while allowing several of the channels to be blocked or even to corrupt the information conveyed through them.

7. Authentication bay

Identifying and authenticating an entity in the physical world by the digital world are the biggest challenges in information security. Having secured robust and reliable identification and authentication of a person, an institute, a company, or a device are the first chain in securing digital representation and processing of information. For example, a bank client needs to be identified and authenticated for performing digital operations on their account. The linkage between the physical entity and the digital representation of an entity allows processing of digital and physical assets in the computers and the Internet.

The need for identification and authentication of an entity started before computers exist. Certificates signed by trusted authorities were used by governments to monitor the activity of the society, to enable law and order. Certificates used to authenticate entities were and are part of business infrastructure. The procedures used to authenticate an entity were and are defined by societies. A newborn child does not need a certificate to be born, obviously when the child is born at home. Moreover, a newborn may not have a certificate with identifying details, including identifying number, without enforcing society's regulations. Some societies pay parents of newborns when they register the child, an attractive payment that almost ensures that newborn will be registered.

In the scope of people, biometric identifications, by using fingerprints, face recognition, iris, and palm, are becoming standard. The identification starts with the registration process in which there is a need to identify and link the person with the biometric information recorded during the registration process. This is an error-prone process that encapsulates the challenge in the authentication bay. There is a need for a trusted authority (e.g., government, banks) or trusted manufacturer (e.g., Apple, Samsung) to collect biometric samples while authenticating the person by other means (e.g., driving license, passport) and digitally link them in a digital record. The actual biometric sampling would be better stored in a form of one-way hash, just like passwords; otherwise, they can be copied and used without the actual involvement of the biometric identification device (e.g., fingerprint reader, camera). Keeping the biometric database private and secure is another challenging task, as once a biometric data is leaked to untrusted entities, the search for confusing biometric data to fake identification can be feasible.

Moreover, current technologies for identifying a person biometrically are not perfect. Biometric identifications have false positives, when a non-authorized person is identified as another authorized person and performs an action they are not allowed to perform. Biometric identifications also have false negatives, when a person is not correctly identified as the person registered and cannot perform actions they are authorized to take. DNA identification will also be possible in the near future; still identical twins share the same DNA.

Having unique attributes is only one facet of the identification and authentication process, as there should be trust in the digital identification and authorization process. For example, consider a program identifying a person having DNA linked to the registered digital record of a person with a certain identity number, and then send an approval on the check. There are several questions to ask on the program actions. Does the program have the means to verify that the input device (e.g., fingerprint, camera) observed the person, or is it a mock-up? Were the input device compromised and a replay attack performed? Another question is whether the program verified the collected data from the input device against the right registration record or was maybe hacked to output approval with no actual checking. This chain of trust is yielded from the trust in the biometric device producer.

In the framework of the Internet of Things (IoT), the identification of things is even more challenging, as devices and items tend to be produced identically. Vehicle networking is now emerging, and the means to identify a car (by another car) is one of the basic ingredients that the trust vehicles have in inter-vehicle communication. Recent works suggested to monolithically sign the car description (e.g., driving license, color, and brand) and the public key associated with the car description in one monolithically signed certificate. The signing authority can be the governmental vehicle registration [10]. The car description should allow for a unique identification by means of an out-of-band channel such as a camera. Note that the identity of a device can be challenging; for example, consider two cars of the same model; if one exchanges the doors of these cars, does that alter the identity of the car? What about changing the engine? And so on.

Another possibility for identifying IoT devices requires trust in the producer, which embeds a unique serial identification number, A unique identifying numbers in unaltered barcode, QR code, RFID, and ROM that can be used as part of the identification and authentication process.

The cloud and blockchain infrastructures enable a new opportunity for representing each person, entity, and organization by a digital avatar. The avatar, being a digital historical record of events, digital assets, and procedures/functions defined to be executed upon given events. The identity linkage between the avatar and the physical entity accumulates trust over time, letting the physical entity monitor the possibility of identity theft, as recorded actions for the avatar can be examined by the actual entity represented by the avatar.

Fake avatars already exist, and they are represented by profiles in social networks, Facebook, LinkedIn, etc., and may interact with persons as bots do. This is one light form of identity theft where there may be no real entity linked to the avatar. Identity theft has been a trust problem in societies from the years of the bible where Jacob represented himself as Esav to Itzhak. Nowadays, the remote actions enabled in the digital interaction make the identity theft phenomena a major concern.

In some cases, e.g., cryptocurrency, anonymity is an important aspect, as cash money, or digital money, appearing in an account had better not carry its history. Thus every coin or bill having an identical value. Blockchain associates an account with a public key, where the matching private key is held by the owner of a wallet. This somewhat anonymous linkage between an entity and digital assets is only by the means of the private key. The vulnerability of such a solution erases the famous cases of lost/stolen private keys.

Private keys are also a means to sign transactions binding the holder (even in court) to the transaction; thus, the way to secure the private key, possibly in enclaved memory, is very important. Moreover, having a quantum-safe signature is a must, as the bidding is a very important aspect of the trust infrastructure, and if the bidding is broken, deniability of actions is possible. A client that transferred a million dollars from their account may rightly claim that someone else preformed the transfer to this account on their behalf, with no permission.

Another aspect of the authentication bay is the usage of passwords. The illusion that passwords can contribute to the security of the communication is misleading. Many of the passwords are subject to dictionary attacks. Users tend to forget and manage passwords in vulnerable storage, leading to many password lists being sold on the black net. The typical password renewal procedure involves password reset invocation and a temporal password sent through email. Such single channel security is another weak chain in the security infrastructure, a weak chain that may dramatically benefit using the multichannel security and authenticity yielded from the overlay security concept.

8. Distributed trust, blockchain, beyond social identity

Certificate authorities are a major source of trust for the public key infrastructure. The certificate authority identifies an entity and signs a certificate that associates a public key with the entity description. The history of the Internet testifies to examples of the vulnerability of the trust associated with certificate authorities. For example, private keys that were used to sign certificates were stolen, and significant percentage of the Internet were not secure [7, 37]. Recently, Estonia, Canada, and other countries started to use distributed trust among several trusted and heterogeneous entities as a source for identification. Such distributed trust is enabled by blockchain technology [14]. Identity, verified by several trusted entities, possibly including governmental, financial, and notary entities, among others, is logged in a distributed fashion.

To communicate with an entity, a search of several participants in the distributed ledger returns contact information for the entity. Using the communication channels in the contact information and secret sharing enables the creation of a symmetric key. The newly created random symmetric key may, in turn, be used in employing efficient advanced encryption standard (AES) over a single communication link. Unlike the functions used in asymmetric encryption, AES is crafted, rather than relying on number theory challenge, and believed to imply quantum-safe encryption. The key length should still be carefully selected to accommodate the quadratic speedup of search of Grover's algorithm [13]. Note that secure hash algorithms (SHA) are crafted, similarly to AES, and are also believed to be quantum safe, reducing the risk of finding an efficient number theory solution for a natural problem, such as discrete logarithm.

9. Quantum-safe signatures

The ability to perform a transaction in an undeniable fashion over the Internet is important, especially when financial transactions are executed. Lamport's one-time signature [21] is not tied to a particular one-way function. Thus, Lamport's signature can employ secure hash function, such as SHA. The use of Merkle trees with multiple private keys in the leaves (leaves that can also be produced by several nested hash functions) and the root of the tree serving as the public key yields an efficient, quantum-safe signature scheme.

In greater detail, the private key is an array of pairs of random numbers. The first random number pair is used to sign the first bit of the message; the second random number pair is used to sign the second bit of the message and so on. Note that, for reasons of efficiency, typically, the hash of the message is signed instead of signing the longer original message. Each random number in each pair is hashed (in fact, any other one-way functions can be used instead of hash), and the resulting array of hashed values serve as the public key. Once the public key is published in a way that links the signing entity to the public key, the construction can serve in signing any single binary string, a string that may be the hash of the original message to be signed. The actual signature is a sequence of random numbers from the private key, one from each pair, attached to the message to be signed. The first random number in the signature is the first (second) random number in the first pair if the first bit to be signed is zero (one, respectively). Similarly, the second random number in the signature is the first (second) random number in the second pair if the first bit to be signed is zero (one, respectively) and so on. Since the array of numbers in the public key are results of one-way hash function, no one but the producer of the public key is able (under standard computation assumptions) to know and expose the right portions of the private key. Hence, the signature is binding.

Still, the need to identify an entity and associate the entity to the public key is the most challenging stage in authentication. Lamport's signature essentially requires such an identification process for each signature. Fortunately, many of Lamport's signatures may share a single public key, which consists of the roots of Merkle tree, one tree for each position of a random number in each pair of the private keys. The first positions, representing the private keys used to sign a zero value of the strings, consist of random numbers, such that such numbers belonging to the first two private keys are concatenated and hashed to yield the value of their common parent in the first Merkle tree. Similarly, for the second positions, the two random numbers are concatenated and hashed to yield the value of their parent in a second Merkle tree and so on. The parent of any such two leaves is concatenated to the hash obtained from the next two random numbers that reside in the same positions in the next two private keys and hashed yielding the value of the grandparent of these four values and so on.

A signature will use one of the leaves, where each leaf is connected by a path to the roots of Merkle trees, one tree for each random number in the leaf. When using a leaf to sign, the appropriate random number in each pair of the leaf is exposed together with the missing hash values that are concatenated in each level of the tree. Thus allowing the verifier to check that indeed any revealed random number leads to the corresponding value of the Merkle tree root public value.

The root value may be stored with the contact information that resides in the blockchain. The contact information with the public value of the root will be added to the distributed ledger after the blockchain participants verify and approve the identity of the contact information and root value owner.

10. Conclusion

Overlay security combined with distributed trust forms an immediate quantum-safe alternative to the public key infrastructure. The existing technologies enable (1) the use of multi-logical/multi-physical channels to create a random secret at will, (2) use of the blockchain distributed ledger as a replacement for single point of failure trusted authority, and to (3) produce quantum-safe signatures.

The suggested changes can gradually, seamlessly, and smoothly emerge over the existing infrastructure without the need to restructure any component of the Internet.

Author details

Shlomi Dolev
Ben-Gurion University of the Negev & Secret Double Octopus Ltd, Israel

*Address all correspondence to: dolev@cs.bgu.ac.il

References

[1] Adrian D, Bhargavan K, Durumeric Z, Pierrick G, Green M, Halderman JA, et al. Imperfect forward secrecy: How Diffie-Hellman fails in practice. In: CCS'15. 2015

[2] Agrawal M, Kayal N, Saxena N. PRIMES is in P. Annals of Mathematics. 2004;**160**(2):781-793

[3] Bennett CH, Brassard G. Quantum cryptography: Public key distribution and coin tossing. In: Proceedings of IEEE International Conference on Computers, Systems and Signal Processing. Vol. 175. New York; 1984. p. 8

[4] Bernstein JB, Heninger N, Lou P, Valenta L. Post-quantum RSA. International Workshop on Post-Quantum Cryptography. 2017. pp. 311-329. A Preview of Bristlecone, Google's New Quantum Processor. Available from: https://ai.googleblog.com/2018/03/a-preview-of-bristlecone-googles-new.html

[5] Blakley GR. Safeguarding cryptographic key. In: Managing Requirements Knowledge, International Workshop on (AFIPS). Vol. 48. 1979. pp. 313-317

[6] Canada's New Partnership with Estonia is a Major Digital Government Milestone 28/5/18 Max Greenwood More can be found here at Techvibs: https://techvibes.com/2018/05/29/canadas-new-partnership-with-estonia-is-a-major-digital-government-milestone

[7] News article, the real security issue behind the Comodo hack. CSO from IDG By Roger A. Grimes. Available from: https://www.csoonline.com/article/2623707/hacking/the-real-security-issue-behind-the-comodo-hack.html

[8] Center for quantum computation & communication technology, Australian research council center of excellence. Available from: http://www.cqc2t.org

[9] Diffie W, Hellman ME. New directions in cryptography. IEEE Transactions on Information Theory. 1976;**22**(6):644-654

[10] Dolev S, Panwar N, Segal M. Certificating vehicle public key with vehicle attributes. 2014. US US9769658B2

[11] D-wave the quantum computing company. Available from: https://www.dwavesys.com/d-wave-two-system

[12] Fedorov AK, Kiktenko E, Lvovsky AI. Quantum computers put blockchain security at risk. Nature. 2018;**7732**(465):563-663

[13] Grover LK. A fast quantum mechanical algorithm for database search. In: STOC. 1996. pp. 212-219

[14] Gheorghiu V, Gorbunov S, Mosca M, Munson M. Quantum Proofing the Blockchain. Blockchain Research Institute: University of Waterloo; 2017

[15] Google Tests Post-Quantum Crypto Quantum Computing Will Shred Current Crypto Systems, Experts Warn Jeremy Kirk • July 11, 2016. Available from: https://www.bankinfosecurity.com/google-adds-quantum-computing-armor-to-chrome-a-9253

[16] Available from: https://ai.googleblog.com/2018/03/a-preview-of-bristlecone-googles-new.html

[17] Herrero-Collantes M, Garcia-Escartin JC. Quantum random number generators. Reviews of Modern Physics. 2017;**89**(1):015004

[18] IBM Raises the Bar with a 50-Qubit Quantum Computer. MIT technology review. Available from: https://www.technologyreview.com/s/609451/ibm-raises-the-bar-with-a-50-qubit-quantum-computer

[19] 2018 CES: Intel advances quantum and neuromorphic computing research. 2018. Available from: https://newsroom.intel.com/news/intel-advances-quantum-neuromorphic-computing-research/#gs.9ud403

[20] A true quantum leap. Introducing the first commercial trapped ion quantum computer. Available from: https://ionq.co

[21] Lamport L. Constructing digital signatures from a one-way function. Technical Report SRI-CSL-98. SRI International Computer Science Laboratory. 1979

[22] Liao SK, Cai WQ, et al. Satellite-to-ground quantum key distribution. Nature. 2017;**549**:43-47

[23] Merkle R. Secure communications over insecure channels. Communications of the ACM. 1978;**21**(4):294-299

[24] Niederhagen R, Waidner M. Practical post-quantum cryptography. White Paper, Fraunhofer Institute for Secure Information Technology SIT. August 18, 2017

[25] Perlner RA, Cooper DA. Quantum resistant public key cryptography: A survey. ID Trust. 2009. pp. 85-93

[26] Post-quantum cryptography. Available from: https://en.wikipedia.org/wiki/Post-quantum.cryptography

[27] Information about Post-quantum cryptography. Available from: https://pqcrypto.org

[28] QPU Specifications. Rigetti Technical Publications. Available from: https://www.rigetti.com/qpu

[29] Rivest RL, Shamir A, Adelman L. A method for obtaining digital signatures and public-key cryptosystems. Communications of the ACM. 1978;**21**(2):120-126

[30] Ren J-G et al. Ground-to-satellite quantum teleportation. Nature. 2017;**549**:70-73

[31] Quantum Algorithm Zoo. Details about the Quantum algorithm Zoo, by Stephen Jordan. Available from: https://math.nist.gov/quantum/zoo/

[32] Building quantum computers designed to scale published in QCI at: https://www.quantumcircuits.com

[33] Shamir A. How to share a secret. Communications of the ACM. 1979;**22**(11):612-613

[34] Shannon C. Communication theory of secrecy systems. Bell System Technical Journal. 1949;**28**(4):656-715

[35] Shor WP. Polynomial-time algorithms for prime factorization and discrete logarithms on a quantum computer. SIAM Review. 1999;**41**(2):303-332

[36] Available from: http://www.sussex.ac.uk/physics/iqt/index.html

[37] 23,000 HTTPS certs will be axed in next 24 hours after private keys leak Trustico, DigiCert come to blows as browsers prepare to snub Symantec-brand SSL by, By John Leyden 1 Mar 2018. Available from: https://www.theregister.co.uk/2018/03/01/trusticodigicert symantec spat/

[38] Zomorodi-Moghadam M, Houshmand M, Houshmand M. Optimizing teleportation cost in distributed quantum circuits. International Journal of Theoretical Physics. 2018;**57**(3):848-861

[39] Zych MD. Quantum safe cryptography based on hash functions: A survey [master's thesis]. Department of Informatics, University of Oslo. 2018

Chapter 6

The MOR Cryptosystem in Classical Groups with a Gaussian Elimination Algorithm for Symplectic and Orthogonal Groups

Sushil Bhunia, Ayan Mahalanobis, Pralhad Shinde and Anupam Singh

Abstract

In this chapter, we study the MOR cryptosystem with symplectic and orthogonal groups over finite fields of odd characteristics. There are four infinite families of finite classical Chevalley groups. These are special linear groups $\mathrm{SL}(d, q)$, orthogonal groups $\mathrm{O}(d, q)$, and symplectic groups $\mathrm{Sp}(d, q)$. The family $\mathrm{O}(d, q)$ splits into two different families of Chevalley groups depending on the parity of d. The MOR cryptosystem over $\mathrm{SL}(d, q)$ was studied by the second author. In that case, the hardness of the MOR cryptosystem was found to be equivalent to the discrete logarithm problem in $\mathbb{F}_{q^d}$. In this chapter, we show that the MOR cryptosystem over $\mathrm{Sp}(d, q)$ has the security of the discrete logarithm problem in $\mathbb{F}_{q^d}$. However, it seems likely that the security of the MOR cryptosystem for the family of orthogonal groups is $\mathbb{F}_{q^{d^2}}$. We also develop an analog of row-column operations in symplectic and orthogonal groups which is of independent interest as an appendix.

Keywords: public-key cryptography, MOR cryptosystem, Chevalley groups, Gaussian elimination, 2010 Mathematics Subject Classification: 94A60, 20H30

1. Introduction

Public-key cryptography is the backbone of this modern society. However with **recent advances in quantum computers** and its possible implication to factoring integers and solving the discrete logarithm problems, it seems that we are left with no secure cryptographic primitive. So it seems prudent that we set out in search for new cryptographic primitives and subsequently new cryptosystems. The obvious question is: how to search and where to look? One can look into several well-known hard problems in Mathematics and hope to create a trap-door function, or one can try to generalize the known, trusted cryptosystems.

This chapter is in the direction of generalizing a known cryptosystem with the hope that something practical and useful will come out of this generalization. A new but arbitrary cryptosystem might not be considered by the community as a secure cryptosystem for decades. So our approach is conservative but practical. Several such approaches were earlier made by many eminent mathematicians. To name a few, Maze et al. [1, 2] developed SAP and Shpilrain and Zapata developed CAKE, both work in non-abelian structures. There is an interesting cryptosystem in the work of Climent et al. [3]. We further recommend the work of Grogoriev et al. [4] and Roman'kov [5].

The cryptosystem that we have in mind is *the MOR cryptosystem* [6–9]. In Section 2, we describe the MOR cryptosystem in details. It is a simple but powerful generalization of the well-known and classic ElGamal cryptosystem. In this cryptosystem, the discrete logarithm problem works in the automorphism group of a group instead of the group. As a matter of fact, it can work in the automorphism group of most algebraic structures. However, we will limit ourselves to finite groups. One way to look at the MOR cryptosystem is that it generalizes the discrete logarithm problem from a cyclic (sub)group to an arbitrary group.

The MOR cryptosystem over $\mathrm{SL}(d, q)$ was studied earlier [6] and cryptanalyzed by Monico [10]. It became clear that working with matrix groups of size d over $\mathbb{F}_q$ and with automorphisms that act by conjugation, like the inner automorphisms, there are two possible reductions of the security to finite fields. It is the security of the discrete logarithm problem in $\mathbb{F}_{q^d}$ or $\mathbb{F}_{q^{d^2}}$ ([6], Section 7). This reduction is similar to the embedding of the discrete logarithm problem in the group of rational points of an elliptic curve to a finite field; the degree of the extension of that field over the field of definition of the elliptic curve is called the *embedding degree*. In the case of $\mathrm{SL}(d, q)$, it became the security of $\mathbb{F}_{q^d}$. The reason that we undertook this study is to see if the security in other classical Chevalley groups is $\mathbb{F}_{q^d}$ or $\mathbb{F}_{q^{d^2}}$.

In cryptography, it is often hard to come up with theorems about security of a cryptosystem. However, at this moment it seems likely that the security of the MOR cryptosystem in orthogonal groups $\mathrm{O}(d, q)$ is $\mathbb{F}_{q^{d^2}}$. The way we implement this cryptosystem is by solving the word problem in generators. It presents **no advantage** to small characteristic. In the light of Joux's [11] improvement of the index-calculus attack in small characteristic, this contribution of the MOR cryptosystem is remarkable.

In summary, the proposed MOR cryptosystem is totally different from the known ElGamal cryptosystems from a functional point of view. Its implementation depends on Gaussian elimination and substitutions (substituting a matrix for a word in generators). However, we do have a concrete and tangible understanding of its security. It is clear from this work that the MOR cryptosystem over classical groups is *not quantum-secure*. However, for other groups like solvable groups, the answer is not known and could be a topic of further research.

1.1 Structure of the chapter

This chapter is an interplay between computational group theory and public-key cryptography, in particular the MOR cryptosystem, and is thus interdisciplinary in nature. In this chapter, we study the MOR cryptosystem using the orthogonal and symplectic groups over finite fields of odd characteristic.

In Section 2, we describe the MOR cryptosystem in some details. We emphasize that the MOR cryptosystem is a natural generalization of the classic ElGamal cryptosystem. In Section 3, we describe the orthogonal and symplectic groups and their automorphisms. In Appendix A, we describe few new algorithms. These algorithms use row-column operations to write an element in classical groups as a word in generators. This is very similar to the Gaussian elimination algorithm for special linear groups. These algorithms are vital to the implementation of the MOR cryptosystem. These algorithms are also of *independent interest in computational group theory*.

1.2 Notations and terminology

It was bit hard for us to pick notations for this chapter. The notations used by a Lie group theorist is somewhat different from that of a computational group theorist. We tried to preserve the essence of notations as much as possible. For example, a Lie group theorist will use $\mathrm{SL}_{l+1}(q)$ to denote what we will denote by $\mathrm{SL}(l+1,q)$ or $\mathrm{SL}(d,q)$. We have used ${}^{T}X$ to denote the transpose of the matrix X. This was necessary to avoid any confusion that might arise when using X^{-1} and ${}^{T}X$ simultaneously. In this chapter, we use $\mathcal{K}$ and $\mathbb{F}_q$ interchangeably, while each of them is **a finite field of odd characteristic**. However, in the appendix the field k is unrestricted. The matrix te_{ij} is used to denote the matrix unit with t in the $(i,j)^{\text{th}}$ place and zero everywhere else. We will often use $x_r(t)$ as generators, a notation used in the theory of Chevalley groups. Here r is a short hand for (i,j) and $x_r(t)$ are defined in **Tables A1, A3, A5,** and **A7**. We often refer to the orthogonal group as $\mathrm{O}(d,q)$, specifically, the split orthogonal group as $\mathrm{O}^{+}(2l,q)$ or $\mathrm{O}^{+}(2l+1,q)$ and the twisted orthogonal group as $\mathrm{O}^{-}(2l,q)$. All other notations used are standard.

2. The MOR cryptosystem

The MOR cryptosystem is a natural generalization of the classic ElGamal cryptosystem. It was first proposed by Paeng et al. [9]. To elaborate the idea behind a MOR cryptosystem, we take a slightly expository route. For the purpose of this exposition, we define **the discrete logarithm problem**. It is one of the most common cryptographic primitive in use. It works in any cyclic (sub)group $G = \langle g \rangle$ but is not secure in any cyclic group.

Definition 2.1 (The discrete logarithm problem). *The discrete logarithm problem in* $G = \langle g \rangle$*, given* g *and* g^{m}*, find* m.

The word "find" in the above definition is bit vague, in this chapter we mean compute m. The hardness to solve the discrete logarithm problem depends on the presentation of the group and is not an invariant under isomorphism. It is believed that the discrete logarithm problem is secure in the multiplicative group of a finite field and the group of rational points of an elliptic curve.

A more important cryptographic primitive, related to the discrete logarithm problem, is the **Diffie-Hellman problem**, also known as the **computational Diffie-Hellman problem.**

Definition 2.2 (Diffie-Hellman problem). *Given* g, g^{m_1}*, and* g^{m_2}*, find* $g^{\mathrm{m}_1\mathrm{m}_2}$.

It is clear; if one solves the discrete logarithm problem, then the Diffie-Hellman problem is solved as well. The other direction is not known.

The most prolific cryptosystem in use today is the ElGamal cryptosystem. It uses the cyclic group $G = \langle g \rangle$. It is defined as follows:

2.1 The ElGamal cryptosystem

A cyclic group $G = \langle g \rangle$ is public.

- **Public-key**: Let g and g^{m} be public.
- **Private-key**: The integer m be private.

Encryption:

To encrypt a plaintext $\mathfrak{M} \in G$, get an arbitrary integer $\mathrm{r} \in [1, |G|]$ and compute g^{r} and g^{rm}. The ciphertext is $(g^{\mathrm{r}}, \mathfrak{M} g^{\mathrm{rm}})$.

Decryption:

After receiving the ciphertext $(g^{\mathrm{r}}, \mathfrak{M} g^{\mathrm{rm}})$, the user uses the private-key m. So she computes g^{mr} from g^{r} and then computes $\mathfrak{M}$.

It is well known that the hardness of the ElGamal cryptosystem is equivalent to the Diffie-Hellman problem ([12], Proposition 2.10).

2.2 The MOR cryptosystem

In the case of the MOR cryptosystem, one works with the automorphism group of a group. An automorphism group can be defined on any algebraic structure, and subsequently a MOR cryptosystem can also be defined on that automorphism group; however, in this chapter we restrict ourselves to finite groups. Furthermore, we look at *classical groups* defined by generators and automorphisms that are defined as actions on those generators.

Let $G = \langle g_1, g_2, \ldots, g_s \rangle$ be a finite group. Let ϕ be a non-identity automorphism.

- Public-key: Let $\{\phi(g_i)\}_{i=1}^{s}$ and $\{\phi^{\mathrm{m}}(g_i)\}_{i=1}^{s}$ be public.
- Private-key: The integer m is private.

Encryption:

To encrypt a plaintext $\mathfrak{M} \in G$, get an arbitrary integer $\mathrm{r} \in [1, |\phi|]$ and compute ϕ^{r} and ϕ^{rm}. The ciphertext is $(\phi^{\mathrm{r}}, \phi^{\mathrm{rm}}(\mathfrak{M}))$.

Decryption:

After receiving the ciphertext $(\phi^{\mathrm{r}}, \phi^{\mathrm{rm}}(\mathfrak{M}))$, the user knows the private-key m. So she computes ϕ^{mr} from ϕ^{r} and then computes $\mathfrak{M}$.

Theorem 2.1 *The hardness to break the above MOR cryptosystem is equivalent to the Diffie-Hellman problem in the group* $\langle \phi \rangle$.

Proof. It is easy to see that if one can break the Diffie-Hellman problem, then one can compute ϕ^{mr} from ϕ^{m} in the public-key and ϕ^{r} in the ciphertext. This breaks the system.

On the other hand, observe that the plaintext is $\phi^{-\mathrm{mr}}(\phi^{\mathrm{mr}}(\mathfrak{M}))$. Assume that there is an oracle that can break the MOR cryptosystem, i.e., given ϕ, ϕ^{m} and a plaintext (ϕ^{r}, g) will deliver $\phi^{-\mathrm{mr}}(g)$. Now we query the oracle s times with the public-key and the ciphertext (ϕ^{r}, g_i) for $i = 1, 2, \ldots, s$. From the output, one can easily find $\phi^{\mathrm{mr}}(g_i)$ for $i = 1, 2, \ldots, s$. So we just witnessed that for ϕ^{m} and ϕ^{r}, one can compute ϕ^{mr} using the oracle. This solves the Diffie-Hellman problem.

In a practical implementation of a MOR cryptosystem, there are two things that matter the most.

a: The number of generators. As we saw that the automorphism ϕ is presented as action on generators. Larger the number of generators, bigger is the size of the public key.

b: Efficient algorithm to solve the word problem. This means that given $G = \langle g_1, g_2, \ldots, g_s \rangle$ and $g \in G$, is there an efficient algorithm to write g as word in $g_1, g_2, \ldots, g_s$? The reason of this importance is immediate—the automorphisms are presented as action on generators, and if one has to compute $\phi(g)$, then the word problem must be solved.

DOI: http://dx.doi.org/10.5772/intechopen.84663

The obvious question is: what are the right groups for the MOR cryptosystem? In this chapter, we pursue a study of the MOR cryptosystem using **finite Chevalley groups** of classical type, in particular, orthogonal and symplectic groups.

3. Description of automorphisms of classical groups

This chapter studies the MOR cryptosystem for orthogonal and symplectic groups over a field of odd characteristics. As we discussed before, MOR cryptosystem is presented as action on generators of the group. Then to use an automorphism on an arbitrary element, one has to solve the word problem in that group with respect to that set of generators.

The generators and the Gaussian elimination algorithm to solve the word problem are described in Appendix A. We will be very brief here.

Let V be a vector space of dimension d over a field $\mathcal{K}$ of odd characteristic. Let $\beta : V \times V \to \mathcal{K}$ be a bilinear form. By fixing a basis of V, we can associate a matrix to β. We shall abuse the notation slightly and denote the matrix of the bilinear form by β itself. Thus $\beta(x,y)={}^T x\beta y$, where x, y are column vectors. We will work with non-degenerate bilinear forms and that means $\det\beta \neq 0$. A symmetric or skew-symmetric bilinear form β satisfies $\beta={}^T\beta$ or $\beta = -{}^T\beta$, respectively.

Definition 3.1 (Orthogonal group). *A square matrix X of size d is called orthogonal if* ${}^TX\beta X = \beta$, *where* β *is symmetric. It is well known that the orthogonal matrices form a group known as the orthogonal group.*

Definition 3.2 (Symplectic group). *A square matrix X of size d is called symplectic if* ${}^TX\beta X = \beta$, *where* β *is skew-symmetric. And the set of symplectic matrices form a symplectic group.*

We write the dimension of V as $d = 2l + 1$ or $d = 2l$ for $l \geq 1$. We fix a basis and index it by $0, 1, \ldots, l, -1, \ldots, -l$ in the odd dimension, and in the case of even dimension where there are two non-degenerate symmetric bilinear forms up to equivalence, we index the bases by $1, 2, \ldots, l, -1, -2, \ldots, -l$ and $1, -1, 2, \ldots, l, -2, \ldots, -l$ for split and twisted forms, respectively. We consider the non-degenerate bilinear forms β on V given by the following matrices:

a: The odd-orthogonal group. The form β is symmetric with $d = 2l + 1$ and

$$\beta = \begin{pmatrix} 2 & 0 & 0 \\ 0 & 0 & I_l \\ 0 & I_l & 0 \end{pmatrix}.$$

b: The symplectic group. The form β is skew-symmetric with $d = 2l$ and

$$\beta = \begin{pmatrix} 0 & I_l \\ -I_l & 0 \end{pmatrix}.$$

c: The split orthogonal group. The form β is symmetric with $d = 2l$ and

$$\beta = \begin{pmatrix} 0 & I_l \\ I_l & 0 \end{pmatrix}.$$

c′: The twisted orthogonal group. The form β is symmetric with $d = 2l$ and

$$\beta = \begin{pmatrix} \beta_0 & 0 & 0 \\ 0 & 0 & I_{l-1} \\ 0 & I_{l-1} & 0 \end{pmatrix},$$

where I_l is the identity matrix of size l over $\mathcal{K}$ and for a fixed non-square $\epsilon \in \mathcal{K}$, $\beta_0 = \begin{pmatrix} 1 & 0 \\ 0 & \epsilon \end{pmatrix}$.

We now describe the automorphism group of the orthogonal and symplectic groups. This helps us in picking the right set of automorphisms for the MOR cryptosystem.

Definition 3.3 (Orthogonal similitude group). *The orthogonal similitude group is defined as the set of matrices X of size d as*

$$\mathrm{GO}(d,q) = \left\{X \in \mathrm{GL}(d,q) | {}^T X\beta X = \mu\beta, \mu \in \mathbb{F}_q^\times\right\},$$

where $d = 2l + 1$ *or* $2l$ *and* β *is of type a, c, or c′, respectively.*

Definition 3.4 (Symplectic similitude group). *The symplectic similitude group is defined as*

$$\mathrm{GSp}(2l,q) = \left\{X \in \mathrm{GL}(2l,q) | {}^T X\beta X = \mu\beta, \mu \in \mathbb{F}_q^\times\right\},$$

where β *is of type b.*

Here μ depends on the matrix X and is called the similitude factor. The similitude factor μ defines a group homomorphism from the similitude group to $\mathbb{F}_q^\times$, and the kernel is the orthogonal group $\mathrm{O}(d,q)$ when β is symmetric and symplectic group $\mathrm{Sp}(2l,q)$ and when β is skew-symmetric, respectively ([13], Section 12). Note that scalar matrices λI for $\lambda \in \mathbb{F}_q^\times$ belong to the center of similitude groups. The similitude groups are analog of what $\mathrm{GL}(d,q)$ is for $\mathrm{SL}(d,q)$. For a discussion of the diagonal automorphisms of Chevalley groups, we need the diagonal subgroups of the similitude groups.

Definition 3.5 (Diagonal group). *The diagonal groups are defined to be the group of non-singular diagonal matrices in the corresponding similitude group and are as follows: in the case of* $GO(2l+1,q)$*, it is*

$$\left\{\mathrm{diag}\left(\alpha, \lambda_1, \ldots, \lambda_l, \mu\lambda_1^{-1}, \ldots, \mu\lambda_l^{-1}\right) | \lambda_1, \ldots, \lambda_l, \alpha^2 = \mu \in \mathbb{F}_q^\times\right\},$$

and in the case of $\mathrm{GO}(2l,q)$ and $\mathrm{GSp}(2l,q)$, it is

$$\left\{\mathrm{diag}\left(\lambda_1, \ldots, \lambda_l, \mu\lambda_1^{-1}, \ldots, \mu\lambda_l^{-1}\right) | \lambda_1, \ldots, \lambda_l, \mu \in \mathbb{F}_q^\times\right\}.$$

Conjugation by these diagonal elements produces diagonal automorphisms in the respective Chevalley groups. To build a MOR cryptosystem, we need to work with the automorphism group of Chevalley groups. In this section we describe the automorphism group of classical groups following Dieudonne [14].

Conjugation automorphisms: If N is a normal subgroup of a group G, then the conjugation maps $n \mapsto gng^{-1}$ for $n \in N$ and $g \in G$ are called conjugation automorphisms of G. In particular, both inner automorphisms and diagonal automorphisms are examples of conjugation automorphisms.

Central automorphisms: Let $\chi : G \to \mathcal{Z}(G)$ be a homomorphism to the center of the group. Then the map $g \mapsto \chi(g)g$ is an automorphism of G, known as the central automorphism. There are no nontrivial central automorphisms for perfect groups, for example, the Chevalley groups $\mathrm{SL}(l+1,\mathcal{K})$ and $\mathrm{Sp}(2l,\mathcal{K})$, $|\mathcal{K}| \geq 4$, and $l \geq 2$. In the case of orthogonal group, the center is of two elements $\{\mathrm{I}, -\mathrm{I}\}$, where I is the identity matrix. This implies that there are at most four central automorphisms in this case.

Field automorphisms: Let $f \in \mathrm{Aut}(\mathcal{K})$. In terms of matrices, field automorphisms amount to replacing each term of the matrix by its image under f.

Graph automorphisms: A symmetry of Dynkin diagram induces such automorphisms. This way we get automorphisms of order 2 for $\mathrm{SL}(l+1,\mathcal{K})$ and $l \geq 2$ and $\mathrm{O}^{+}(2l,\mathcal{K})$ and $l \geq 4$. We also get an automorphisms of order 3 for $\mathrm{O}^{+}(4,\mathcal{K})$.

In the case of $\mathrm{SL}(d,q)$ for $d \geq 3$, the map $x \mapsto A^{-1T}x^{-1}A$, where

$$A = \begin{pmatrix} 0 & \cdots & 0 & 0 & 0 & 1 \\ 0 & \cdots & 0 & 0 & -1 & 0 \\ 0 & \cdots & 0 & 1 & 0 & 0 \\ 0 & \cdots & -1 & 0 & 0 & 0 \\ \vdots & ⋰ & \vdots & \vdots & \vdots & \vdots \\ (-1)^{l-1} & \cdots & 0 & 0 & 0 & 0 \end{pmatrix}$$

explicitly describes the graph automorphism.

In the case of $\mathrm{O}(2l,q)$ for $l \geq 5$, the graph automorphism is given by $x \mapsto B^{-1}xB$ where B is a permutation matrix obtained from identity matrix of size $2l \times 2l$ by switching the lth row and $-l^{\text{th}}$ row. This automorphism is a conjugating automorphism.

Theorem 3.1 (Dieudonne). *Let $\mathcal{K}$ be a field of odd characteristic and $l \geq 2$.*

1. For the group $\mathrm{SL}(l+1,\mathcal{K})$, any automorphism is of the form $\iota\gamma\theta$ where ι is a conjugation automorphism defined by elements of $\mathrm{GL}(l+1,\mathcal{K})$ and γ is a graph automorphism for the special linear group.

2. For the group $\mathrm{O}^{+}(d,\mathcal{K})$, any automorphism is of the form $c_\chi\iota\theta$ where c_χ is a central automorphism and ι is a conjugation automorphism by elements of $\mathrm{GO}^{+}(d,\mathcal{K})$ (this includes the graph automorphism of even-orthogonal groups).

3. For the group $\mathrm{O}^{-}(d,\mathcal{K})$, any automorphism is of the form $\iota\theta$, where ι is a conjugation automorphism by elements of $\mathrm{GO}^{-}(d,\mathcal{K})$.

4. For the group $\mathrm{Sp}(2l,\mathcal{K})$, any automorphism is of the form $\iota\theta$ where ι is a conjugation automorphism by elements of $\mathrm{GSp}(2l,\mathcal{K})$.

In all cases θ denotes a field automorphism.

For a proof of the above theorem, see [26], Theorems 30 and 36. In the above theorem, conjugation automorphisms are given by conjugation by elements of a larger group, and it includes the group of inner automorphisms. We introduce diagonal automorphisms to make it more precise. The conjugation automorphisms ι can be written as a product of ι_g and η where ι_g is an inner automorphism and η is a diagonal automorphism.

Diagonal automorphisms: In the definition of the conjugating automorphism, when the conjugating element is from the similitude group but not in the group we get a diagonal automorphism. In the case of special linear groups, diagonal automorphisms are given by conjugation by diagonal elements of $\mathrm{PGL}(l+1,q)$ on $\mathrm{PGL}(l+1,q)$. In the case of symplectic and orthogonal groups, diagonal automorphisms are given by conjugation by corresponding diagonal group elements defined in Definition 3.5.

4. Security of the proposed MOR cryptosystem

The purpose of this section is to show that for a secure MOR cryptosystem over the classical Chevalley and twisted orthogonal groups, we have to look at automorphisms that act by conjugation like the inner automorphisms. There are other automorphisms that also act by conjugation, like the diagonal automorphism and the graph automorphism for odd-order orthogonal groups. Then we argue what is the hardness of our security assumptions. We denote the split orthogonal group by $O^{+}(2l,q)$ and twisted orthogonal group by $O^{-}(2l,q)$. Now onwards $O(2l,q)$ means either split or twisted orthogonal group and we will specify whenever required.

Let ϕ be an automorphism of one of the classical Chevalley groups G: $SL(l+1,q)$, $O(2l+1,q)$, $Sp(2l,q)$, or $O(2l,q)$. From Theorem 3.1, we know that $\phi = c_\chi \iota \eta \gamma \theta$ where c_χ is a central automorphism, ι is an inner automorphism, η is a diagonal automorphism, γ is a graph automorphism, and θ is a field automorphism.

The group of central automorphisms are too small and the field automorphisms reduce to a discrete logarithm in the field $\mathbb{F}_q$. So there is no benefit of using these in a MOR cryptosystem. Also there are not many graph automorphisms in classical Chevalley and twisted orthogonal groups other than special linear groups and odd-order orthogonal groups. In the odd-order orthogonal groups, these automorphisms act by conjugation. Recall here that our automorphisms are presented as action on generators. It is clear ([6], Section 7) that if we can recover the conjugating matrix from the action on generators, the security is a discrete logarithm problem in $\mathbb{F}_{q^d}$, or else the security is a discrete logarithm problem in $\mathbb{F}_{q^{d^2}}$.

So from these we conclude that for a secure MOR cryptosystem, we must look at automorphisms that act by conjugation, like the inner automorphisms. Inner automorphisms form a normal subgroup of $\mathrm{Aut}(G)$ and usually constitute the bulk of automorphisms. If ϕ is an inner automorphism, say $\iota_g : x \mapsto gxg^{-1}$, we would like to determine the conjugating element g. For the special linear group, it was done in [6]. We will follow the steps there for the present situation too. However, before we do that, let us digress briefly to observe that $G \to \mathrm{Inn}(G)$ given by $g \mapsto \iota_g$ is a surjective group homomorphism. Thus if G is generated by $g_1, g_2, \ldots, g_s$, then $\mathrm{Inn}(G)$ is generated by $\iota_{g_1}, \ldots, \iota_{g_s}$. Let $\phi \in \mathrm{Inn}(G)$. If we can find $g_j, j \in \{1, 2, \ldots, s\}$ generators, such that $\phi = \prod_j \iota_{g_j}$, then $\phi = \iota_g$ where $g = \prod_j g_j$. This implies that our problem is equivalent to solving the word problem in $\mathrm{Inn}(G)$. Note that solving word problem depends on how the group is presented and it is not invariant under group homomorphisms. Thus the algorithm described earlier to solve the word problem in the classical Chevalley and twisted orthogonal groups does not help us in the present case.

In what follows, we will use generators $x_r(t)$, where $r = (i,j);\quad i \neq j,\quad 1 \le i,j \le d$ for the special linear group. For symplectic group $r = (i,j); i,j \in \{\pm1, \pm2, \ldots, \pm l\}$. For the even-orthogonal group, $r = (i,j); i,j \in \{\pm1, \pm2, \ldots, \pm l\};\ \pm i \neq \pm j$. For the odd-orthogonal group $r = (i,j);\ -l \le i \le l$ and $j \in \{\pm1, \pm2, \ldots \pm l\};\ \pm i \neq \pm j$. These are the Chevalley generators for the Chevalley groups we are dealing with and are described in details in **Tables A1, A5, A3, and A7** in the Appendix.

4.1 Reduction of security

In this subsection, we show that for special linear and symplectic groups, the security of the MOR cryptosystem is the hardness of the discrete logarithm problem in $\mathbb{F}_{q^d}$. This is the same as saying that we can find the conjugating matrix up to a scalar multiple. We further show that the method that works for special linear and symplectic groups does not work for orthogonal groups.

Let ϕ be an automorphism that works by conjugation, i.e., $\phi = \iota_g$, for some g, and we try to determine g.

Step 1: The automorphism ϕ is presented as action on generators $x_r(t)$.

Thus $\phi(x_r(t)) = g(I + te_r)g^{-1} = I + tge_rg^{-1}$. This implies that we know ge_rg^{-1} for all possible r. We first claim that we can determine $N = gD$ where D is sparse, in fact, diagonal in the case of special linear and symplectic groups.

In the case of special linear groups, write $g = [G_1, \ldots, G_i, \ldots, G_d]$, where G_i are column vectors of g. Then $ge_{i,j} = [G_1, \ldots, G_d]e_{i,j} = [0, \ldots, 0, G_i, 0\ldots, 0]$ where G_i is at the jth place. Multiplying this with g^{-1} on the right, i.e., computing $ge_{i,j}g^{-1}$, determines G_i up to a scalar multiple d_i (say). Thus, we know $N = gD$ where $D = \text{diag}(d_1, \ldots, d_{l+1})$.

For the symplectic groups, we do the similar computation with the generators $I + te_{i,-i}$ and $I + te_{-i,i}$. Write g in the column form as $[G_1, \ldots G_l, G_{-1}, \ldots, G_{-l}]$. Now,

1. $[G_1, \ldots G_l, G_{-1}, \ldots, G_{-l}]e_{i,-i} = [0, \ldots, 0, G_i, 0, \ldots, 0]$ where G_i is at $-i$th place. Multiplying this further with g^{-1} gives us scalar multiple of G_i, say d_iG_i.

2. $[G_1, \ldots G_l, G_{-1}, \ldots, G_{-l}]e_{-i,i} = [0, \ldots, 0, G_{-i}, 0, \ldots, 0]$ where G_{-i} is at ith place. Multiplying this with g^{-1} gives us scalar multiple of G_{-i}, say $d_{-i}G_i$.

Thus we get $N = gD$ where D is a diagonal matrix $\text{diag}(d_1, \ldots, d_l, d_{-1}, \ldots, d_{-l})$.

Step 2: Compute $N^{-1}\phi(x_r(t))N = D^{-1}g^{-1}\left(gx_r(t)g^{-1}\right)gD = I + D^{-1}e_rD$ which is equivalent to computing $D^{-1}e_rD$.

In the case of special linear groups, we have D a diagonal. Thus by computing $D^{-1}e_{i,j}D$, we determine $d_i^{-1}d_j$ for $i \neq j$ and form a matrix $\text{diag}\left(1, d_2^{-1}d_1, \ldots, d_l^{-1}d_1\right)$, and multiplying this to N, we get d_1g. Hence we can determine g up to a scalar matrix.

For symplectic groups, we can do similar computation as D is diagonal. First compute $D^{-1}\left(e_{i,j} - e_{-j,-i}\right)D$ to get $d_i^{-1}d_j$ and $d_{-i}^{-1}d_{-j}$ for $i \neq j$. Now compute $D^{-1}e_{i,-i}D, D^{-1}e_{-i,i}D$ to get $d_id_{-i}^{-1}, d_{-i}d_i^{-1}$. We form a matrix

$$\text{diag}\left(1, d_2^{-1}d_1, \ldots, d_l^{-1}d_1, d_{-1}^{-1}d_{-2}.d_{-2}^{-1}d_2.d_2^{-1}d_1, \ldots, d_{-l}^{\ 1}d_{-1}.d_{-1}^{-1}d_1\right)$$

and multiply it to $N = gD$ to get d_1g. Thus we can determine g up to a scalar multiple say ag. Similarly we can determine g^{m} up to a scalar multiple say bg^{m}. Now, compute $(ag)^{q-1} = g^{q-1}$ and $(bg^{\text{m}})^{q-1} = (g^{\text{m}})^{q-1}$, and then we can recover m by solving the discrete logarithm in the matrices using Menezes and Wu's idea [15]. However, if we choose g such that $g^{q-1} = 1$, then it seems that we might avoid this line of attack. We can bypass this argument by recovering the scalars a and b, and then to determine m, we compute the discrete logarithm in $\langle g \rangle$ using Menezes and Wu's idea. We prove the following proposition.

Proposition 4.1 *Given any $g \in \text{Sp}(d, q)$ up to scalar multiple ag, $a \in \mathbb{F}_q$. If $\gcd(d, q-1) = 1$, we can determine the scalar a. Otherwise one can find the scalar a by solving a discrete logarithm problem in $\mathbb{F}_q$.*

Proof. We can recover the scalar a as follows: Let $\{\lambda_1, \ldots, \lambda_d\}$ be a set of eigenvalues of g, and then the eigenvalues of ag are $\{a\lambda_1, \ldots, a\lambda_d\}$. Set $\alpha = a\lambda_1 \cdots a\lambda_d$ and thus $\alpha = a^d$ as $\lambda_1 \cdots \lambda_d = det(g) = 1$. Suppose $\gcd(d, q-1) = \zeta$, using extended Euclidean algorithm, we find u and v such that $ud + v(q-1) = \zeta$. Next, computing α^u, we get $a^{ud} = a^{\zeta - v(q-1)} = a^{\zeta}$. Thus, if $\gcd(d, q-1) = 1$, then we have recovered the scalar a; otherwise we can recover the scalar by solving the discrete logarithm problem in $\mathbb{F}_q$.

Thus, if $\gcd(d, q-1) = 1$, then using the above proposition, we can recover the scalars a and b from ag and bg^{m}, respectively. Otherwise one needs to solve discrete logarithm problem in $\mathbb{F}_q$ to recover the scalars. Now, we can recover g and g^{m} from ag and bg^{m} just by multiplying with scalar matrices $a^{-1}I$ and $b^{-1}I$, respectively. Finally, we recover m using Menezes and Wu's idea. Thus, if we choose g such that

$g^{q-1} = 1$ and $\gcd(d, q-1) \neq 1$, then to solve the discrete logarithm in $\langle \phi \rangle$, one needs to solve the discrete logarithm in $\mathbb{F}_q$ and $\mathbb{F}_{q^d}$.

However, in the case of orthogonal groups, we show that one cannot recover g up to a diagonal matrix using the above approach, and hence the above reduction attack does not work.

Theorem 4.1 *Let $g \in \mathrm{GO}(d,q)$. Consider the conjugation automorphism $\phi : \mathrm{O}(d,q) \to \mathrm{O}(d,q)$. Let $\{x_r\}$ be a set of Chevalley generators of $\mathrm{O}(d,q)$ described in Appendix A. Suppose that the public-key is presented as an action of ϕ on $\{x_r\}$, then it is impossible to recover a matrix gD, where D is a diagonal matrix using the above reduction.*

Proof. We prove the theorem for $\mathrm{O}^+(d,q)$, d even, and the theorem follows for other cases similarly. Let $d = 2l$ and we write g in columns form as $g = [C_1, ..., C_l, C_{-1}, ..., C_{-l}]$. We compute $ge_r g^{-1}$ which gives the following equations:

1. Note that $g(e_{i,j} - e_{-j,-i})g^{-1} = [0, ..., 0, C_i, 0, ..., 0, C_{-j}, 0, ..., 0]g^{-1}$, where C_i is at jth place and C_{-j} is at $-i^{\text{th}}$ place. After multiplying by g^{-1}, we get a matrix whose all columns are linear combinations of columns C_i and C_{-j}.

2. Note that $g(e_{i,-j} - e_{j,-i})g^{-1} = [0, ..., 0, C_i, 0, ..., 0, C_j, 0, ..., 0]g^{-1}$, where C_i is at $-j^{\text{th}}$ place and C_j is at $-i^{\text{th}}$ place. After multiplying by g^{-1}, we get a matrix whose all columns are linear combinations of columns C_i and C_j.

3. Note that $g(e_{-i,j} - e_{-j,i})g^{-1} = [0, ..., 0, C_{-i}, 0, ..., 0, C_{-j}, 0, ..., 0]g^{-1}$, where C_{-i} is at j^{th} place and C_{-j} is at i^{th} place. After multiplying by g^{-1}, we get a matrix whose all columns are linear combinations of columns C_{-i} and C_{-j}.

Suppose one can construct a matrix B from columns obtained above such that $B = gD$, where D is diagonal, then we can see that $d_i C_i = a_i C_j + b_j C_k$ for some i, j, k which is a contradiction as $\det(g) \neq 0$. Thus, it is not possible to construct a matrix B such that $B = gD$, where D is diagonal.

This conclusively proves that the attack on the special linear groups and symplectic groups will not work for most orthogonal groups.

For orthogonal groups, the best we can do is the following: We can construct N such that $N = g(D_1 + PD_2)$, where D_1 and D_2 are diagonal and P is a permutation matrix. We demonstrate the construction of N in the case of a split orthogonal group $\mathrm{O}^+(2l, q)$; similar construction works for other cases as well. Computing $ge_r g^{-1}$ gives the following equations:

1. $[G_1, ...G_l, G_{-1}, ..., G_{-l}](e_{i,j} - e_{-j,-i})g^{-1} = [0, ..., 0, G_i, 0, ..., 0, G_{-j}, 0, ..., 0]g^{-1}$, where G_i is at jth place and G_{-j} is at $-i^{\text{th}}$ place. This gives us a linear combination of the columns G_i and G_{-j}.

2. $[G_1, ...G_l, G_{-1}, ..., G_{-l}](e_{i,-j} - e_{j,-i})g^{-1} = [0, ..., 0, G_i, 0, ..., 0, G_j, 0, ..., 0]g^{-1}$, where G_i is at $-j^{\text{th}}$ place and G_j is at $-i^{\text{th}}$ place. This will give us a linear combination of the columns G_i and G_j.

3. $[G_1, ...G_l, G_{-1}, ..., G_{-l}](e_{-i,j} - e_{-j,i})g^{-1} = [0, ..., 0, G_{-i}, 0, ..., 0, G_{-j}, 0, ..., 0]g^{-1}$, where G_{-i} is at jth place and G_{-j} is at ith place. This will give us a linear combination of the columns G_{-i} and G_{-j}.

We construct a matrix N as follows: For each $i = 1, \ldots, l-1$, compute $g(I + e_{i,i+1} - e_{-(i+1),-i})g^{-1} - I$ whose each column is a linear combination of C_i and $C_{-(i+1)}$. Choose one of its column say $r_i C_i + s_i C_{-(i+1)}$ for each $i = 1, \ldots, l-1$. Similarly compute $g(I + e_{i+1,i} - e_{-i,-(i+1)})g^{-1} - I$ and choose $r_{-i}C_{-i} + s_{-i}C_{(i+1)}$ for each $i = 1, \ldots, l-1$. Further, we compute $g(I + e_{1,-l} - e_{l,-1})g^{-1} - I$ to get $r_l C_l + s_l C_1$ and $g(I + e_{-1,l} - e_{-l,1})g^{-1} - I$ to get $r_{-l}C_{-l} + s_{-l}C_{-1}$. We set $N = [r_1 C_1 + s_1 C_{-2}, \ldots, r_{l-1} C_{l-1} + s_{l-1}C_{-l}, r_l C_l + s_l C_1, r_{-1}C_{-1} + s_{-1}C_2, \ldots, r_{-(l-1)}C_{-(l-1)} + s_{-(l-1)}C_l, r_{-l}C_{-l} + s_{-l}C_{-1}]$. Now it is easy to note that $N = g(D_1 + PD_2)$, where $D_1 = \text{diag}(r_1, \ldots, r_l, r_{-1}, \ldots, r_{-l})$, $D_2 = \text{diag}(s_1, \ldots, s_l, s_{-1}, \ldots, s_{-l})$, and P are permutation matrix corresponding to the permutation of indexing set $1 \to -2 \to 3 \to -4 \to \cdots \to l-1 \to -l \to -1 \to 2 \to -3 \to 4 \to \cdots \to -(l-1) \to l \to 1$.

Thus we get $N = g(D_1 + PD_2)$, where D_1 and D_2 are diagonal and P is a permutation matrix. This is not a diagonal matrix. One can do a similar computation for the odd-orthogonal group and twisted orthogonal group as well.

Remark 4.1 *An observant reader would ask the question: why does this attack works for the special linear and symplectic groups but not for orthogonal groups? The answer lies in a closer look at the generators (elementary matrices) for these groups.*

In the special linear groups, the generators are the elementary transvections of the form $I + te_{i,j}$ where $i \neq j$ and $t \in \mathbb{F}_q$. Then the attack goes on smoothly as we saw earlier. However, when we look at generators of the form $I + te_{i,j} - te_{-j,-i}$, where $t \in \mathbb{F}_q$ and $i \neq j$, conjugating by them, it gets us a linear sum of the ith and jth column, not scalar multiple of one particular column. This stops the attack from going forward. However in the symplectic groups, there are generators of the form $I + e_{i,-i}$ and $I + e_{-i,i}$ for $1 \leq i \leq l$. These generators make the attack possible for the symplectic groups. However there are no such generators for orthogonal groups, and so this attack turns out to be impossible for orthogonal groups.

5. The case for two-generators and prime fields

One serious objection against a MOR cryptosystem is the size of the key ([10], Section 7). The reason is that in a MOR cryptosystem, the automorphisms are presented as action on generators. Now the bigger the number of generators, the larger the key-size.

On the other hand, many of the finite simple groups can be generated by two elements. However, a set of generators is not enough. We must be able to compute the image of an arbitrary element. When the automorphism is presented as action on generators, we need an efficient solution to the word problem in order to do that. We have demonstrated in Appendix A that there is one set of generators, the elementary matrices, for which the word problem is easy.

The theme of this section is that for symplectic and even-order split orthogonal groups, there are two generators and for the odd-orthogonal group there are three generators. Over the **prime field of odd characteristic**, one can easily compute the word corresponding to the elementary matrices for these generators.

So one can present the automorphisms ϕ and ϕ^m as action on these few generators and then compute the action of these automorphisms on the elementary matrices later. This substantially reduces the key-size. To do this we use the technique of *straight line programs*, which is popular in computational group theory. These are programs, but in practice are actually easy to use formulas. Say, for example, we want to compute $x_{i,j}(t)$ for some $t \in \mathbb{F}_q$. We have loaded matrices $w^{i-1}x_{1,2}(\cdot)w^{(i-1)}$ in the memory in such a way that this formula takes as input t and put it in the (1, 2) position of the matrix $x_{1,2}(\cdot)$ and do the matrix multiplication. This is one straight line program. Since these programs are loaded in the memory, computation is much faster. This is somewhat similar to a time-memory trade-off. We have built a series of these straight line programs, where one straight line program can use other straight line programs and have written down the length of these programs. The length is nothing but the number of matrices in the formula.

Using the symplectic group in the MOR cryptosystem is straightforward. However, using orthogonal groups is little tricky because of the presence of λ in the output of the Gaussian elimination algorithm (see Section A.2.3). It is well known that the elementary matrices, without w_i—the row interchanges matrices and generates Ω, the commutator subgroup of a orthogonal group. However in between the commutator and the whole group, there is another important subgroup, $W\Omega = \langle \Omega, w_i \rangle$ for some i. From the algorithmic point of view, it is the subgroup of all the matrices for which the λ is a square. Now once the λ is a square and we can efficiently compute the square root, we can write this matrix down as product of elementary matrices, and it is easy to implement in the MOR cryptosystem. It is well known that if $p \equiv 3(\text{mod}4)$, then it is easy to compute the square root. Only for this reason, in the latter part of this section and for orthogonal groups, we concentrate on $p \equiv 3\ (\text{mod}4)$.

5.1 Symplectic group Sp $(2l, p)$

Let p be an odd prime. It is known [16] that the group Sp$(2l,p)$ is generated by two elements:

$$x = x_{1,2}(1) \tag{1}$$

$$w = \begin{pmatrix} 0 & 1 \\ -I_{2l-1} & 0 \end{pmatrix} \tag{2}$$

We will refer these two elements as **Steinberg generators**. However in the context of the MOR cryptosystem, we need to know how to go back and forth between these two generating sets—Steinberg generators and elementary matrices (see **Table A3**). To write w as a product of elementary matrices is easy, just put this generator through our Gaussian elimination algorithm. Here we demonstrate the other way round, that is, how to write elementary matrices as a product of x and w. In what follows, we denote the length of SLPs by $L(\delta, i)$, where $\delta = j - i$ and $1 \le i < j \le l$.

$$\begin{array}{lll} \delta = 1, & x_{i,j}(t) = & w^{i-1}x_{1,2}(t)w^{-(i-1)}, \\ \delta = 2, & x_{i,j}(t) = & [x_{i,j-1}(t), x_{j-1,j}(1)], \\ \delta = 3, & x_{i,j}(t) = & [x_{i,j-1}(t), x_{j-1,j}(1)], \\ \vdots & \vdots & \vdots \\ \delta = l-1, & x_{i,j}(t) = & [x_{i,j-1}(t), x_{j-1,j}(1)]. \end{array}$$

Here

$$L(\delta, i) = \begin{cases} 2i - 1 & \text{for } \delta = 1, \\ 2L(\delta - 1) + 4(i + \delta) - 6 & \text{for } \delta = 2, 3, \ldots, l - 1. \end{cases}$$

Now $w^l = (-1)^{l-1}\begin{pmatrix} 0 & I_l \\ -I_l & 0 \end{pmatrix}$ and $x_{j,i}(t) = w^l x_{i,j}(-t) w^{-l}$, so length of this SLP is $L(\delta, i) + 2l$. Hence we get all $x_{i,j}(t)$ for $1 \le i \ne j \le l$. Number of SLP is l. Next observe the following:

Elements	Indices	Equation	Length	
$x_{1,-l}(t)$		$w x_{l-1,l}(t) w^{-1}$	$2l-1$	
$x_{1,-i}(t)$	$2 \le i \le l-1$	$[x_{i,l}(t), x_{1,-l}(1)]$	$2(L(l-i,i)+2l-1)$	
$x_{i,-j}(t)$	$2 \le i \le l-1$ $(i+1 \le j \le l)$	$[x_{i,1}(t), x_{1,-j}(1)]$	$2(L(i-1,1)+4l-1)$ $2(L(i-1,1)+2L(l-j,j)+6l-2)$	$j=l$ $j \ne l$
$x_{i,-i}(t)$	$i = 1, 2, \ldots, l-1$	$\left[x_{i,i+1}\left(\frac{t}{2}\right), x_{i,-(i+1)}(1)\right]$	$2(2L(l-2,1)+10l-5)$ $2(L(1,i)+2L(i-1,1)+$ $4L(l-(i+1),i+1)+12l-4)$	$i=l-1$ $i \ne l-1$
$x_{l,-l}(t)$		$\left[x_{l,l-1}\left(\frac{t}{2}\right), x_{l-1,-l}(1)\right]$	$2(2L(l-2,1)+12l-5)$	

So we generate all $x_{i,-j}(t)$ for $1 \le i < j \le l$ and $x_{i,-i}(t)$ for $1 \le i \le l$. Now $w^l x_{i,-j}(t) w^{-l} = x_{-i,j}(t)$ for $1 \le i < j \le l$ and $w^l x_{i,-i}(t) w^{-l} = x_{-i,i}(t)$ for $1 \le i \le l$, then we get $x_{-i,j}(t)$ and $x_{-i,i}(t)$. Total number of SLPs is $l + (3+1) + (2+1) = l + 7$. Hence we generate all the elementary matrices (**Table A3**) using only two generators x and w. Hence $\mathrm{Sp}(2l, p)$ is generated by only two generators x and w.

5.2 Split orthogonal group $O^{+}(2l, p)$

Let $p \equiv 3 \pmod 4$ be a prime. It is known [16] that the group $O^{+}(2l, p)$ is generated by two elements:

$$x = x_{1,2}(1), \tag{3}$$

$$w = \left(\begin{array}{ccc|ccc} 0 & \cdots & 0 & 0 & \cdots & 1 \\ -1 & \cdots & 0 & 0 & \cdots & 0 \\ \vdots & \ddots & \vdots & \vdots & \ddots & \vdots \\ \cdots & -1 & 0 & 0 & \cdots & 0 \\ \hline 0 & \cdots & 1 & 0 & \cdots & 0 \\ 0 & \cdots & 0 & -1 & \cdots & 0 \\ \vdots & \ddots & \vdots & \vdots & \ddots & \vdots \\ 0 & \cdots & 0 & \cdots & -1 & 0 \end{array}\right) \tag{4}$$

We will refer these two elements as **Steinberg generators**. As we discussed earlier, in context of the MOR cryptosystem, we need to know how to go back and forth between these two generating sets—Steinberg generators and elementary matrices (**Table A1**). To write w as a product of elementary matrices is easy, just put this generator through our Gaussian elimination algorithm. Here we demonstrate the other way round, that is, how to write elementary matrices as a product of x and w. In what follows, we denote the length of SLPs by $L(\delta, i)$, where $\delta = j - i$ and $1 \le i < j \le l$.

$$\begin{aligned}
\delta = 1, \quad & x_{i,j}(t) = && w^{i-1}x_{1,2}(t)w^{-(i-1)},\\
\delta = 2, \quad & x_{i,j}(t) = && [x_{i,j-1}(t), x_{j-1,j}(1)],\\
\delta = 3, \quad & x_{i,j}(t) = && [x_{i,j-1}(t), x_{j-1,j}(1)],\\
\vdots \quad & \quad \vdots && \vdots\\
\delta = l-1, \quad & x_{i,j}(t) = && [x_{i,j-1}(t), x_{j-1,j}(1)].
\end{aligned}$$

Here

$$L(\delta, i) = \begin{cases} 2i-1 & \text{for } \delta = 1,\\ 2L(\delta-1) + 4(i+\delta) - 6 & \text{for } \delta = 2, 3, \ldots, l-1. \end{cases}$$

Now $w^l = (-1)^l \begin{pmatrix} 0 & I_l \\ I_l & 0 \end{pmatrix}$ and $x_{j,i}(t) = w^l x_{i,j}(-t)w^{-l}$, so length of this SLP is $L(\delta, i) + 2l$. Hence we get all $x_{i,j}(t)$ for $1 \le i \ne j \le l$. The number of SLPs is l. Next observe the following:

Elements	Indices	Equation	Length	
$x_{1,-l}(t)$		$wx_{l-1,l}(t)w^{-1}$	$2l-1$	
$x_{1,-i}(t)$	$2 \le i \le l-1$	$[x_{i,l}(t), x_{1,-l}(1)]$	$2(L(l-i,i)+2l-1)$	
$x_{i,-j}(t)$	$2 \le i \le l-1$	$[x_{i,1}(t), x_{1,-j}(1)]$	$2(L(i-1,1)+2L(l-j,j)+6l-2)$	$j \ne l$
	$(i+1 \le j \le l)$		$2(L(i-1,1)+4l-1)$	$j = l$

So we generate all $x_{i,-j}(t)$ for $i > j$. Now $w^l x_{i,-j}(t) w^{-l} = x_{-i,j}(t)$, and we get $x_{-i,j}(t)$ and the total number of SLPs is $l+4$. It is shown by Ree [17] that elementary matrices $x_{i,j}(t)$ generate $\Omega(2l, p)$, the commutator subgroup of $O(2l, p)$. Hence we generate $\Omega(2l, p)$, using only two elements x and w. Since we generate $x_{i,j}(t)$ and $w_{i,j}$ as a product of $x_{i,j}(t)$ and $w = w_{1,2}(1)w_{2,3}(1)\cdots w_{l-1,l}(1)w_l$, so we are able to generate w_l. Here $w_{i,j}(t) = x_{i,j}(t)x_{j,i}(-t^{-1})x_{i,j}(t)$ for $i \ne j$ and $w_l = I - e_{l,l} - e_{-l,-l} + e_{l,-l} + e_{-l,l}$. Now we know $w_{l-1} = w_l w_{l,l-1}(1) w_{l-1,-l}(1)$, so we generate w_{l-1}. Hence by induction, we generate $w_i = w_{i+1}w_{i+1,i}(1)w_{i,-(i+1)}(1)$ for $i = l-1, \ldots, 1$. Here $w_{i,-j}(t) = x_{i,-j}(t)(1)x_{-i,j}(t^{-1})x_{i,-j}(t)$, for $i < j$. Hence we generate all the elementary matrices (**Table A1**) using only two generators x and w. So we generate a new subgroup $W\Omega(2l, p)$ of $O(2l,p)$, which is a normal subgroup of $O(2l, p)$. Our algorithm output matrix is $d(\lambda) = \mathrm{diag}\left(1, 1, \ldots, \lambda, 1, 1, \ldots, \lambda^{-1}\right)$. If $\lambda \in F_p^{\times 2}$, say $\lambda \equiv t^2 (\mathrm{mod}\, p)$, then $t \equiv \lambda^{\frac{p+1}{4}} (\mathrm{mod}\, p)$, since $p \equiv 3 (\mathrm{mod}\ 4)$. Then

$$\begin{aligned}
d(\lambda) &= \mathrm{diag}\left(1, \ldots, t^2, 1, \ldots, , t^{-2}\right)\\
&= w_{l-1,l}(1)\mathrm{diag}\left(1, \ldots, t^2, 1, 1, \ldots, , t^{-2}, 1\right)w_{l-1,l}(-1)\\
&= w_{l-1,l}(1)w_{l-1,l}(t)w_{l-1,l}(-1)w_{l-1,-l}(t)w_{l-1,-l}(-1)w_{l-1,l}(-1).
\end{aligned}$$

Hence we generate $W\Omega(2l, p)$ using only two generators x and w.

5.3 Orthogonal group O(2*l*+1, *p*)

Let $p \equiv 3$ (mod4) be a prime. It is known [16] that the group $O(2l+1, p)$ is generated by these elements:

$$x = x_{0,1}(1), \tag{5}$$

$$w = \begin{pmatrix} -1 & 0 & 0 \\ 0 & 0 & -1 \\ 0 & -I_{2l-1} & 0 \end{pmatrix}, \tag{6}$$

$$w_l = \quad I - e_{l,l} - e_{-l,-l} + e_{l,-l} + e_{-l,l}. \tag{7}$$

We will refer these three elements as **Steinberg generators**. However in context of the MOR cryptosystem, we need to know how to go back and forth between these two generating sets—Steinberg generators and elementary matrices (**Table A5**). To write w as a product of elementary matrices is easy, just put this generator through our Gaussian elimination algorithm. Here we demonstrate the other way round, that is, how to write elementary matrices as a product of w and x. First we compute, $x_{0,i}(t) = w^{i-1}x_{0,1}(1)w^{-(i-1)}$ which is of length $2i-1$ for $1 \le i \le l$. Now

$$w^l = (-1)^l \begin{pmatrix} 1 & 0 & 0 \\ 0 & 0 & I_l \\ 0 & I_l & 0 \end{pmatrix}$$

and $x_{i,0}(t) = w^l x_{0,i}(-t)w^{-l}$ for $1 \le i \le l$, and length of this SLP is $2l + 2i - 1$. So we get $x_{i,0}(t)$ and $x_{0,i}(t)$ for $i = 1, 2, \ldots, l$. Again we have $x_{1,2}(t) = \left[x_{1,0}\left(\frac{t}{2}\right), x_{0,2}(1)\right]$ and length of this SLP is $4l + 8$. In what follows, we denote the length of SLPs by $L(\delta, i)$, where $\delta = j - i$ and $1 \le i < j \le l$.

$$\begin{aligned}
\delta = 1, &\quad x_{i,j}(t) = && w^{i-1}x_{1,2}(t)w^{-(i-1)}, \\
\delta = 2, &\quad x_{i,j}(t) = && \left[x_{i,j-1}(t), x_{j-1,j}(1)\right], \\
\delta = 3, &\quad x_{i,j}(t) = && \left[x_{i,j-1}(t), x_{j-1,j}(1)\right], \\
\vdots \quad &\qquad \vdots && \quad \vdots \\
\delta = l-1, &\quad x_{i,j}(t) = && \left[x_{i,j-1}(t), x_{j-1,j}(1)\right].
\end{aligned}$$

Here

$$L(\delta, i) = \begin{cases} 2i + 4l + 6 & \text{for } \delta = 1, \\ 2L(\delta - 1, i) + 4(i + \delta + 2l + 2) & \text{for } \delta = 2, 3, \ldots, l-1. \end{cases}$$

As $x_{j,i}(t) = w^l x_{i,j}(-t)w^{-l}$, so the length of this SLP is $L(\delta, i) + 2l$. Hence we generate all $x_{i,j}(t)$ for $1 \le i \ne j \le l$ and the number of SLPs is $3 + (l-1) + 1 = l + 3$. Next observe the following:

Elements	Indices	Equation (SLP)	Length	
$x_{1,-l}(t)$		$wx_{l-1,l}(t)w^{-1}$	$6l + 6$	
$x_{1,-i}(t)$	$2 \le i \le l-1$	$[x_{i,l}(t), x_{1,-l}(1)]$	$24l + 20$	$i = l-1$
			$2L(l-i, i) + 12(l+1)$	$i \ne l-1$
$x_{i,-j}(t)$	$2 \le i \le l-1$ $(i+1 \le j \le l)$	$[x_{i,1}(t), x_{1,-j}(1)]$	$2L(i-1,1) + 4L(l-j-\delta, j-\delta) + 4(7l+6)$	$j < l-1$
			$2L(i-1,1) + 4(7l+5)$	$j = l-1$
			$2L(i-1,1) + 10l + 6$	$j = l$

So we generate all $x_{i,-j}(t)$ for $i<j$. Now $w^l x_{i,-j}(t)w^{-l} = x_{-i,j}(t)$, and we have $x_{-i,j}(t)$. The total number of SLPs is $l+7$. It is shown in Ree [17] that elementary matrices $x_{i,j}(t)$ generate $\Omega(2l+1,p)$, the commutator subgroup of $O(2l+1,p)$ which is of index 4. So we generate $\Omega(2l+1,p)$, using only two generators x and w. Now we know $w_{l-1} = w_l w_{l,l-1}(1) w_{l-1,-l}(1)$, so we generate w_{l-1}. Hence inductively we can generate $w_i = w_{i+1} w_{i+1,i}(1) w_{i,-(i+1)}(1)$ for $i = l-1, \ldots, 1$. Here $w_{i,j}(t) = x_{i,j}(t)x_{j,i}(-t^{-1})x_{i,j}(t)$ for $i \neq j$ and $w_{i,-j}(t) = x_{i,-j}(t)x_{-i,j}(t^{-1})x_{i,-j}(t)$ for $i<j$. Hence we generate all the elementary matrices (**Table A5**) using only two generators x and w and an extra element w_l. Hence we generate a new subgroup $W\Omega(2l+1,p)$ of the orthogonal group $O(2l+1,p)$, containing Ω, which is indeed a normal subgroup of $O(2l+1,p)$. In our algorithm the output matrix is $d(\lambda) = \mathrm{diag}\left(1,1,\ldots,\lambda,1,\ldots,\lambda^{-1}\right)$. If $\lambda \in F_p^{\times 2}$, say $\lambda \equiv t^2 (\mathrm{mod}p)$, here $t \equiv \lambda^{\frac{p+1}{4}} (\mathrm{mod}p)$, since $p \equiv 3\ (\mathrm{mod}4)$. Then

$$
\begin{aligned}
d(\lambda) &= \mathrm{diag}\left(1,1,\ldots,t^2,1,\ldots,,t^{-2}\right)\\
&= w_{l-1,l}(1)\mathrm{diag}\left(1,1,\ldots,t^2,1,1,\ldots,,t^{-2},1\right)w_{l-1,l}(-1)\\
&= w_{l-1,l}(1)w_{l-1,l}(t)w_{l-1,l}(-1)w_{l-1,-l}(t)w_{l-1,-l}(-1)w_{l-1,l}(-1).
\end{aligned}
$$

Hence we generate $W\Omega(2l+1,p)$ using x, w and w_l.

Remark 5.1 *Let* $d(\zeta) = \mathrm{diag}\left(1,1,\ldots,\zeta,1,\ldots,\zeta^{-1}\right)$, *where* ζ *is non-square in* $\mathbb{F}_p^{\times}$. *The group* $\langle W\Omega, d(\zeta)\rangle$ *is the orthogonal group.*

5.4 Twisted orthogonal group $O^{-}(2l,p)$

We use the following generators which we refer as Steinberg generators.

$$x = x_{1,2}(1),$$

$$x' = x_{-1,2}(1),$$

$$w = \begin{pmatrix} -I_2 & 0 & 0 \\ 0 & 0 & -1 \\ 0 & -I_{2l-3} & 0 \end{pmatrix},$$

$$w_l = I - e_{l,l} - e_{-l,-l} - e_{l,-l} - e_{-l,l},$$

$$x_1(t,s),\ \text{where } t \in \mathbb{F}_p^{\times}, s \in \mathbb{F}_p \text{ and } x_2.$$

In the context of MOR cryptosystem, we need to know how to go back and forth between these generators and elementary matrices (**Table A7**). The procedure is almost similar to the case of $O^{+}(2l,p)$. Again, note that $x = x_{1,2}$, $x' = x_{-1,2}$, $x_1(t,s)$, and x_2 are elementary matrices. Thus, we just need to write w as a product of elementary matrices. However, computing w is fairly easy, just put this generator through our Gaussian elimination algorithm in Appendix A. Here we demonstrate the other way round, that is, how to write elementary matrices as a product of w, x, and x'. First, we compute $x_{1,i}(t) = w^{i-1}x_{1,2}(1)w^{-(i-1)}$ which is of length $2i-1$ for $2 \leq i \leq l$. Now we compute $x_{i,1}(t)$ using the relation $x_{i,1}(t) = w^{l-1}x_{1,i}(-t)w^{-(l-1)}$ for

$2 \leq i \leq l$, where $w^{l-1} = (-1)^{l-1} \begin{pmatrix} I_2 & 0 & 0 \\ 0 & 0 & I_{l-1} \\ 0 & I_{l-1} & 0 \end{pmatrix}$ and length of this SLP is $2(l-1) + 2i - 1$. Thus, we get $x_{i,1}(t)$ and $x_{1,i}(t)$, for $i = 2, \ldots, l$. Similarly we compute $x_{i,-1}(t)$ and $x_{-1,i}(t)$ using the relations $x_{-1,i}(t) = w^{i-1}x_{-1,2}(1)w^{-(i-1)}$ and $x_{i,-1}(t) = w^{l-1}x_{-1,i}(-t)w^{-(l-1)}$ for $2 \leq i \leq l$, and length of this SLP are $2i-1$ and $2(l-1) + 2i - 1$, respectively. Next, we compute $x_{2,3}(t)$ using the commutator formula $x_{2,3}(t) = \left[x_{2,1}\left(\frac{t}{2}\right), x_{1,3}(1)\right]$, and length of this SLP is $4(l-1) + 8$. In what follows, we denote the length of SLPs by $L(\delta, i)$, where $\delta = j - i$ and $2 \leq i < j \leq l$.

$$\begin{array}{lll} \delta = 1, & x_{i,j}(t) = & w^{i-1}x_{2,3}(t)w^{-(i-1)}, \\ \delta = 2, & x_{i,j}(t) = & \left[x_{i,j-1}(t), x_{j-1,j}(1)\right], \\ \delta = 3, & x_{i,j}(t) = & \left[x_{i,j-1}(t), x_{j-1,j}(1)\right], \\ \vdots & \vdots & \vdots \\ \delta = l-1, & x_{i,j}(t) = & \left[x_{i,j-1}(t), x_{j-1,j}(1)\right]. \end{array}$$

Here

$$L(\delta, i) = \begin{cases} 2i + 4(l-1) + 6 & \text{for } \delta = 1, \\ 2L(\delta - 1, i) + 4(i + \delta + 2(l-1) + 2) & \text{for } \delta = 2, 3, \ldots, l-2. \end{cases}$$

As $x_{j,i}(t) = w^{l-1}x_{i,j}(-t)w^{-(l-1)}$, so length of this SLP is $L(\delta, i) + 2(l-1)$. Hence, we get all $x_{i,j}(t)$ for $2 \leq i \neq j \leq l$ and the number of SLPs is $l + 2$. Next, we compute the remaining elementary matrices using the commutator formula and are listed in the table; let $r = l - 1$.

Elements	Indices	Equation (SLP)	Length	
$x_{1,-l}(t)$		$wx_{l-1,l}(t)w^{-1}$	$6(l-1)+6$	
$x_{1,-i}(t)$	$2 \leq i \leq l-1$	$[x_{i,l}(t), x_{1,-l}(1)]$	$24(l-1)+20$	$i = l-1$
			$2L(r-i,i) + 12(r+1)$	$i \neq l-1$
$x_{i,-j}(t)$	$2 \leq i \leq r-1$	$[x_{i,1}(t), x_{1,-j}(1)]$	$2L(i-1,1) + 4(7r+6) + 4L(r-j-\delta, j-\delta)$	$j < l-1$
	$(i+1 \leq j \leq l)$		$2L(i-1,1) + 4(7r+5)$	$j = l-1$
			$2L(i-1,1) + 10r + 6$	$j = l$

Thus, we have generated all $x_{i,-j}(t)$ for $i < j$. Now, using the formula $w^l x_{i,-j}(t)w^{-l} = x_{-i,j}(t)$, we get $x_{-i,j}(t)$ and the total number of SLPs required is $l + 6$. Now we know $w_{l-1} = w_l w_{l,l-1}(1)w_{l-1,-l}(1)$, so we generate w_{l-1}. Hence by induction we can generate $w_i = w_{i+1}w_{i+1,i}(1)w_{i,-(i+1)}(1)$, for $i = l-1, \ldots, 2$. Here $w_{i,j}(t) = x_{i,j}(t)x_{j,i}(-t^{-1})x_{i,j}(t)$, for $i \neq j$, and $w_{i,-j}(t) = x_{i,-j}(t)x_{-i,j}(t^{-1})x_{i,-j}(t)$, for $i < j$. Hence we generate all the elementary matrices defined in **Table A7** using generators $x, x', x_1(t,s), x_2$, and w and an extra element w_l. In our algorithm the output matrix is $d(\lambda) = \text{diag}\left(1, 1, 1, \ldots, \lambda, 1, \ldots, \lambda^{-1}\right)$. If $\lambda \in F_p^{\times 2}$, say $\lambda \equiv t^2 (\text{mod}\, p)$, here $t \equiv \lambda^{\frac{p+1}{4}} (\text{mod}\, p)$, since $p \equiv 3 \ (\text{mod } 4)$.

$$\begin{aligned} \text{Then } d(\lambda) &= \text{diag}\left(1, 1, 1, \ldots, t^2, 1, \ldots, , t^{-2}\right) \\ &= w_{l-1,l}(1)\text{diag}\left(1, 1, 1, \ldots, t^2, 1, 1, \ldots, , t^{-2}, 1\right)w_{l-1,l}(-1) \\ &= w_{l-1,l}(1)w_{l-1,l}(t)w_{l-1,l}(-1)w_{l-1,-l}(t)w_{l-1,-l}(-1)w_{l-1,l}(-1). \end{aligned}$$

Remark 5.2 *Let $d(\zeta) = \mathrm{diag}\left(1, 1, 1, \ldots, \zeta, 1, \ldots, \zeta^{-1}\right)$, where ζ is non-square in $\mathbb{F}_p^{\times}$. Then as a consequence of our Gaussian elimination algorithm in Appendix A, we can see that x, x', $x_1(t, s)$, x_2, w and w_l along with $d(\zeta)$ generate the twisted orthogonal group.*

6. Conclusion

This section is similar to ([6], Section 8). A useful public-key cryptosystem is a delicate dance between speed and the security. So one must talk about speed along with security.

The implementation of the MOR cryptosystem that we have in mind uses the row-column operations. Let $\langle g_1, g_2, \ldots, g_s \rangle$ be a set of generators for the orthogonal or symplectic group as described before. As is the custom with a MOR cryptosystem, the automorphisms ϕ and ϕ^m are presented as action on generators, i.e., we have $\phi(g_i)$ and $\phi^m(g_i)$ as matrices for $i = 1, 2, \ldots, s$.

To encrypt a message in this MOR cryptosystem, we compute ϕ^r. We do that by *square-and-multiply* algorithm. For this implementation, squaring and multiplying is almost the same. So we will refer to both squaring and multiplication as multiplication. Note that multiplication is composed of automorphisms.

The implementation that we describe in this chapter can work in parallel. Each instance computes $\phi^r(g_i)$ for $i = 1, 2, \ldots, s$. First thing that we do is write the matrix of $\phi(g_i)$ as a word in generators. So essentially the map ϕ becomes a map $g_i \mapsto w_i$ where w_i is a word in generators of some fixed length. Then multiplication becomes essentially a replacement, replace all instances of g_i by w_i. This can be done very fast. However, the length of the replaced word can become very large. The obvious question is how soon are we going to write this word as a matrix. This is a difficult question to answer at this stage and depends on available computational resources.

Once we decide how often we change back to matrices, how are we going to change back to matrices? There can be a fairly easy *time-memory* trade-offs. Write all words up to a fixed length and the corresponding matrix as a pre-computed table and use this table to compute the matrices. Once we have matrices, we can multiply them together to generate the final output. There are also many obvious relations among the generators of these groups. One can just store and use them. The best strategy for an efficient implementation is yet to be determined. It is clear now that there are many interesting and novel choices.

The benefits of this MOR cryptosystem are:

- This can be implemented in parallel easily.
- This implementation does not depend on the size of the characteristic of the field. This is an important property in light of Joux's recent improvement of the index-calculus attacks [11].

For parameters and complexity analysis of this cryptosystem, we refer to ([6], Section 8). Assume that we take a prime of size 2^{160} and we are using two generators presentation of ϕ for the even-orthogonal group. Then the security is the discrete logarithm problem in $\mathbb{F}_{p^{d^2}}$. Now if we take $d = 4$, then the security is better than $\mathbb{F}_{2^{2560}}$. Our key-size is about 8000 bits. Comparing with Monico ([10], Section 7), where he says an ElGamal will have about 6080 bits, our system is quite comparable. Moreover, the MOR cryptosystem is better suited to handle large primes and can be easily parallelized.

Acknowledgements

We are thankful to the editor and referees for their valuable comments which has improved the paper substantially. This work was supported by a SERB research grant. This chapter contains part of the PhD thesis of the first and the third author, directed by the second and the fourth author at IISER Pune.

Appendix A. Solving the word problem in G

In computational group theory, one is always looking for algorithms that solve the word problem. When G is a special linear group, one has a well-known algorithm to solve the word problem—the Gaussian elimination algorithm. One observes that the effect of multiplying an element of the special linear group by an elementary matrix (also known as elementary transvection) from left or right is either a row or a column operation, respectively. Using this algorithm one can start with any matrix $g \in \mathrm{SL}(l+1, k)$ and get to the identity matrix, thus writing g as a product of elementary matrices ([18], Proposition 6.2). One of the **objective of this appendix** is to discuss a similar algorithm for orthogonal and symplectic groups, with a set of generators that we will call **elementary matrices in their respective groups**. Similar algorithms can be found in the works of Brooksbank [19, 20] and Costi [21]. However, we have no restrictions on the cardinality or characteristic of the field k.

We first describe the elementary matrices and the row-column operations for the respective groups. These row-column operations are nothing but multiplication by elementary matrices from left and right, respectively. Here elementary matrices used are nothing but Chevalley generators which follows from the theory of Chevalley groups.

The basic idea of the algorithm is to use the fact that multiplying any orthogonal matrix by any one of the generators enables us to perform row or column operations. The relation ${}^{T}g\beta g = \beta$ gives us some compact relations among the blocks of g which can be used to make the algorithm faster. To make the algorithm simple, we will write the algorithm for $\mathrm{O}(2l+1, k)$, $\mathrm{O}^{+}(2l, k)$, and $\mathrm{O}^{-}(2l, k)$ separately.

A.1 Groups in which Gaussian elimination works

- Symplectic groups: Since all non-degenerate skew-symmetric bilinear forms are equivalent ([22], Corollary 2.12), we have a Gaussian elimination algorithm for all symplectic groups over an arbitrary field.

- Orthogonal groups:

    - Since non-degenerate symmetric bilinear forms over a finite field of odd characteristics are classified ([22], p. 79) according to the β (see Section 3), we have a Gaussian elimination algorithm for all orthogonal groups over a finite field of odd characteristics.

    - Since non-degenerate quadratic forms over a perfect field of even characteristics can be classified ([23], p. 10) according to quadratic forms $Q(x)$ defined in ([24], Section 4.2), we have a Gaussian elimination algorithm for all orthogonal groups over a perfect field of even characteristics.

- Furthermore, we have Gaussian elimination algorithm for orthogonal groups that are given by the above bilinear forms or quadratic forms over arbitrary fields. This algorithm also works for bilinear or quadratic forms that are equivalent to the above forms.

A.2 Gaussian elimination for matrices of even size—orthogonal group $O^+(d,k)$ and symplectic group

Recall that the bilinear forms β are the following:

- For symplectic group, $\mathrm{Sp}(d,k)$, $d = 2l$, and $\beta = \begin{pmatrix} 0 & I_l \\ -I_l & 0 \end{pmatrix}$.

- For orthogonal group, $O^+(d,k)$, $d = 2l$, and $\beta = \begin{pmatrix} 0 & I_l \\ I_l & 0 \end{pmatrix}$.

Note that any isometry g satisfies ${}^Tg\beta g = \beta$. The main reason our algorithm works is the following: Recall that a matrix $g = \begin{pmatrix} A & B \\ C & D \end{pmatrix}$, where A, B, C, and D are matrices of size l, is orthogonal or symplectic if ${}^Tg\beta g = \beta$ for the respective β. After some usual calculations, for orthogonal group it becomes

$$\begin{pmatrix} {}^TCA+{}^TAC & {}^TCB+{}^TAD \\ {}^TDA+{}^TBC & {}^TDB+{}^TBD \end{pmatrix} = \begin{pmatrix} 0 & I_l \\ I_l & 0 \end{pmatrix} \tag{A.1}$$

The above equation implies among other things, ${}^TCA+{}^TAC = 0$. This implies that ${}^TAC$ is skew-symmetric. In an almost identical way, one can show, if g is symplectic, ${}^TAC$ is symmetric. The working principle of our algorithm is simple—use the symmetry of ${}^TAC$. The problem is, for arbitrary A and C, it is not easy to use this symmetry. In our case we were able to reduce A to a diagonal matrix, and then it is relatively straightforward to use this symmetry. We will explain the algorithm in details later. First of all, let us describe the elementary matrices and the row-column operations for orthogonal and symplectic groups. The genesis of these elementary matrices lies in the Chevalley basis of simple Lie algebras. We will not go into details of Chevalley's theory in this appendix. Furthermore, we do not need to, the algorithm that we produce will show that these elementary matrices are generators for the respective groups.

Next we present the elementary matrices for the respective groups and then the row-column operations in a tabular form.

A.2.1 Elementary matrices (Chevalley generators) for orthogonal group $O^+(d,k)$ of even size

Following the theory of root system in a simple Lie algebra, we index rows by $1, 2, \ldots, l, -1, -2, \ldots, -l$. For $t \in k$, the elementary matrices are defined as follows (**Tables A1** and **A2**):

Let us note the effect of multiplying g by elementary matrices. We write

Char(k)		Elementary matrices	
	$x_{i,j}(t)$	$I + t(e_{i,j} - e_{-j,-i})$	$i \neq j$
Both	$x_{i,-j}(t)$	$I + t(e_{i,-j} - e_{j,-i})$	$i<j$
	$x_{-i,j}(t)$	$I + t(e_{-i,j} - e_{-j,i})$	$i<j$
	w_i	$I - e_{i,i} - e_{-i,-i} + e_{i,-i} + e_{-i,i}$	$1 \leq i \leq l$

Table A1.
Elementary matrices for $O^+(2l, k)$.

	Row operations		Column operations
ER1	ith↦ith + tjth row	EC1	jth↦jth + tith column
	$-j$th↦ $-j$th $- t(-i)$th row		$-i$th↦ $-i$th $- t(-j)$th column
ER2	ith↦ith + $t(-j)$th row	EC2	$-i$th↦ $-i$th $- tj$th column
	jth↦jth $- t(-i)$th row		$-j$th↦ $-j$th + tith column
ER3	$-i$th↦ $-i$th $- tj$th row	EC3	jth↦jth + $t(-i)$th column
	$-j$th↦ $-j$th + tith row		ith↦ith $- t(-j)$th column
w_i	Interchange ith and $(-i)$th row		Interchange ith and $(-i)$th column

Table A2.
The row-column operations for $O^+(2l, k)$.

Char(k)		Elementary matrices	
	$x_{i,j}(t)$	$I + t(e_{i,j} - e_{-j,-i})$	$i \neq j$
Both	$x_{i,-j}(t)$	$I + t(e_{i,-j} + e_{j,-i})$	$i<j$
	$x_{-i,j}(t)$	$I + t(e_{-i,j} + e_{-j,i})$	$i<j$
	$x_{i,-i}(t)$	$I + te_{i,-i}$	$1 \leq i \leq l$
	$x_{-i,i}(t)$	$I + te_{-i,i}$	$1 \leq i \leq l$

Table A3.
Elementary matrices for $Sp(2l, k)$.

$g \in O^+(2l, k)$ as $g = \begin{pmatrix} A & B \\ C & D \end{pmatrix}$, where A, B, C, and D are $l \times l$ matrices.

A.2.2 Elementary matrices (Chevalley generators) for symplectic group

For $t \in k$, the elementary matrices are defined as follows (**Table A3**):

Let us note the effect of multiplying g by elementary matrices. We write $g \in Sp(2l, k)$ as $g = \begin{pmatrix} A & B \\ C & D \end{pmatrix}$, where A, B, C, and D are $l \times l$ matrices (**Table A4**).

A.2.3 Gaussian elimination for $Sp(2l, k)$ and $O^+(2l, k)$

Step 1: Use ER1 and EC1 to make A into a diagonal matrix. This makes A into a diagonal matrix and changes other matrices A, B, C, and D. For the sake of notational convenience, we keep calling these changed matrices as A, B, C, and D as well.

	Row operations		Column operations
ER1	ith$\mapsto i$th $+ tj$th row	EC1	jth$\mapsto j$th $+ ti$th column
	$-j$th$\mapsto -j$th $+ t(-i)$th row		$-i$th$\mapsto -i$th $+ t(-j)$th column
ER2	ith$\mapsto i$th $+ t(-j)$th row	EC2	$-i$th$\mapsto -i$th $+ tj$th column
	jth$\mapsto j$th $+ t(-i)$th row		$-j$th$\mapsto -j$th $+ ti$th column
ER3	$-i$th$\mapsto -i$th $+ tj$th row	EC3	jth$\mapsto j$th $+ t(-i)$th column
	$-j$th$\mapsto -j$th $+ ti$th row		ith$\mapsto i$th $+ t(-j)$th column
ER1a	ith$\mapsto i$th $+ t(-i)$th row	EC1a	$-i$th$\mapsto -i$th $+ ti$th column
ER2a	$-i$th$\mapsto -i$th $+ ti$th row	EC2a	ith$\mapsto i$th $+ t(-i)$th column
w_i	Interchange ith and $(-i)$th rows		Interchange ith and $(-i)$th columns
	with a sign change in the ith row		with a sign change in the ith column

Table A4.
The row-column operations for symplectic groups.

Step 2: There are two possibilities. One, the diagonal matrix A is of full rank, and two, the diagonal matrix A is of rank $\mathfrak{r}$ less than l. This is clearly identifiable by looking for zeros in the diagonal of A.

Step 3: Make $\mathfrak{r}$ rows of C, corresponding to the non-zero entries in the diagonal of A zero by using ER3. If $\mathfrak{r} = l$, we have C as zero matrix. If not let us assume that ith row is zero in A. Then we interchange the ith row with the $-i^{\text{th}}$ row in g. We do this for all zero rows in A. The new C is a zero matrix. We claim that the new A must have a full rank. This follows from Equation A.1; in particular ${}^{T}CB + {}^{T}AD = I_l$. If C is zero matrix, then A is invertible. Now make A a diagonal matrix by using Step 1. Then one can make A a matrix of the form $\text{diag}(1, \ldots, 1, \lambda)$, where $\lambda \in k^{\times}$ using ER1 ([18], Proposition 6.2). Once A is diagonal and C a zero matrix, the equation ${}^{T}CB + {}^{T}AD = I_l$ makes D a diagonal matrix of full rank.

Step 4: Use ER2 to make B a zero matrix. The matrix g becomes a diagonal matrix of the form
$\text{diag}(1, \ldots, 1, \lambda, 1, \ldots, 1, \lambda^{-1})$, where $\lambda \in k^{\times}$.

Step 5: (Only for symplectic groups) Reduce the λ to 1 using Lemma A.1.

Lemma A.1 *For* $\text{Sp}(2l, k)$, *the element* $\text{diag}(1, \ldots, 1, \lambda, 1, \ldots, 1, \lambda^{-1})$ *is a product of elementary matrices.*

Proof. Observe that
$(I + \lambda e_{l,-l})(I - \lambda^{-1} e_{-l,l})(I + \lambda e_{l,-l}) = I - e_{l,l} - e_{-l,-l} + \lambda e_{l,-l} - \lambda^{-1} e_{-l,l}$ and denote it by $w_l(\lambda)$, and then the diagonal element is $w_l(\lambda) w_l(-1)$.

Remark A.1 *As we saw in the above algorithm, we will have to interchange i^{th} and $-i^{th}$ rows for $i = 1, 2, \ldots, l$. This can be done by pre-multiplying with a suitable matrix.*

Let I be the $2l \times 2l$ identity matrix over k. To swap ith and $-i$th row in $\text{O}^{+}(2l, k)$, swap ith and $-i$th rows in the matrix I. We will call this matrix w_i. It is easy to see that this matrix w_i is in $\text{O}^{+}(2l, k)$ and is of determinant -1. Pre-multiplying with w_i does the row interchange we are looking for.

In the case of symplectic group $\text{Sp}(2l, k)$, we again swap two rows ith and $-i$th in I. However we do a sign change in the ith row and call it w_i. Simple computation with our chosen β shows that the above matrices are in $\text{O}^{+}(2l, k)$ and $\text{Sp}(2l, k)$, respectively.

However there is one difference between orthogonal and symplectic groups. In symplectic group, w_i can be generated by elementary matrices because $w_i = x_{i,-i}(1)x_{-i,i}(-1)x_{i,-i}(1)$. In the case of orthogonal groups, that is not the case. This is clear that the elementary matrices come from the Chevalley generators and those generates Ω, the commutator of the orthogonal group. All matrices in Ω have determinant 1. However w_i has determinant -1. So we must add w_i as an elementary matrix for $O^+(2l, k)$.

Remark A.2 *This algorithm proves every element in the symplectic group is of determinant 1. Note the elementary matrices for the symplectic group are of determinant 1, and we have an algorithm to write any element as product of elementary matrices. So this proves that the determinant is 1.*

Remark A.3 *This algorithm proves if X is an element of a symplectic group then so is* ${}^{T}X$*. The argument is similar to the above; here we note that the transpose of an elementary matrix in symplectic groups is an elementary matrix.*

A.3 Gaussian elimination for matrices of odd size—the odd-orthogonal group

In this case, matrices are of odd size and there is only one family of group to consider; it is the odd-orthogonal group $O(2l+1, k)$. This group will be referred to as the odd-orthogonal group.

A.3.1 Elementary matrices (Chevalley generators) for $O(2l+1, k)$

Following the theory of Lie algebra, we index rows by 0, 1, ..., l, -1, ..., $-l$. These elementary matrices are listed in **Table A5**.

Elementary matrices for the odd-orthogonal group in even characteristics differ from that of odd characteristics. In above table we made that distinction and listed them separately in different rows according to the characteristics of k. If char(k) is even, we can construct the elements w_i, which interchanges the ith row with $-i^{th}$ row as follows:

$$w_i = (I + e_{0,i} + e_{-i,i})(I + e_{0,-i} + e_{i,-i})(I + e_{0,i} + e_{-i,i}) = I + e_{i,i} + e_{-i,-i} + e_{i,-i} + e_{-i,i}.$$

Otherwise, we can construct w_i, which interchanges the ith row with $-i^{th}$ row with a sign change in i^{th}, $-i^{th}$ and 0th row in odd-orthogonal group as follows:

Char(k)		**Elementary matrices**	
Both	$x_{i,j}(t)$	$I + t(e_{i,j} - e_{-j,-i})$	$i \neq j$
	$x_{i,-j}(t)$	$I + t(e_{i,-j} - e_{j,-i})$	$i<j$
	$x_{-i,j}(t)$	$I + t(e_{-i,j} - e_{-j,i})$	$i<j$
Odd	$x_{i,0}(t)$	$I + t(2e_{i,0} - e_{0,-i}) - t^2 e_{i,-i}$	$1 \leq i \leq l$
	$x_{0,i}(t)$	$I + t(-2e_{-i,0} + e_{0,i}) - t^2 e_{-i,i}$	$1 \leq i \leq l$
Even	$x_{i,0}(t)$	$I + te_{0,-i} + t^2 e_{i,-i}$	$1 \leq i \leq l$
	$x_{0,i}(t)$	$I + te_{0,i} + t^2 e_{-i,i}$	$1 \leq i \leq l$

Table A5.
Elementary matrices for $O(2l+1, k)$.

$$w_i = x_{0,i}(-1)x_{i,0}(1)x_{0,i}(-1) = I - 2e_{0,0} - e_{i,i} - e_{-i,-i} - e_{i,-i} - e_{-i,i}.$$

The Gaussian elimination algorithm for $O(2l+1,k)$ follows the earlier algorithm for symplectic and even-orthogonal group closely, except that we need to take care of the zero row and the zero column. We write an element $g \in O(2l+1,k)$ as $g = \begin{pmatrix} \alpha & X & Y \\ E & A & B \\ F & C & D \end{pmatrix}$, where A, B, C, and D are $l \times l$ matrices, X and Y are $1 \times l$ matrices, E and F are $l \times 1$ matrices, $\alpha \in k$ and $\beta = \begin{pmatrix} 2 & 0 & 0 \\ 0 & 0 & I_l \\ 0 & I_l & 0 \end{pmatrix}$. Then from the condition ${}^Tg\beta g = \beta$, we get the following relations:

$$2^TXX + {}^TAC + {}^TCA = 0 \tag{A.2}$$

$$2\alpha^TX + {}^TAF + {}^TCE = 0 \tag{A.3}$$

$$2\alpha Y + {}^TED + {}^TFB = 0 \tag{A.4}$$

$$2^TXY + {}^TAD + {}^TCB = I_l \tag{A.5}$$

Let us note the effect of multiplying g by elementary matrices (**Table A6**).

	Row operations		Column operations
ER1	ith$\mapsto i$th $+ tj$th row	EC1	jth$\mapsto j$th $+ ti$th column
(both)	$-j$th$\mapsto -j$th $- t(-i)$th row	(both)	$-i$th$\mapsto -i$th $- t(-j)$th column
ER2	ith$\mapsto i$th $+ t(-j)$th row	EC2	$-i$th$\mapsto -i$th $- tj$th column
(both)	jth$\mapsto j$th $- t(-i)$th row	(both)	$-j$th$\mapsto -j$th $+ ti$th column
ER3	$-i$th$\mapsto -i$th $- tj$th row	EC3	jth$\mapsto j$th $+ t(-i)$th column
(both)	$-j$th$\mapsto -j$th $+ ti$th row	(both)	ith$\mapsto i$th $- t(-j)$th column
ER4	0th$\mapsto$0th $- t(-i)$th row	EC4	0th$\mapsto$0th $+ 2ti$th column
(odd)	ith$\mapsto i$th $+ 2t$0th $- t^2(-i)$th row	(odd)	$(-i)$th$\mapsto(-i)$th $- t$0th $- t^2i$th column
ER5	0th$\mapsto$0th $+ ti$th row	EC5	0th$\mapsto$0th $- 2t(-i)$th column
(odd)	$(-i)$th$\mapsto(-i)$th $- 2t$0th $- t^2i$th row	(odd)	ith$\mapsto i$th $+ t$0th $- t^2(-i)$th column
ER6	0th$\mapsto$0th $+ t(-i)$th row	EC6	$(-i)$th$\mapsto(-i)$th $+ t$0th $+ t^2i$th column
(even)	ith$\mapsto i$th $+ t^2(-i)$th row	(even)	
ER7	0th$\mapsto$0th $+ ti$th row	EC7	ith$\mapsto i$th $+ t$0th $+ t^2(-i)$th column
(even)	$(-i)$th$\mapsto(-i)$th $+ t^2i$th row	(even)	
w_i	Interchange ith and $(-i)$th rows	w_i	Interchange ith and $(-i)$th column
(odd)	with a sign change in ith, $-i$th and 0th rows	(odd)	with a sign change in ith, $-i$th and 0th columns
w_i (even)	Interchange ith and $(-i)$th row	w_i (even)	Interchange ith and $(-i)$th column

Table A6.
The row-column operations for $O(2l+1,k)$.

A.3.2 Gaussian elimination for $O(2l+1, k)$

Step 1: Use ER1 and EC1 to make A into a diagonal matrix, but in the process, it changes other matrices A, B, C, D, E, F, X, and Y. For the sake of notational convenience, we keep calling these changed matrices as A, B, C, D, E, F, X, and Y as well.

Step 2: Now there will be two cases depending on the rank $\mathfrak{r}$ of matrix A. The rank of A can be easily determined using the number of non-zero diagonal entries. Use ER3 and non-zero diagonal entries of A to make corresponding $\mathfrak{r}$ rows of C zero.

1. If $\mathfrak{r} = l$ then C becomes zero matrix.

2. If $\mathfrak{r} < l$ then *interchange* all zero rows of A with corresponding rows of C using w_i so that the new C becomes a zero matrix.

Once C becomes zero, note that Relation A.2 if $\text{char}(k)$ is odd or Relation $Q(g(v)) = Q(v)$ if $\text{char}(k)$ is even guarantees that X becomes zero. Relation A.5 guarantees that A has full rank l which also makes D a diagonal with full rank l. Thus Relation A.3 shows that F becomes zero as well. Then use Step 1 to reduce $A = \text{diag}(1, \ldots, 1, \lambda)$, where $\lambda \in k^{\times}$.

Step 3: Now if $\text{char}(k)$ is even, then Relation A.4 guarantees that E becomes zero as well. If $\text{char}(k)$ is odd, then use ER4 to make E a zero matrix.

Step 4: Use ER2 to make B a zero matrix. For $\text{char}(k)$ even the relation $Q(g(v)) = Q(v)$ guarantees that Y is a zero matrix, and for $\text{char}(k)$ odd Relation A.4 implies that Y becomes zero.

Thus the matrix g reduces to $\text{diag}(\pm 1, 1, \ldots, \lambda, 1, \ldots, \lambda)$, where $\lambda \in k^{\times}$.

Remark A.4 *Let k be a perfect filed of characteristics 2. Note that we can write the diagonal matrix* $\text{diag}(1, \ldots, 1, \lambda, 1, \ldots, 1, \lambda^{-1})$ *as a product of elementary matrices as follows:*

$$\text{diag}(1, \ldots, 1, \lambda, 1, \ldots, 1, \lambda^{-1}) = x_{l,-l}(t)x_{-l,l}(-t^{-1})x_{l,-l}(t), \quad \text{where } t^2 = \lambda,$$

and hence we can reduce the matrix g to identity.

A.4 Gaussian elimination in twisted orthogonal groups

In this section we present a Gaussian elimination algorithm for twisted orthogonal groups. The size of the matrix is even; the bilinear form used is c′ from Section 3.

A.4.1 Elementary matrices (Chevalley generators) for twisted orthogonal groups $O^{-}(2l, k)$

In this section, we describe row-column operations for twisted Chevalley groups. These groups are also known as the Steinberg groups. An element $g \in O^{-}(2l, k)$ is denoted as $g = \begin{pmatrix} A_0 & X & Y \\ E & A & B \\ F & C & D \end{pmatrix}$, where A, B, C, and D are $(l-1) \times (l-1)$ matrices, X and Y are $2 \times (l-1)$ matrices, E and F are $(l-1) \times 2$ matrices, and A_0 is a 2×2 matrix. In the Gaussian elimination algorithm that we discuss, we reduce X, Y, E, F, B, and C to zero and A and D to diagonal matrices.

However, unlike the previous cases, we were unable to reduce A_0 to an identity matrix. However, for odd characteristics we were able to reduce A_0 to a two-parameter subgroup.

We now talk about the output of the algorithm. In the output we will have a 2×2 block (also called A_0) which will satisfy ${}^{T}A_0\beta_0 A_0 = \beta_0$, where $\beta_0 = \begin{pmatrix} 1 & 0 \\ 0 & \epsilon \end{pmatrix}$ for odd characteristics and ε is a non-square. Then A_0 is a orthogonal matrix given by the bilinear form β_0. Now if we write $A_0 = \begin{pmatrix} a & b \\ c & d \end{pmatrix}$, then we get the following equations:

$$a^2 + c^2\epsilon = 1, \quad ab + cd\epsilon = 0, \quad b^2 + d^2\epsilon = \epsilon.$$

Considering the fact that $\det(A_0) = \pm 1$, one more equation $ad - bc = \pm 1$ and this leads to two cases either $a = d$ and $b = -c\epsilon$ or $a = -d$ and $b = c\epsilon$. Recall that, since ϵ is not a square, $d \neq 0$. Then if $c = 0$, then there are four choices for A_0 and these are $A_0 = \begin{pmatrix} \pm 1 & 0 \\ 0 & \pm 1 \end{pmatrix}$.

To summarize, the output of the algorithm A_0 will have one of the following forms

$$\begin{pmatrix} t & -s\epsilon \\ s & t \end{pmatrix} \text{or} \begin{pmatrix} t & s\epsilon \\ s & -t \end{pmatrix}, \text{ where } \quad t^2 + s^2\epsilon = 1, \qquad \text{(A.6)}$$

and $t \in k^{\times}, s \in k$, and ϵ are non-square. There are now two ways to describe the algorithm: one is to leave A_0 as it is in the output of the algorithm, and the other is to include these matrices as generators. For the purpose of uniform exposition, we chose the latter and included the following two generators

Char(k)		**Elementary matrices**	
	$x_{i,j}(t)$	$I + t(e_{i,j} - e_{-j,-i})$	$i \neq j$
Both	$x_{i,-j}(t)$	$I + t(e_{i,-j} - e_{j,-i})$	$i<j$
	$x_{-i,j}(t)$	$I + t(e_{-i,j} - e_{-j,i})$	$i<j$
	w_i	$I - e_{i,i} - e_{-i,-i} + e_{i,-i} + e_{-i,i}$	$2 \leq i \leq l$
	$x_{i,1}(t)$	$I + t(e_{1,i} - 2e_{-i,1}) - t^2 e_{-i,i}$	$2 \leq i \leq l$
	$x_{1,i}(t)$	$I + t(-e_{1,-i} + 2e_{i,1}) - t^2 e_{i,-i}$	$2 \leq i \leq l$
	$x_{i,-1}(t)$	$I + t(e_{-1,i} - 2\varepsilon e_{-i,-1}) - \varepsilon t^2 e_{-i,i}$	$2 \leq i \leq l$
Odd	$x_{-1,i}(t)$	$I + t(-e_{-1,-i} + 2\varepsilon e_{i,-1}) - \varepsilon t^2 e_{i,-i}$	$2 \leq i \leq l$
	$x_1(t,s)$	$I + (t-1)e_{1,1} - (t+1)e_{-1,-1} + s(e_{-1,1} + \varepsilon e_{1,-1})$	$t^2 + \varepsilon s^2 = 1$
	x_2	$I - 2e_{-1,-1}$	
	$x_{1,-i}(t)$	$I + te_{1,-i} + te_{i,-1} + \alpha t^2 e_{i,-i}$	$2 \leq i \leq l$
Even	$x_{-1,-i}(t)$	$I + te_{-1,-i} + te_{i,1} + \alpha t^2 e_{i,-i}$	$2 \leq i \leq l$
	x_{A_0}	$I + (t-1)e_{1,1} + (s-1)e_{-1,-1} + pe_{1,-1} + re_{-1,1}$	$ts + pr = 1$

Table A7.
Elementary matrices for $O^{-}(2l,k)$.

$$x_1(t,s) = I + (t-1)e_{1,1} - (t+1)e_{-1,-1} + s(e_{-1,1} + \epsilon e_{1,-1}); \quad t^2 + \epsilon s^2 = 1,$$
$$x_2 = I - 2e_{-1,-1},$$

in the list of elementary matrices in **Table A7**. In the case of even characteristics, no such reduction is possible, and we included the matrix $\begin{pmatrix} t & p \\ r & s \end{pmatrix}$ in the list of generators with the condition that the determinant is 1.

The elementary matrices for $O^-(2l,k)$ depend on the characteristics of k. We describe them separately in the following table. Let α be an Arf-invariant, $2 \le i,j \le l$ and $t \in K$ and $\xi \in k^\times$.

Let us note the effect of multiplying g by elementary matrices. Elementary matrices for the twisted orthogonal group in even characteristics differ from that of odd characteristics, so in the following tables (**Tables A8** and **A9**), we made that distinction and listed them separately in different rows according to the characteristics of k.

	Row operations
ER1 (both)	ith$\mapsto i$th $+ tj$th row and $-j$th$\mapsto -j$th $- t(-i)$th row
ER2 (both)	ith$\mapsto i$th $+ t(-j)$th row and jth$\mapsto j$th $- t(-i)$th row
ER3 (both)	$-i$th$\mapsto -i$th $- tj$th row and $-j$th$\mapsto -j$th $+ ti$th row
ER4 (odd)	1st$\mapsto$1st $- t(-i)$th row and ith$\mapsto i$th $+ 2t$1st $- t^2(-i)$th row
ER5 (odd)	1st$\mapsto$1st $+ ti$th row and $(-i)$th$\mapsto(-i)$th $- 2t$1st $- t^2i$th row
ER6 (odd)	(-1)th$\mapsto(-1)$th $- t(-i)$th row and ith$\mapsto i$th $+ 2\varepsilon t(-1)$th $- \varepsilon t^2(-i)$th row
ER7 (odd)	(-1)th$\mapsto(-1)$th $+ ti$th row and $(-i)$th$\mapsto(-i)$th $- 2\varepsilon t(-1)$th $- \varepsilon t^2 i$th row
ER8 (even)	1st$\mapsto$1st $+ t(-i)$th row and ith$\mapsto i$th $+ t(-1)$th $+ \alpha t^2(-i)$th row
ER9 (even)	(-1)th$\mapsto(-1)$th $+ t(-i)$th row and ith$\mapsto i$th $+ t$1st $+ \alpha t^2(-i)$th row
w_i (both)	Interchange ith and $(-i)$th row

Table A8.
The row operations for $O^-(2l,k)$.

	Column operations
EC1(both)	jth$\mapsto j$th $+ ti$th column and $-i$th$\mapsto -i$th $- t(-j)$th column
EC2 (both)	$-i$th$\mapsto -i$th $- tj$th column and $-j$th$\mapsto -j$th $+ ti$th column
EC3 (both)	jth$\mapsto j$th $+ t(-i)$th column and ith$\mapsto i$th $- t(-j)$th column
EC4 (odd)	1st$\mapsto$1st $+ 2ti$th column and $(-i)$th$\mapsto(-i)$th $- t$1st $- t^2i$th column
EC5 (odd)	1st$\mapsto$1st $- 2t(-i)$th column and ith$\mapsto i$th $+ t$1st $- t^2(-i)$th column
EC6 (odd)	(-1)th$\mapsto(-1)$th $+ (2\varepsilon t)i$th column and $(-i)$th$\mapsto(-i)$th $- t(-1)$th $- \varepsilon t^2 i$th column
EC7 (odd)	(-1)th$\mapsto(-1)$th $- 2\varepsilon t(-i)$th column and ith$\mapsto i$th $+ t(-1)$th $- \varepsilon t^2(-i)$th column
EC8 (even)	(-1)th$\mapsto(-1)$th $+ ti$th column and $(-i)$th$\mapsto(-i)$th $+ t$1st $+ \alpha t^2 i$th column
EC9 (even)	1st$\mapsto$1st $+ ti$th column and $(-i)$th$\mapsto(-i)$th $+ t(-1)$th $+ \alpha t^2 i$th column
w_i (both)	Interchange ith and $(-i)$th column

Table A9.
The column operations for $O^-(2l,k)$.

Note that any isometry g satisfies ${}^T g\beta g = \beta$. The main reason the following algorithm works is the closed condition ${}^T g\beta g = \beta$ which gives the following relations:

$$ {}^T A_0\beta_0 A_0 + {}^T FE + {}^T EF = \beta_0, \tag{A.7}$$

$$ {}^T A_0\beta_0 X + {}^T FA + {}^T EC = 0, \tag{A.8}$$

$$ {}^T A_0\beta_0 Y + {}^T FB + {}^T ED = 0, \tag{A.9}$$

$$ {}^T X\beta_0 X + {}^T CA + {}^T AC = 0, \tag{A.10}$$

$$ {}^T X\beta_0 Y + {}^T CB + {}^T AD = I_{l-1}. \tag{A.11}$$

A.4.2 The Gaussian elimination algorithm for $\mathbf{O}^-(2l, k)$

Step 1: Use ER1 and EC1 to make A into a diagonal matrix, but in the process, it changes other matrices A_0, A, B, C, D, E, F, X, and Y. For the sake of notational convenience, we keep calling these changed matrices as A_0, A, B, C, D, E, F, X, and Y as well.

Step 2: Now there will be two cases depending on the rank $\mathfrak{r}$ of the matrix A. The rank of A can be easily determined by the number of non-zero diagonal entries.

Step 3: Use ER3 and non-zero diagonal entries of A to make corresponding $\mathfrak{r}$ rows of C zero.

- If $\mathfrak{r} = l - 1$ then C becomes zero matrix.
- If $\mathfrak{r} < l - 1$ then interchange all zero rows of A with corresponding rows of C using w_i, so that the new C becomes a zero matrix.
- Once C becomes zero one, can note that the relation ${}^T X\beta_0 X + {}^T CA + {}^T AC = 0$ if char(k) is odd or the relation $Q(g(v)) = Q(v)$ and the fact that $\alpha t^2 + t + \alpha$ is irreducible when char(k) is even guarantees that X becomes zero. Then the relation ${}^T X\beta_0 Y + {}^T CB + {}^T AD = I_{l-1}$ guarantees that A has full rank $l - 1$ which also makes D a diagonal with full rank, and the relation ${}^T A_0\beta_0 X + {}^T FA + {}^T EC = 0$ shows that F is zero. Now we diagonalize A again to the form diag$(1, \ldots, 1, \lambda)$, where $\lambda \in k^\times$ as in Step 1.

Step 4: Use EC4 and EC6 when char(k) is odd or use EC8 and EC9 when char(k) is even to make E zero. Note that the relation ${}^T A_0\beta_0 A_0 + {}^T FE + {}^T EF = \beta_0$ shows that A_0 is invertible. Thus the relation ${}^T A_0\beta_0 Y + {}^T FB + {}^T ED = 0$ guarantees that Y becomes zero.

Step 5: Use ER2 to make B a zero matrix. Thus the matrix g reduces to $g = \text{diag}(A_0, 1, \ldots, \lambda, 1, \ldots, \lambda^{-1})$. Now if char$(k)$ is odd, then go to Step 6; otherwise go to Step 7.

Step 6: Using the relation ${}^T A_0\beta_0 A_0 = \beta_0$, it is easy to check that A_0 has the form $\begin{pmatrix} t & -\epsilon s \\ s & t \end{pmatrix}$ or $\begin{pmatrix} t & \epsilon s \\ s & -t \end{pmatrix}$. If the determinant of A_0 is -1, multiply g by x_2 to get new g of the above form such that A_0 has determinant 1. Now using the elementary matrix $x_1(t, s)$, we can reduce g to diag$(I_2, 1, \ldots, \lambda, 1, \ldots, \lambda^{-1})$.

Step 7: Using elementary matrix x_{A_0}, we can reduce g to $\operatorname{diag}(I_2, 1, \ldots, \lambda, 1, \ldots, \lambda^{-1})$.

Lemma A.2 *Let k be a field of characteristics 2 and let* $g = \begin{pmatrix} A_0 & X & Y \\ E & A & B \\ F & 0 & D \end{pmatrix}$, *where* $A = \operatorname{diag}(1, 1, \ldots, 1, \lambda)$, *be an element of* $O^-(2l, k)$ *then* $X = 0$.

Proof. Let $\{e_1, e_{-1}, e_2, \ldots, e_l, e_{-2}, \ldots, e_{-l}\}$ be the standard basis of the vector space V. Recall that for a column vector $x = (x_1, x_{-1}, x_2, \ldots, x_l, x_{-2}, \ldots, x_{-l})^t$, the action of the quadratic form Q is given by $Q(x) = \alpha(x_1^2 + x_{-1}^2) + x_1x_{-1} + \ldots + x_lx_{-l}$, where $\alpha t^2 + t + \alpha$ is irreducible over $k[t]$. By definition, for any $g \in O^-(2l, k)$, we have $Q(g(x)) = Q(x)$ for all $x \in V$. Let $X = \begin{pmatrix} x_{11} \cdots x_{1(l-1)} \\ x_{21} \cdots x_{2(l-1)} \end{pmatrix}$ be a $2 \times (l-1)$ matrix. Computing $Q(g(e_i)) = Q(e_i)$ for all $2 \le i \le l$, we can see that $\alpha(x_{1i}^2 + x_{2i}^2) + x_{1i}x_{2i} = 0$. If $x_{2i} = 0$ then we can see that $x_{1i} = 0$. Suppose $x_{2i} \neq 0$ for some i, then we rewrite the equation by dividing it by x_{2i} as $\alpha\left(\frac{x_{1i}}{x_{2i}}\right)^2 + \frac{x_{1i}}{x_{2i}} + \alpha = 0$, which is a contradiction to the fact that $\alpha t^2 + t + \alpha$ is irreducible over $k[t]$. Thus, $x_{2i} = 0$ for all $2 \le i \le l$ and hence $X = 0$. •

A.5 Time complexity of the above algorithms

We establish that the worst-case time complexity of the above algorithm is $\mathcal{O}(l^3)$. We mostly count the number of field multiplications.

Step 1: We make A a diagonal matrix by row-column operations that has complexity $\mathcal{O}(l^3)$.

Step 2: In making both C and B zero matrix, we multiply two rows by a field element and additions. In the worst case, it has to be done $\mathcal{O}(l)$ times and done $\mathcal{O}(l^2)$ many times. So the complexity is $\mathcal{O}(l^3)$.

Step 3: In odd-orthogonal group and twisted orthogonal group, we clear X, Y, E, F, this clearly has complexity $\mathcal{O}(l^2)$.

Step 4: This step has only a few operations that is independent of l.

Then clearly, the time complexity of our algorithm is $\mathcal{O}(l^3)$.

We have implemented the above algorithms in Magma [25]. For details of that implementation along with performance analysis of our algorithm, we refer to Bhunia et al. ([24], Section 8).

Author details

Sushil Bhunia[1], Ayan Mahalanobis[2]*, Pralhad Shinde[2] and Anupam Singh[2]

1 IISER Mohali, India

2 IISER Pune, Pune, India

*Address all correspondence to: ayan.mahalanobis@gmail.com

References

[1] Monico C, Maze G, Rosenthal J. A public key cryptosystem based on action by semigroups. In: Proceedings of IEEE International Symposium on Information Theory. 2002

[2] Monico C, Maze G, Rosenthal J. Public key cryptography based on semigroup actions. Advances in Mathematics of Communications. 2007; **1**(4):489-506

[3] Climent J-J, Navarro PR, Tortosa L. An extension of the noncommutative Bergman's ring with a large number of noninvertible elements. Applicable Algebra in Engineering, Communication and Computing. 2014;**25**(5):347-361

[4] Grigoriev D, Kojevnikov A, Nikolenko SJ. Algebraic cryptography: New constructions and their security against provable break. St. Petersburg Mathematical Journal. 2009;**20**(6): 937-953

[5] Roman'kov V. Two general schemes of algebraic cryptography. Groups-Complexity-Cryptology. 2019, to appear

[6] Mahalanobis A. A simple generalization of the ElGamal cryptosystem to non-abelian groups II. Communications in Algebra. 2012; **40**(9):3583-3596

[7] Mahalanobis A. The MOR cryptosystem and finite p-groups. In: Contemporary Mathematics. Vol. 633. AMS; 2015. pp. 81-95

[8] Mahalanobis A, Singh A. Gaussian elimination in split unitary groups with an application to public-key cryptography. Journal of Algebra Combinatorics Discrete Structures and Applications. 2017;**4**(3):247-260

[9] Paeng S-H, Ha K-C, Kim JH, Chee S, Park C. New public key cryptosystem using finite non-Abelian groups. In: Kilian J, editor. Crypto 2001. LNCS. Vol. 2139. Springer-Verlag; 2001. pp. 470-485

[10] Monico C. Cryptanalysis of matrix-based MOR system. Communications in Algebra. 2016;**44**:218-227

[11] Barbulescu R, Gaudry P, Joux A, Thome E. A heuristic quasi-polynomial algorithm for discrete logarithm in finite fields of small characteristic. In: Eurocrypt2014. 2014. pp. 1-16

[12] Hoffstein J, Pipher J, Silverman JH. An Introduction to Mathematical Cryptography. Springer; 2008

[13] Knus M-A, Merkurjev A, Rost M, Tignol J-P. The Book of Involutions (English Summary) with a Preface in French by J. Tits. Vol. 44. American Mathematical Society Colloquium Publications; 1998

[14] Dieudonne J. On the automorphisms of the classical groups with a supplement by Loo-Keng Hua. Memoirs of the American Mathematical Society. 1951

[15] Menezes AJ, Yi-Hong W. The discrete logarithm problem in GL (n, q). Ars Combinatoria. 1997;**47**:23-32

[16] Steinberg R. Generators of simple groups. Canadian Journal of Mathematics. 1962;**14**:277-283

[17] Ree R. On some simple groups defined by C. Chevalley. Transactions of the American Mathematical Society. 1957;**84**:392-400

[18] Alperin JL, Bell RB. Groups and Representations. New York: Springer-Verlag; 1995

[19] Brooksbank P. Constructive recognition of classical groups in their

natural representation. Journal of Symbolic Computation. 2003;**35**:195-239

[20] Brooksbank P. Fast constructive recognition of black-box unitary groups. LMS Journal of Computation and Mathematics. 2003;**6**:162-197

[21] Costi E. Constructive membership testing in classical groups [PhD thesis]. Queen Mary, Univ. of London; 2009

[22] Grove LC. Classical groups and geometric algebra. Vol. 39. American Mathematical Society, Graduate Studies in Mathematics; 2002

[23] Carter R. Simple groups of Lie type. In: Pure and Applied Mathematics. Vol. 28. John Wiley & Sons; 1972

[24] Bhunia S, Mahalanobis A, Shinde P, Singh A. Gaussian elimination in symplectic and orthogonal groups. In: Tech. Report. IISER Pune; 2017. Available from: https://arxiv.org/abs/1504.03794

[25] Bosma W, Cannon J, Playoust C. The magma algebra system. I. The user language. Journal of Symbolic Computation. 1997;**24**(3-4):235-265

[26] Steinberg R. Lectures on Chevalley Groups. University Lecture Series, Vol. 66, American Mathematical Society; 2016